This book is dedicated to my daughter
Anne Marie Simms

Contents

COMPOSER RESOURCE MANUALS

In response to the growing need for bibliographic guidance to the vast literature on significant composers, Garland is publishing an extensive series of research guides. This ongoing series encompasses more than 50 composers; they represent Western musical tradition from the Renaissance to the present century.

Each research guide offers a selective, annotated list of writings, in all European languages, about one or more composers. There are also lists of works by the composers, unless these are available elsewhere. Biographical sketches and guides to library resources, organizations, and specialists are presented. As appropriate to the individual composer, there are maps, photographs or other illustrative matter, glossaries, and indexes.

Preface

This book contains a bibliographic survey of research into the life and works of Alban Berg (1885-1935). Like other contributions to the Garland Composer Resource Series, it is primarily a selective, annotated bibliography of writings about a major composer intended to summarize research that has already been done and to provide a practical guide to future studies of both general and specialized types.

Organization and Contents

The book begins with a chapter containing a brief biography, survey of works, and discussion of trends in research. This should be helpful as a source of background information concerning issues mentioned in titles and abstracts found later in the bibliography. The next two chapters are devoted to a list of all of Berg's published compositions and published writings about music. The body of the book is then encountered in Chapters 4 through 9, which contain selective citations of writings concerning Berg.

The organization of these last six chapters is topical, placing together writings on each of Berg's major works. Sources that deal with more than one work or with aspects of the composer's life, oeuvre, and cultural milieu are located separately in Chapter 9. In light of this organization it is important that any subject search begin with the Index.

Each item in the bibliography is provided with complete publication data, in a standard, concise form. For periodical articles, an issue number is given only if needed to locate the item. When found, it follows the volume number, the two separated by a slash. Inclusive page numbers follow a colon. In order to eliminate redundancy, reprints and translations of an item are added as annotations to the citation of the earliest version. Books are provided with International Standard Book Numbers (ISBNs) and Library of Congress call numbers. Readers are cautioned, however, against the assumption that Library of Congress call numbers are exactly duplicated by other libraries. Even libraries using principles of cataloging of the Library of Congress often deviate from Library of Congress call numbers, especially toward the end of the call number.

Short abstracts that outline the subject of an item are added to virtually all citations. A few citations lack abstracts, an indication that they have not been seen by the author of this guide. A discography is not found in this study. The interested reader is referred instead to J. F. Weber's *Alban Berg* (no. 1038), which is a comprehensive discography of Berg's music to 1979. References to more recent discographies are found in the Index.

Principles of Selection

The 1,000 books and articles cited in this study represent less than half of all published writings on Berg. The following principles of selectivity have been followed in order to make this survey shorter and easier to use, although no less a comprehensive guide to important research. In general, items have not been included if they are of these types:

1. unpublished materials (including unpublished dissertations);
2. reviews, except for a selection of easy-to-find reviews of books concerning Berg;
3. theses or dissertations, except for published Ph.D. dissertations (which are included);
4. very brief articles;
5. articles in daily newspapers;
6. articles in popular or general-readership magazines;
7. articles from program booklets or theater or concert periodicals;
8. material from textbooks;
9. record liner notes;
10. lexicographic notices, except for the most often used;
11. articles in Eastern European or Asian languages;

12. discussions in books or articles that do not primarily concern Berg (e.g., books on Schoenberg, Webern, twelve-tone composition, or the Society for Private Musical Performances);
13. items published after 1994.

The exclusion of reviews of performances or recordings of Berg's music has been necessary in order to make the size of this volume manageable. These items rarely contain original material concerning the music itself. A selection of reviews concerning early performances of Berg's works, including the 1925 premiere of *Wozzeck* and the 1937 premiere of *Lulu*, and reviews that report on research have been retained.

Articles in Eastern European and Asian languages have been omitted partly due to practical considerations, since these sources will be difficult to locate and to read by users of this guide. With very few exceptions, their content duplicates material also found in English and German sources. A few articles that have uniquely important content written in Eastern European languages are included, as, for example, an article by János Breuer (no. 707) which is the only published transcription of Alexander Jemnitz's correspondence with Berg. All books in Eastern European languages on Berg are included. There has been no systematic attempt to include items published after 1994, although a few major studies on Berg announced for appearance after this date, such as Patricia Hall's book on *Lulu* (no. 355), are cited. Since major literature indexes—most importantly RILM—were not available for writings published after 1992, it is likely that some articles concerning Berg appearing in 1993 and 1994 have been omitted. Users of this guide wishing to update its contents should consult indexes such as RILM beginning with 1993.

Abbreviations

ABS   *Alban Berg Studien* (Vienna: Alban Berg-Stiftung and Universal Edition, 1980–)

AGS   Theodor W. Adorno, *Gesammelte Schriften*, 20 volumes (Frankfurt: Suhrkamp Verlag, 1970-86)

BMW   *Beiträge zur Musikwissenschaft*

BSN   *International Alban Berg Society Newsletter*

HJM   *Hamburger Jahrbuch für Musikwissenschaft*

JAMS *Journal of the American Musicological Society*

JASI *Journal of the Arnold Schoenberg Institute*

MA   *Music Analysis*

MBA   *Musikblätter des Anbruch/Anbruch*

MEL   *Melos*

MF   *Die Musikforschung*

MK   *Musik-Konzepte*

ML   *Music and Letters*

MQ   *Musical Quarterly*

MR   *Music Review*

MT   *Musical Times*

NZM   *Neue Zeitschrift für Musik*

ÖMZ   *Österreichische Musikzeitschrift*

PNM   *Perspectives of New Music*

RM   *La revue musicale*

RMA   *Proceedings/Journal of the Royal Musical Association*

SMZ   *Schweizerische Musikzeitung/Revue musicale suisse*

UMI   Ann Arbor, Michigan: University Microfilms

ALBAN BERG

Alban Berg in the early 1920s
(courtesy of the Arnold Schoénberg Institute)

1

Alban Berg:
The Making of a Classic Composer

Alban Berg is now recognized as a classic figure in the history of music. His entire oeuvre is performed repeatedly around the world, recorded regularly, studied in well over a thousand books and articles, enjoyed and pondered by the serious musical public everywhere. His music has been influential upon, indeed indispensable to, other major composers. Operas including Zimmermann's *Die Soldaten* and Rihm's *Jakob Lenz* could probably not have been written without *Wozzeck*; the brilliant virtuosity of Boulez's *Éclat* would be hard to imagine without the Chamber Concerto, the pathos-laden music of George Rochberg without the Orchestral Pieces, the quotation collages of Berio and Kagel without the Violin Concerto, or the provocative eclecticism of Alfred Schnittke without *Lulu* and *Der Wein*.

But Berg's vast importance—so obvious in the present day—became generally known only long after the composer's death in 1935. Before the 1960s and 1970s he was widely regarded as a minor figure who left relatively few works which were either imitations of Schoenberg or confused by allegiances to both the romantic and modern periods. His teacher, Arnold Schoenberg, although sensitive to Berg's talent, was almost certainly unaware of his student's true importance. Following World War II, as works by Schoenberg and Webern became models for the emerging European and American avant-garde, relatively few observers rated Berg's oeuvre at the same high level as others in the Second Viennese School, finding it more of a romantic atavism than a model for the future.

But gradually Berg's true position in the future of music forced its way out. His ultimate recognition came almost solely from the inherent greatness of the works themselves—their power, exerted independently of fashions and personalities, to grasp and hold the musical imagination. A vivid reflection of this change in perception is contained in the specialized literature that is the main subject of this volume. Writing in 1920 the pianist Eduard Erdmann—one of the first interpretors of Berg's Piano Sonata—could only compare the work to Schoenberg's. Erdmann found its style derived from Schoenberg's Chamber Symphony although lacking in Schoenberg's "sweep of imagination." In 1951 Hans Keller dismissed *Wozzeck* as an inferior copy of works by Schoenberg. By the 1980s, however, such evaluations had become unthinkable among reputable music critics. More typical of the present day is George Perle's 1982 assessment of *Lulu* as "one of the supreme masterpieces of its genre in the entire repertory."

Writings about Berg have left a record of discoveries and insights into the man and his music. Before turning to a report on this body of research, a brief sketch of his life and work will help to put his oeuvre into context.

Berg's Life

Albano Maria Johannes Berg was born in central Vienna on 9 February 1885. His father, Conrad Berg (1846–1900), ran a book and art shop. His mother, Johanna (née Braun, 1851–1926), was artistic and cultivated the trait in her children. Berg and his three siblings—Hermann (1872–1921), Karl (called Charley, 1881–1952), and Smaragda (1886–1954)—grew up in a comfortable and artistic family environment. Summers were usually spent in the family's villa, "Berghof," in the mountainous region of Carinthia in southern Austria.

Berg's circumstances took a perilous turn in 1900, when his father died suddenly from a heart attack. The remainder of his adolescence was marked by poor health, financial uncertainty, failures in school, and emotional crises. One of these was prompted by the birth out of wedlock in December 1902 of a daughter, named Albine, whose mother, Marie Scheuchl, was a domestic at the Berghof. Willi Reich has written that feelings of guilt and depression led Berg shortly thereafter to attempt suicide. But despite personal problems, the years from 1900 to 1904 witnessed important musical growth. Berg had developed into a competent pianist, and he had begun to compose songs, which were often performed privately by those in his family.

In 1904 Berg became the private student of Arnold Schoenberg, giving both his artistic and personal life a strict guidance that it had lacked to that time. Berg received lessons from Schoenberg until about 1910, although Schoenberg permanently remained an awesome presence in Berg's life, influencing not only his career and artistic direction but acting as a stern father figure who tended to be censorious. His studies with Schoenberg were methodical and extensive, beginning with harmony, moving to counterpoint (at which Berg was especially gifted), finally turning to free composition.

At about the same time that he began his studies with Schoenberg, Berg also began an apprenticeship as an accountant in the Austrian civil service. In 1905 he took over the management of rental properties that his mother had inherited, allowing him to resign from the civil service. But he was determined to be a professional musician, as his imagination was now fired by modern art and literature and by the new directions in music represented by his teacher, Schoenberg. Berg formed a close friendship with other Schoenberg students, especially with Anton Webern, who enjoyed a much warmer personal relationship with the master than Berg ever was to have.

In 1907 Berg was introduced to an aspiring opera singer, Helene Nahowski, with whom he fell passionately in love. On 3 May 1911, despite the reservations of her father, the two were married and took up residence in Hietzing, a suburb of Vienna. During the period of his tumultuous courtship, he composed his first important works: a Piano Sonata, Op. 1; String Quartet, Op. 3; and songs of far greater originality than his earlier essays in this genre. But he had no success in arranging for performances, outside of appearances on several concerts of Schoenberg's students, nor could he attract significant critical attention to his efforts. One of the concerts arranged by Schoenberg had an especially damaging effect upon his self-confidence. This was sponsored by the Akademischer Verband für Literatur und

Musik in Vienna, on 31 March 1913, when two of his Orchestral
Songs, Op. 4, together with works by Webern, Schoenberg,
Mahler, and Zemlinsky, were to be heard. In the middle of
Berg's selections, the audience erupted in protest against their
recondite modernism. The police were summoned, and the
remainder of the concert was cancelled, leaving Berg bitterly
dejected. Indeed, prior to the mid-1920s Berg seemed unable to
emerge from Schoenberg's shadow and establish himself as an
original and important voice in modern music.

Like most musicians in Schoenberg's circle, Berg's patriotism
at the beginning of World War I was keen. Ready to fight for the
Hapsburg Monarchy, he entered the Austrian military service in
1915 and was stationed near the Hungarian border. But his
enthusiasm for military life quickly turned to revulsion—later
reflected in his opera *Wozzeck*—and his poor health led to his
being restationed at the war ministry in Vienna. Berg was left an
antimilitarist, bitterly disillusioned by the society that had
produced the war and its devastating aftermath.

Following the war, he was appointed by Schoenberg as a
leader and manager of the Society for Private Musical
Performances, an idealistic organization for the performance of
modern music in Vienna. Although repeatedly interrupted by
poor health, Berg worked tirelessly for the Society until its
demise in 1921. It brought him a small measure of attention as
a composer since his Four Songs, Op. 2; String Quartet, Op. 3;
and Clarinet Pieces, Op. 5, were performed in its concerts. But
his hopes for a significant career in music seemed no brighter
than before, and around 1920, with Schoenberg's encouragement,
he considered redirecting his work toward that of a writer about
music. In that year he accepted the editorship of the modern
music journal *Musikblätter des Anbruch* and soon began to write
a biography of Schoenberg. He backed out of both undertakings
in order to devote himself to completing *Wozzeck*, although the
essays that began to appear in 1920 show his skill as a writer and
musical analyst.

In 1922 *Wozzeck* was at last completed and published at
Berg's own expense (with assistance from Mahler's widow,
Alma). There were no immediate prospects for a performance,
although the originality of the work provoked several polemics

in the musical press. In 1923 his reputation as a composer began to improve. In April he entered into a contract with the Viennese publisher Universal Edition, which brought out all of his music from that point. His String Quartet was heard in August at the Salzburg Festival of the International Society for Contemporary Music, and the work received praise in several newspapers. Erich Kleiber, the new director of the Berlin Staatsoper, expressed interest in staging *Wozzeck* in the German capital, a prospect that was advanced by Hermann Scherchen's performance in Frankfurt in June of 1924 of a suite of extracts from the opera. The way was finally cleared for the Berlin premiere of *Wozzeck*, which occurred on 14 December 1925. Although controversial, the work was a success and established Berg as a major composer in his own right.

Berg now experienced the prerogatives of an internationally celebrated artist, travelling to performances throughout Europe, receiving a monthly stipend from his publisher, and later even purchasing a new automobile. In 1932 he also acquired a villa, the "Waldhaus," near the old Berghof, for use as a summer retreat. Beginning in 1925, Berg adopted Schoenberg's twelve-tone method of composition, but he interpreted the method in a distinctive way and adapted it to music that was far more eclectic in style than Schoenberg's.

In May of 1925 Berg visited the home in Prague of Herbert and Hanna Fuchs-Robettin. Berg's introduction to them came through their mutual friend Alma Mahler, whose husband, Franz Werfel, was Hanna's brother. Although Berg was always filled with respect for and devotion to his wife, he apparently felt at this time the need for a renewal of the intimacy that earlier had inspired his music. This desire led to a powerful infatuation with Hanna. Berg's way of composing had long relied upon hidden symbols to connect his music to his innermost personal life. Numbers, letters formed by note names, and melodic quotations outlined an inner poetic meaning that was often unrelated to, even contradictory of, the outer layer of expression suggested by text, dedication, or external programmatic connotation. Hanna Fuchs now became the muse to all of his remaining compositions, which were laden with secretive references to her and to himself. In a remarkable letter to her dated October 1931, Berg describes his constant yearning for her, saying that he is now forced to act out a false and shallow existence except in his thoughts of her, wherein lies the inspiration for such works as *Lulu*. The reader is reminded of the letters of 1907–1908 from Béla Bartók to his muse, Stefi Geyer, in which the woman herself seems scarcely to exist apart from a beloved, obsessional ideal that is at the very root of the composer's creativity.

The success of *Wozzeck* made Berg think almost immediately of composing another opera. He considered various literary works as prospective subjects, settling in 1928 upon Frank Wedekind's Lulu plays (*Erdgeist* and *Die Büchse der Pandora*). As in *Wozzeck* he needed to shorten the source plays to make them suitable as a libretto, but in the new opera his revisions departed so extensively from his literary source as to constitute a distinctive version. Work on the new opera was interrupted by two lucrative commissions—a concert aria (*Der Wein*) for the soprano Ruzena Herlinger and a violin concerto for the American virtuoso Louis Krasner. The latter work has a funereal character, and it is dedicated to Manon Gropius, daughter of Alma Mahler and Walter Gropius, who died in April 1935 at the age of eighteen. Since Berg's correspondence of 1935 speaks of intimations of his own death, the work may also refer obliquely to his personal feelings of mortality, comparable to Mahler's "Der Abschied" from *Das Lied von der Erde* and numerous other great last works.

Berg's final years were troubled. With the rise of the Nazis in Germany, there were ever fewer performances of *Wozzeck*, and the type of music that he composed was then under outright attack throughout the German-speaking world. Schoenberg had fled Europe for America in 1933, and Berg's health was worse then ever. In the summer of 1935 he began to suffer from painful, recurrent abscesses. In November he remarked to friends that he could not live much longer. On 17 December he was hospitalized, whereupon blood poisoning was diagnosed. A series of heart attacks ensued, and the composer died on 24 December 1935 with Helene at his side. The circumstances leading to Berg's death were reported to Schoenberg in detail by several members of their circle. A letter from Erwin Stein, dated

17 January 1936, is especially informative: "Helene said that he [Berg] pushed free of his restraints, reared himself up, spread his arms and said repeatedly, 'Es ist genug!' Poor Helene, to have had to witness this. 'This is Lulu's last victim,' she remarked."

Only a few major performances of Berg's music remained in the offing before war again descended upon Europe. The Violin Concerto was premiered in Barcelona, although Webern—scheduled to conduct—was too distracted to do so. Most problematic of all was *Lulu*, since before his death the composer had not quite finished the scoring of Act 3 nor had time to make general revisions. Schoenberg offered to finish the work, but when he saw the unflattering caricature of the Jewish banker Puntschu in Act 3, he declined. An incomplete version, limited to Acts 1 and 2 plus orchestral selections from Act 3, was first heard in Zurich in 1937.

Following the war, Berg's music gradually returned to center stage in international modern music circles. *Wozzeck* was performed ever more widely in the 1950s, including stagings at Covent Garden in 1952 and at the Metropolitan Opera in New York in 1959. *Lulu* remained an enigma since Helene Berg, who lived until 1976, now refused to have the third act completed, published, or the opera performed as a whole. Only after her death and in spite of stipulations in her will was the entire work performed, with Act 3 completed and the whole opera revised by the Viennese composer Friedrich Cerha. The first complete performance took place in Paris in 1979.

Berg's Music

Berg's music followed the same stylistic evolution as that of his teacher, Schoenberg, although their works are not especially similar in specifics of style or structure. The early pieces by both composers are in the German late-romantic idiom, which Schoenberg used until about 1908 and Berg until about 1910. After this time both composers wrote atonal music (a term they rejected on semantic grounds). Schoenberg concisely defined atonality as a style that "treats dissonances like consonances and renounces a tonal centre." In his radio dialogue "What Is Atonality?" Berg adduced other characteristic features of such music: traditional forms are still encountered, thematic work is central to its expansion, counterpoint is intensified, phrasing is irregular, and rhythm and meter are proselike.

In the early 1920s Schoenberg developed a "twelve-tone" compositional method that allowed him to have systematic control over the harmonic and melodic structure of his otherwise atonal music. Berg adopted aspects of this method beginning with the 1925 song setting of "Schließe mir die Augen beide," although he had already referred to certain elements of Schoenberg's method in the Chamber Concerto (1923–25). Like every other major composer who has written twelve-tone music—Webern, Stravinsky, Krenek, Hauer, Boulez, Copland, and Britten among them—Berg developed his own distinctive interpretation of the method and produced music that was unique in style. As with Schoenberg, Berg used the twelve-tone method in music that had a more traditional tone than had been apparent earlier, conforming to an international movement of the 1920s and 30s in which traditional musical materials, forms, and styles gained favor.

Berg's music can thus be divided into three periods—tonal/romantic, atonal, and twelve-tone. Many characteristics are shared commonly by the music of all three: the presence of reinterpreted classical forms (including sonata-allegro form, variational forms, and ternary or otherwise symmetrical schema), organic unity based on continuous variations upon initial motivic or thematic shapes, eclectic harmonic structures based on triadic, whole-tone, and quartal collections of notes, and ever-present referential or rhetorical gestures including quotations, latent semantic symbols, or programmatic narratives.

Music of the first of these three periods is mainly devoted to the genre of song, as exemplified by the Seven Early Songs; Four Songs, Op. 2; and numerous early songs published posthumously. Under Schoenberg's tutelage, instrumental composition was also undertaken, resulting in the Piano Sonata, Op. 1, among other works. In all of these pieces, elements of the late-romantic German idiom are plain: an enriched harmonic vocabulary in which whole-tone formations are especially characteristic, an attenuated sense of key, dense and contrapuntal textures, hyperemotive expressivity, irregular phrasing and proselike rhythm, and extensive motivic development. Berg often chose poetry by late nineteenth-century German writers that shared an overstated, emotive tone with the music, and he was especially fond of poetry that referred to sleep and dreams. The lyric element in these songs is often suppressed in favor of a declamatory vocal line, and ternary forms are most typical.

In his second or atonal period (1910–23) Berg's music is more equally divided between vocal and instrumental genres. His works are also more eclectic than those in the earlier style, as he experimented with a succession of different idioms: In the Four Pieces for clarinet and piano, Op. 5, he tried his hand at the "aphoristic" manner of his friend Webern, in which a piece was radically abbreviated and concentrated. The Orchestral Pieces, Op. 6, make overt references to the symphonic style of Mahler, despite the absence of traditional tonal plans. The String Quartet, Op. 3, is Schoenbergian in its complex linearity, pervasively dissonant harmonies, and far-reaching motivic work.

The opera *Wozzeck* is the masterpiece of this period, and it is a work in which Berg asserts his own artistic and expressive vision. Although highly original, the overall dramaturgical conception is indebted to Debussy's *Pelléas et Mélisande* in its succession of dramatic tableaux connected by orchestral interludes and in its direct adoption of a preexistent spoken play as a libretto. The background of Wagnerian musical rhetoric is also evident in the use of an elaborate leitmotivic apparatus. The music is again eclectic, mixing elements of tonality, atonality, ultrachromaticism, lyricism, declamation, strict and free forms. In his own statements about the opera Berg chose to emphasize its traditional elements, especially the presence in the various scenes and interludes of forms drawn from classical instrumental music.

Berg's twelve-tone method, to which he turned in 1925 and used in all later works, was uniquely his own. He devised new ways of generating forms of a tone row beyond transposition, inversion, and retrograde motion, he sometimes used multiple basic series in a piece, he freely introduced non-twelve-tone pitch structures, and he preferred tone rows exhibiting familiar substructures (e.g., diatonic scalar patterns or triadic subsets). His twelve-tone works—"Schließe mir die Augen beide," Lyric Suite for string quartet, concert aria *Der Wein*, Violin Concerto, and opera *Lulu*—also reveal traditional styles: They tend to be more melodious, regular in phrasing and rhythm, relaxed in texture, and euphonious than were his earlier atonal compositions.

Trends in Research

Until the late 1950s published research on Alban Berg was generally limited to the work of the composer's friends and students, including Theodor Adorno (1903–69), Willi Reich (1898–1980), and Erwin Stein (1885–1958). The first important book on Berg was Reich's *Alban Berg* (no. 919) of 1937. During the last years of Berg's life, Reich had been preparing a study of his teacher, and following Berg's untimely death a sense of urgency entered into his work. The resulting volume was a collaboration among Reich, who provided biographical information, Adorno, and Ernst Krenek, who wrote the analytic portions. As in virtually all of Reich's other studies of composers, this book was to a considerable extent documentary, incorporating writings by the composer himself. Reich was also the author in the 1930s of the first detailed English-language analytic studies of *Wozzeck* and *Lulu* (nos. 237 and 429). He immigrated permanently to Switzerland in 1938 and, following the war, wrote two additional documentary monographs on Berg (nos. 917 and 918). Ironically, he was not in the forefront of the new discoveries concerning Berg in the 1960s and 70s and, in fact, came under pointed criticism for mythologizing Berg in his pioneering works.

The growth in Berg's reputation as a composer in the 1950s and 60s was accompanied by the appearance of important new sources of information. A general study in 1957 by Hans Redlich (no. 908) contained a new and detailed analysis of the music and dispensed with Reich's documentary approach, although Redlich's work was not spared an ample measure of criticism from Stein, Reich, and others who had known the composer personally. The appearance in 1965 of a volume of letters from Berg to his wife (no. 67) greatly added to an understanding of the man, although Berg's widow was faulted for denying scholars access to the original documents, suppressing letters contained in an abortive earlier edition, and failing to place the letters in an informative context. Theodor Adorno's 1968 book on Berg (no. 667) was also a disappointment to many, as it was largely a compilation of earlier published writings and did not reveal Adorno's intimate personal knowledge of the composer nor contain new insights about the music.

A new era in Berg research began in the 1960s, led by George Perle and other scholars in America and England. It was characterized by the study of two issues: atonal and twelve-tone pitch structures and the incomplete state of *Lulu*. New insights into the first of these areas of research had been provided earlier by Milton Babbitt, who studied the resources of twelve-tone music by applying ideas from mathematics, especially from set theory. Babbitt's methods were taken in new directions by Allen Forte, David Lewin, and George Perle, among others, but only Perle significantly addressed works by Berg, the others turning more to Schoenberg and Webern for examples. Perle's *Serial Composition and Atonality* (1962) gave considerable attention to Berg's twelve-tone method, especially as it applied to *Lulu*. Perle's interest in this opera inevitably led him to attack the restriction upon completing and performing its third act, although Perle's campaign proved futile so long as Helene Berg was alive.

The late 1970s was the heyday for Berg research. Major studies of Berg by Mosco Carner (no. 714) and Douglas Jarman (no. 801) appeared. By the end of the decade *Lulu* had at last been performed and published in its entirety, and, following the passing in 1976 of Berg's widow, sensitive details about Berg's relations with Hanna Fuchs-Robettin and their impact upon his music were brought into the open. In 1977 Berg's manuscripts that had remained in Mrs. Berg's possession were deposited at the Austrian National Library and were opened to serious scholars from around the globe.

The 1980s were not lacking for major advances in Berg research. Of great importance was the appearance of catalogs of the Berg collection at the Austrian National Library (nos. 785 and 786), the first issue of Berg's *Sämtliche Werke*, hitherto unpublished early songs and piano music, selections from the

Berg-Schoenberg correspondence (704), and Perle's monographic studies of *Wozzeck* and *Lulu*, which summarized decades of his involvement with these two works.

The future for Berg research remains bright and challenging. Perhaps the most basic need in understanding Berg's music is the location of a generally acceptable analytic model for posttonal music. None currently exists, at least none that receives broad support from leading analysts in Europe and America. Berg's personal and artistic relationship with Schoenberg is an important and complex issue that still remains open. Berg's correspondence with Webern, still largely unpublished, may well prove more revealing of the man than his letters with Schoenberg. His enigmatic relations with women, so important for his creative impulse, may still be studied fruitfully.

Many important documents concerning Berg will probably emerge in the future, including letters by Berg and, most important, musical manuscripts that his widow gave away. Berg also gave numerous interviews for European newspapers during the last decade of his life, and these are still largely unaccounted for. But these and other future directions in Berg research will of necessity build upon the work that has already been done.

2

Music by Berg

This chapter contains citations of Berg's published musical works, chronologically arranged and divided into original compositions and arrangements. A partial survey of unpublished or fragmentary pieces is found in Rosemary Hilmar (no. 785). Citations of arrangements of Berg's music are limited to those arrangements prepared or overseen by the composer himself, and a few of the early musical manuscripts published in facsimile are omitted. The enumeration of publications is selective, including only first editions, major revisions, and other important printings. Works of doubtful authenticity are enclosed in parentheses, and titles not given by Berg are placed in brackets.

Original Compositions

1. *Jugendlieder: 23 Ausgewählte Lieder*/Songs of Youth: 23 Selected Songs. 2 volumes. Edited by Christopher Hailey. Vienna: Universal Edition (identifying nos. 18143, 18144), 1985, 1987. Composed: ca. 1901–1908.

Volume 1 (1901–1904, contents presented here in alphabetical order by title):

Abschied (Elimar von Monsterberg-Muenckenau)
Am Abend (Emanuel Geibel)
Es wandelt, was wir schauen (Joseph von Eichendorff)
Ferne Lieder (Friedrich Rückert)
Geliebte Schöne (Heinrich Heine)
Grabschrift (Ludwig Jakobowski)
Grenzen der Menschheit (Goethe)
Herbstgefühl (Siegfried Fleischer)

Ich liebe dich! (Christian Grabbe)
Ich will die Fluren meiden (Friedrich Rückert)
Im Morgengrauen (Karl Stieler)
Liebe (Rainer Maria Rilke)
Lied des Schiffermädels (Otto Julius Bierbaum)
Schattenleben (Martin Greif)
Schlummerlose Nächte (Martin Greif)
Sehnsucht I (Paul Hohenberg)
Sehnsucht II (Heinrich Heine)
Sehnsucht III (Paul Hohenberg)
Spielleute (Henrik Ibsen)
Sternefall (Karl Wilhelm)
Vielgeliebte schöne Frau (Heinrich Heine)
Vorüber! (Franz Wisbacher)
Wo der Goldregen steht (F. Lorenz)

Volume 2   (1904–1908):

Am Strande (Georg Scherer)
Augenblicke (Robert Hamerling)
Er klagt, daß der Frühling (Arno Holz)
Erster Verlust (Goethe)
Eure Weisheit (Johannes Georg Fischer)
Flötenspielerin (Peter Altenberg)
Fraue, du Süße (Ludwig Finckh)
Hoffnung (Peter Altenberg)
Leukon (Johann Wilhelm Ludwig Gleim)
Mignon (Goethe)
Die Näherin (Rainer Maria Rilke)
Regen (Johannes Schlaf)
So regnet es (Cäsar Flaischlen)
Die Sorglichen (Gustav Falke)
Spaziergang (Alfred Mombert)
Das stille Königreich (Karl Busse)
Süss sind mir (Karl Ernst Knodt)
Tiefe Sehnsucht (Detlev von Liliencron)
Traum (Frida Semler)
Traurigkeit (Peter Altenberg)
Über den Bergen (Karl Busse)
Verlassen (Bohemian folk text)

Winter (Johannes Schlaf)

2. *Frühe Klaviermusik: Ausgewählte Stücke*/Early Piano Music: Selected Pieces. 2 volumes. Edited by Rudolf Stephan. Vienna: Universal Edition (18145, 18146), 1990, 1985. Composed ca. 1907–1908.

Volume 1:

Menuet, F major
Piece, F minor
Piece, C minor
Piece, B minor
Kleiner Walzer, G major
Theme and Variation, A minor
Theme and Variation, F minor
Piece, C# minor
Impromptu, E major
Piece, C minor

Volume 2:

12 Variationen über ein eigenes Thema/12 Variations on an Original Theme. Composed 1908. First performance Vienna 1908. Facsimile of the composer's manuscript in Redlich (no. 908).

3. *Zwei Lieder: Schließe mir die Augen beide, 1900–1925*/Two Songs: "Close Both My Eyes" (Theodor Storm) for voice and piano. Two settings, composed 1907 and 1925.
Publications: *Die Musik* 22 (1930): 347–54. Revised edition, edited by Hans F. Redlich, English text by Eric Smith, Vienna: Universal Edition (12241), 1955.

4. *Sieben frühe Lieder für eine Singstimme und Klavier*/Seven Early Songs for voice and piano. Composed ca. 1905–1908. First performance Vienna 1907 (nos. 2–4).
Publication: Vienna and Leipzig: Universal Edition (8853), 1928.

1. Im Zimmer (Johannes Schlaf)
2. Die Nachtigall (Theodor Storm)

3. Liebesode (Otto Hartleben)
4. Traumgekrönt (Rainer Maria Rilke)
5. Sommertage (Paul Hohenberg)
6. Nacht (Karl Hauptmann)
7. Schilflied (Nikolaus Lenau)

4a. *Sieben frühe Lieder.* Arranged in 1928 for voice and orchestra. First performance Vienna 1928.
Publication: (score) Vienna: Universal Edition (12479), 1928.

5. *Sonate für Klavier*/Piano Sonata, Op. 1. Composed 1907–1908. First performance Vienna 1911.
Publications: Berlin: Verlag der Schlesinger'schen Buch- und Musikhandlung (Rob. und Wilh. Lienau); Vienna: Carl Haslinger (S.9539), n.d. (1910). New revised edition, Berlin: Lienau; Vienna: Haslinger, 1925.

1. Mäßig bewegt

6. *An Leukon*/To Leukon. Song for voice and piano (Johann Gleim, "Rosen pflücke, Rosen blühn"). Composed ca. 1908.
Publications: Reich 1963 (no. 918): 102–103; Reich 1965 (no. 918): 110–111; Berg (no. 1), volume 2: 48–49.

7. *Vier Lieder für eine Singstimme mit Klavier*/Four Songs for voice and piano, Op. 2. Composed 1909–10. First performances Vienna and Dresden 1919.
Publications: Berlin: Verlag der Schlesingerschen Buch- und Musikhandlung (Rob. und Wilh. Lienau); Vienna: Carl Haslinger (S.9540), n.d. (1910). Revised version, Vienna: Haslinger, 1920. New revised version, Vienna: Universal Edition (S.9540), 1928. Song no. 4 in *Der blaue Reiter*, 238–39, edited by Vasili Kandinsky and Franz Marc (Munich: Piper, 1912).

1. Schlafen, schlafen, nichts als schlafen (Friedrich Hebbel)
2. Schlafend trägt man mich (Alfred Mombert)
3. Nun ich der Riesen Stärksten (Mombert)
4. Warm die Lüfte (Mombert)

8. *Streichquartett/*String Quartet, Op. 3. Composed 1910. First performance Vienna 1911.

Publications: (scores) Berlin: Verlag der Schlesingersche Buch- und Musikhandlung (Rob. Lienau); Vienna: Carl Haslinger (A.B.2), 1920. Second revised version, Vienna and New York: Universal Edition (7538, miniature score 7537), 1925.

Parts: Berlin: Verlag der Schlesingersche Buch- und Musikhandlung (Rob. Lienau); Vienna: Carl Haslinger (A.B.3), 1920.

1. Langsam
2. Mäßige Viertel

9. *Fünf Orchesterlieder nach Ansichtskartentexten von Peter Altenberg/*Five Orchestral Songs to Picture Postcard Texts by Peter Altenberg, Op. 4. Composed 1912. First performance Vienna 1913 (probably songs nos. 2 and 3), Rome 1952 or 1953 (complete cycle).

Publications: (score) Vienna: Universal Edition (14325), 1953, English version by A. Kitchin.

Piano-vocal arrangement: song no. 5 in *Menschen: Zeitschrift neuer Kunst* 4/5–6 (1921): 87–92, reprinted in MQ 34 (1948): 487–511. Full cycle, Vienna: Universal Edition (12126), 1953.

1. Seele wie bist du schöner
2. Sahst du nach dem Gewitterregen
3. Über die Grenzen des All
4. Nichts ist gekommen
5. Hier ist Friede

9a. *Hier ist Friede, Op. 4, no. 5: Eigenhändiges Arrangement des Orchesterliedes für Klavier, Harmonium, Violine und Violoncello/*Here is Peace, Op. 4, no. 5, autograph arrangement of the orchestral song for piano, harmonium, violin, and cello.

Publication: (facsimile of the composer's manuscript score) Vienna: Universal Edition (19322), 1989.

10. *Symphonie-Fragmente/*Symphony Fragments. In Alban Berg, *Sämtliche Werke*. Edited by Rudolf Stephan. Vienna: Alban

Berg-Stiftung in der Universal Edition (18142), 1984. Composed 1913.

Contains sketches, fragments, and a short score of an incomplete symphony that may have included a passacaglia movement. Transcriptions and facsimiles are given.

11. *Vier Stücke für Klarinette und Klavier*/Four Pieces for clarinet and piano, Op. 5. Composed 1913. First performance Vienna 1919.

Publications: Berlin: Verlag der Schlesinger'schen Buch- und Musikhandlung (Robert Lienau); Berlin: Carl Haslinger (identifying no. 1), 1920. New edition, Vienna and New York: Universal Edition (7485), 1924.

1. Mäßig
2. Sehr langsam
3. Sehr rasch
4. Langsam

12. *Drei Orchesterstücke*/Three Orchestral Pieces, Op. 6. Composed 1914–15. First performance Berlin 1923 (movement 1–2), Oldenburg 1930 (complete work).

Publications: (scores) facsimile of the composer's manuscript, Vienna and New York: Universal Edition (7396), 1923. "New version 1929," Vienna: Universal Edition (7396, 12194), 1954.

1. Präludium
2. Reigen
3. Marsch

13. *Georg Büchner's Wozzeck: Oper in 3 Aufzügen (15 Szenen)*/Georg Büchner's *Wozzeck*: Opera in 3 Acts (15 scenes), Op. 7. Composed 1917–22. First performance Berlin 1925.

Publications: (scores) Vienna and Leipzig: Universal Edition (7379), 1926. Revision by Hans E. Apostel, English text by Eric Blackall and Vida Harford, Vienna: Universal Edition (12100), 1955.

Piano-vocal arrangements (by Fritz Heinrich Klein): no place: Eigentum des Komponisten (AB4), n.d. (1922). Vienna and Leipzig: Universal Edition (7382), 1926. Revised edition with additional markings for the vocal parts provided by the composer, Vienna and Leipzig: Universal Edition (7382), 1929. Revision by Hans E. Apostel, English text by Eric Blackall and Vida Harford, Vienna: Universal Edition (7382), 1955.

13a. *Drei Bruchstücke für Gesang mit Orchester aus der Oper Wozzeck (nach Georg Büchners Drama).* . . . *Ausgabe für konzertmäßige Aufführungen*/Three Fragments for voice and orchestra from the opera *Wozzeck* (based on Georg Büchner's Drama). . . . Edition for concert performances. Arranged 1924. First performance Frankfurt 1924.

Publications: (score) Vienna and New York: Universal Edition (7660), 1924.

Piano-vocal arrangement (by Fritz Heinrich Klein): Vienna and New York: Universal Edition (7662), 1924.

1. Aus dem I. Akt, 2.–3. Scene
2. Beginn des III. Aktes
3. Aus dem III. Akt, 4.–5. Scene

14. *Kammerkonzert für Klavier und Geige mit Begleitung von dreizehn Bläsern*/Chamber Concerto for piano and violin accompanied by thirteen wind instruments. Composed 1923–25. First performance Berlin 1927.

Publications: (score) facsimile of the composer's manuscript, Vienna and New York: Universal Edition (8393), 1925.

Arrangement for two pianos and violin (by Fritz Heinrich Klein): Vienna and New York: Universal Edition (8439, 8439a), 1926.

1. Thema scherzoso con variazioni
2. Adagio
3. Rondo ritmico con introduzione

14a. *Adagio. II. Satz aus dem Kammerkonzert vom Komponisten bearbeitet für Violine, Klarinette in B, und Klavier*/Adagio. Second movement from the Chamber Concerto arranged by the composer for violin, clarinet in B♭, and piano. Arranged 1935. First performance Vienna 1935.

Publication: (score and parts) Vienna: Universal Edition (12242), 1956.

15. *Lyrische Suite für Streichquartett*/Lyric Suite for string quartet. Composed 1925–26. First performance Vienna 1927.

Publication: (score and parts), Vienna and Leipzig: Wiener Philharmonischer Verlag in der Universal Edition (U.E.8780, W.Ph.V.173), 1927.

1. Allegretto gioviale
2. Andante amoroso
3. Allegro misterioso/Trio estatico
4. Adagio appassionato
5. Presto delirando/Tenebroso
6. Largo desolato

15a. *Drei Stücke aus der Lyrischen Suite*/Three Pieces from the Lyric Suite arranged for string orchestra. Arranged 1928. First performance Berlin 1929.

Publication: (score) Vienna and Leipzig: Universal Edition (ES 41), 1928.

1. Andante amoroso
2. Allegro misterioso/Trio estatico
3. Adagio appassionato

16. *Le Vin. Der Wein. Air de concert avec orchestre. Konzertarie mit Orchester*/Wine: concert aria with orchestra. Composed 1929. First performance Königsberg 1930.

Publications: (score) Vienna and Leipzig: Universal Edition (9957), 1930.

Piano-vocal arrangement (by Erwin Stein): Vienna and Leipzig: Universal Edition (9957), 1930.

17. *Kanon "In deines Lebens fünfzig Jahren"*/Canon "In the fifty years of your life." Four part canon in honor of the performance of Schoenberg's *Von heute auf morgen* and the fiftieth anniversary of the Frankfurt Opera. Composed 1930. First performance Frankfurt 1930.

Publications: Program book for the first performance ("50 Jahre Opernhaus"), Frankfurt, 1930; facsimile of the composer's autograph manuscript, Vienna: Universal Edition (18895), 1987; Reich 1963 (no. 918): 108; Reich 1965 (no. 918): 116; Berg (no. 68): 312.

18. *Violinkonzert*/Violin Concerto. Composed 1935. First performance Barcelona 1936.

Publications: (score) Vienna, London: Philharmonia Partituren in der Universal Edition (12195, Philharmonia no. 426), 1936.

Arrangement for violin and piano (by Rita Kurzmann, revised by Alban Berg): Vienna: Universal Edition (10903, 10903a), 1936.

1. Andante—Allegretto
2. Allegro—Adagio

19. *Lulu. Oper in drei Akten nach Frank Wedekinds Tragödien "Erdgeist" und "Büchse der Pandora"*/Lulu. Opera in three acts based on Frank Wedekind's tragedies *Earth Spirit* and *Pandora's Box*. Composed 1927–35 (incomplete). First performance Zurich 1937 (Acts 1–2), Paris 1979 (opera in three acts completed by Friedrich Cerha).

Publications: (scores) Acts 1–2, edited by Hans E. Apostel, Vienna: Universal Edition (12864, 13640a), 1964. Revised by Friedrich Cerha, Vienna: Universal Edition (12864, 13640a), 1985. Act 3, revised and completed by Friedrich Cerha, Vienna: Universal Edition (12864, 13640b), 1978.

Piano-vocal arrangements (by Erwin Stein): Acts 1–2, Vienna: Universal Edition (10745), 1936, revised by Friedrich Cerha, Vienna: Universal Edition (10745a), 1978. Act 3, revised and completed by Friedrich Cerha, Vienna: Universal Edition (10745b), 1978 (updated 1985).

19a. *Symphonische Stücke aus der Oper Lulu. Nach den Tragödien "Erdgeist" und "Büchse der Pandora" von Frank Wedekind*/Symphonic Pieces from the opera *Lulu*. Based on the tragedies *Earth Spirit* and *Pandora's Box* by Frank Wedekind. Arranged 1934. First performance Berlin 1934.

Publication: (score) Vienna: Universal Edition (10228), 1935.

1. Rondo
2. Ostinato
3. Lied der Lulu
4. Variationen
5. Adagio

19b. *Lied der Lulu*/Lulu's Song (from Act 2, scene 1 of the opera).

Publications: (score) facsimile edition from the composer's autograph manuscript presented to Anton Webern, edited by Franz Patzer for the Wiener Stadt- und Landesbibliothek, Vienna: Universal Edition, 1985.

Piano-vocal arrangement (by Erwin Stein): Vienna: Universal Edition (10229), 1935.

Arrangements

20. Franz Schreker. *Der ferne Klang.* Piano-vocal score arranged by Alban Berg (with possible contributions by Josef von Wöss). Arranged 1911.

Publication: Vienna: Universal Edition (3096), 1911.

21. *Gurre-Lieder von Jens Peter Jacobsen (Deutsch von Robert Franz Arnold) für Soli, Chor und Orchester von Arnold Schönberg. Klavierauszug von Alban Berg*/Songs from Gurre by Jens Peter Jacobsen (German by Robert Franz Arnold) for solo voices, chorus, and orchestra by Arnold Schoenberg. Piano-vocal score by Alban Berg. Arranged 1912.

Publication: Vienna and Leipzig: Universal Edition (3696), 1912. Also *Einzelausgaben* of four songs—Waldemar's "So tanzen die Engel," Tove's "Nun sag ich," Waldemar's "Du wunderliche Tove," and the Song of the Wood Dove—Vienna and Leipzig: Universal Edition (5330–5333), 1914.

(22. *Arnold Schönbergs Verklärte Nacht.* . . . *Bearbeitung für Streichorchester*/Arnold Schoenberg's *Transfigured Night.* . . .) Arrangement for string orchestra. Arranged ca. 1917.
    Publications: (score) Berlin: Verlag Dreililien, 1917.
    Parts: Vienna: Universal Edition [6066a–g], n.d.

According to the report by Rosemary Hilmar (no. 785), the Berg Collection in the Austrian National Library contains a copy of the first edition of Schoenberg's *Verklärte Nacht* with additions in Berg's hand making the work usable for string orchestra. Whether this is evidence that Berg himself took part in preparing the published arrangement of Schoenberg's Sextet is unknown (although unlikely).

23. *Entrückung (Stefan George).* *IV. Satz aus dem II. Streichquartett Op. 10 von Arnold Schönberg. Für eine Sopranstimme und Klavier.* *Klavierauszug von Alban Berg*/Rapture (Stefan George). Fourth movement from the Second String Quartet, Op. 10, by Arnold Schoenberg. For soprano and piano. Piano-vocal score by Alban Berg. Arrangement ca. 1920.
    Publication: Vienna and Leipzig: Universal Edition (6863), 1921.

24. *Litanei (Stefan George).* *III. Satz aus dem II. Streichquartett op. 10 von Arnold Schönberg.* *Für eine Sopranstimme und Klavier.* *Klavierauszug von Alban Berg*/Litany (Stefan George). Third movement from the Second String Quartet, op. 10, by Arnold Schoenberg. For soprano and piano. Piano-vocal score by Alban Berg. Arranged ca. 1920.
    Publication: Vienna and Leipzig: Universal Edition (6862), 1921.

25. Johann Strauss. *Wein, Weib und Gesang: Walzer*/Wine, Woman, and Song: Waltz, Op. 333. Arranged for small ensemble by Alban Berg. Arranged 1921. First performance Vienna 1921.
    Publication: (score) Vienna: Universal Edition (17103), 1977.

3

Berg's Published Writings, Interviews, Lectures, and Libretti

The citations in this chapter are arranged in chronological order by date of publication. Titles are drawn from first editions; if an item lacked a title in the earliest edition, a bracketed title is supplied by the compiler of this guide. Works of doubtful authenticity are enclosed in parentheses.

(26. "Arnold Schönbergs Fis-Moll-Quartett: Eine technische Analyse.") *Erdgeist* 4/7 (1909): 225–34. Reprinted in JASI 16 (1993): 295–304. In German.

English translation: "Arnold Schoenberg's F# Minor Quartet: A Technical Analysis," translated by Mark DeVoto, JASI 16 (1993): 305–21.

> The analysis, which deals with thematic and formal aspects of Schoenberg's String Quartet no. 2, was published preceding a performance of the work in Vienna in 1909. The article is a collaborative work ("from the composer's circle") to which Berg may have made at most a minor contribution.

27. [Index to *Harmonielehre* by Arnold Schoenberg]. Vienna: Universal Edition, 1911.

28. "Dem Lehrer." In *Sammelband: Arnold Schönberg*. Munich: Piper, 1912. Reprinted Munich and Zurich: Piper; Wels: Welsermühl, 1980. Berg's article reprinted in Reich 1937 (no. 919): 137; Reich 1959 (no. 917): 15–16; Reich 1963 (no. 918): 35–36, Berg (no. 68): 35–36. In German.

English translation: "To the Teacher," in Reich 1965 (no. 918): 36–37.

French translation: "Au maître," in Pousseur (no. 64): 26–27.

Italian translation: "Al maestro—1912" in Mancini (no. 837): 73–74.

Brief tribute to Schoenberg as teacher. "Genius has always been didactic. Its speech is instructive, its activities are exemplary, its works are revelations," Berg writes.

29. *Arnold Schönberg: Gurrelieder. Führer.* Leipzig, Vienna: Universal Edition, 1913. Reprinted in Reich 1959 (no. 917): 24–25 (Foreword only); Berg (no. 68): 37–142; Alban Berg, *Sämtliche Werke*, part 3, volume 1: 1–81, edited by Rudolf Stephan and Regina Busch (Vienna: Universal Edition, 1994). In German.

English translation: "Arnold Schoenberg: Gurrelieder. Guide," translated by Mark DeVoto, JASI 16 (1993): 24–233.

Berg wrote his Guide to *Gurrelieder* to coincide with the premier performance of the work in Vienna in 1913. He describes his objectives in the Foreword: "I have tried to speak with cool objectivity, about the different things in the music as they appear: in one place about harmonic structure . . ., in other places about the construction of motives, themes, melodies, and transitions; about the form and synthesis of large musical structures, about contrapuntal combinations, choral writing, voice-leading, and finally about the nature of the instrumentation."

30. *Arnold Schönberg: Gurrelieder. Führer (kleine Ausgabe).* Leipzig, Vienna: Universal Edition, 1914. Reprinted in Alban Berg, *Sämtliche Werke*, part 3, volume 1: 1–81, edited by Rudolf Stephan and Regina Busch (Vienna: Universal Edition, 1994). In German.

An extensively abbreviated version of no. 29.

31. [Miscellaneous writings for the K. K. Kriegsministerium, 1916–18].

Berg was assigned during the later part of his wartime
military service as scrivener for the Austrian War Ministry.
In a letter to his wife of 12 June 1917, he tells of a recently
published 30–page Ordinance that he had written—"a
substitute for creative work," he said. It is unlikely that Berg
was author, strictly speaking, of this or of any other military
documents.

**32. *Arnold Schönberg: Kammersymphonie, Op. 9: Thematische
Analyse.*** Vienna, Leipzig: Universal Edition, n.d. (1918).
Reprinted in Berg (no. 68): 143–60; Berg, *Sämtliche Werke*, part 3,
volume 1: 119–31, edited by Rudolf Stephan and Regina Busch
(Vienna: Universal Edition, 1994). In German.

English translation: "Arnold Schoenberg: Chamber
Symphony, Op. 9. Thematic Analysis," translated by Mark
DeVoto, JASI 16 (1993): 236–68.

Berg's thematic guide was intended for the knowledgeable
musical amateur. It deals in general with the large-scale
form of Schoenberg's Chamber Symphony and the
application of thematic materials within this form.

33. [Verein für musikalische Privataufführungen in Wien:
prospectuses and miscellaneous publications]. In German.

"Prospekt des Vereins für musikalische Privataufführungen,"
no place: no publisher, no date (February 1919). Reprinted in
Reich 1937 (no. 919): 138–41; Rufer 1956 (no. 950): 207; Reich 1963
(no. 918): 44–46; Berg (no. 68): 173–76. English translation:
"Society for Private Musical Performances in Vienna," in Reich
1965 (no. 918): 46–49; Smith (no. 985): 245–48; Nicolas Slonimsky,
Music since 1900, 1024–27, fifth edition (New York: Schirmer
Books, 1994). French translation: "La Société Viennoise
d'Exécutions Musicales Privées," in Pousseur (no. 64): 33–37.

"Prospekt des Vereins für musikalische Privataufführungen,
September 1919," no place: no publisher. Reprinted in Hilmar
1978 (no. 780): 184–86; MK 36 (1984): 2–7; Berg (no. 68): 177–81.

Berg was almost certainly the author of these two
anonymous prospectuses concerning the Society for Private
Musical Performances, as well as of *Mitteilungen* to members

of the Society during its first two seasons (1918–20). The prospectus of February 1919 contains a statement of the aims of the Society—to present modern music in well-prepared performances that can be frequently repeated and heard without applause or review. The prospectus of September 1919 is more detailed in its exposition of principles, adding that the Society is allied to no particular style of modern music and being more specific about rules of membership. There is also a report on the preceding season of the Society, listing the composers and performers who were heard.

34. "Die musikalische Impotenz der 'neuen Aesthetik' Hans Pfitzners." MBA 2 (1920): 399–408. Reprinted in Reich 1937 (no. 919): 181–92; Reich 1963 (no. 918): 194–206; Berg (no. 68): 191–204. In German.

English translation: "The Musical Impotence of Hans Pfitzner's 'New Aesthetic'," in Reich 1965 (no. 918): 205–18.

French translations: "Alban Berg interprète de Schumann," *Contrepoints* 6 (1949): 43–64; "L'impuissance musicale de la 'Nouvelle esthétique' de Hans Pfitzner," in Pousseur (no. 64): 44–64.

Berg attacks the negative attitude toward modern music expressed in Hans Pfitzner's polemic *Die neue Ästhetik der musikalischen Impotenz* (1919). There, Pfitzner had postulated that the greatness of works like Schumann's "Träumerei" from *Kinderszenen* could not be adequately explained. Their beauty was instead intuitively apparent to all those with a sense for music, just as these people could accurately conclude that modern music was devoid of beauty. Berg holds, on the contrary, that an objective analysis of this or other works can contribute to the listener's appreciation of their aesthetic value. His own detailed analysis of the Schumann piece especially addresses the interrelations among and ingenious use of motifs. Rather than performing a similar analysis on a beautiful modern work, Berg concludes by using Pfitzner's own methods against Pfitzner's song "Nachts," Op. 26, no. 2.

35. *Pelleas und Melisande (Nach dem Drama von Maurice Maeterlinck). Symphonische Dichtung für Orchester von Arnold Schönberg, Op. 5. Kurze thematische Analyse.* Vienna, Leipzig: Universal Edition, n.d. (1920). Reprinted in Berg (no. 68): 161–72; Alban Berg, *Sämtliche Werke*, part 3, volume 1: 83–96, edited by Rudolf Stephan and Regina Busch (Vienna: Universal Edition, 1994). In German.

English translations: "Pelleas and Melisande (After the Play by Maurice Maeterlinck). Symphonic Poem for Orchestra by Arnold Schoenberg, Op. 5. Brief Thematic Analysis," translated by Mark DeVoto, JASI 16 (1993): 270–92; "Pelleas and Melisande. . .," translated by Derrick Puffett (no. 902): 250–64.

Berg cites the primary themes from Schoenberg's tone poem, gives them labels, and observes their recurrences within a symphonic form. Passages from the play are quoted. This 1920 analysis was drawn from a considerably longer analysis, found in the 1994 edition of Berg's *Sämtliche Werke*, pp. 97–118.

36. [*Wozzeck*, selected libretti]. *Georg Büchners Wozzeck: Oper in drei Akten (15 Szenen) Op. 7.* Vienna and New York: Universal Edition (7383), 1923. Reprinted in Csampai and Holland (no. 103): 35–76; Hanselmann (no. 134): 51–153. In German.

English translation: *Georg Büchner's Wozzeck: Opera in Three Acts (15 Scenes) Op. 7.* Translated by Eric Blackall and Vida Harford (London: A. A. Kalmus; Bryn Mawr: T. Presser) 1952. Reprinted in John (no. 156): 60–110.

French translations: *Wozzeck: Texte de l'opéra*, translated by Pierre-Jean Jouve (Monaco: Editions du Rocher), 1964; reprinted in Jouve and Fano (no. 162); *Wozzeck*, translated by Michel Vallois, *L'avant-scène opéra* (no. 80), 19–87.

Italian translations: *Wozzeck*, in Carapezza (no. 96); *Wozzeck*, translated by M. T. Mandelari, in Petazzi (no. 884).

37. "Die musikalischen Formen in meiner Oper *Wozzeck*." *Die Musik* 16 (1924): 587–89. Reprinted in Reich 1937 (no. 919): 178–80; Berg (no. 68): 264–67; Csampai and Holland (no. 103): 150–53. In German.

English translation: "The Musical Forms in My Opera *Wozzeck*," in Jarman, *Alban Berg: Wozzeck* (no. 155): 149–52.

French translation: "A propos des formes musicales employées dans *Wozzeck*," in Pousseur (no. 64): 113–17.

Italian translations: "Le forme musicale nella mia opera *Wozzeck*," in Rognoni 1966 (no. 944): 452–54; "A proposito delle forme musicali utilizzate nel Wozzeck—1924," in Mancini (no. 837): 75–78.

A response to Emil Petschnig's article "Atonales Opernschaffen" (no. 223) in which Berg clarifies aspects of the classical forms used in the opera.

38. "Warum ist Schönbergs Musik so schwer verständlich?" MBA 6 (1924): 329–41. Reprinted in Reich 1937 (no. 919): 142–55; Reich 1963 (no. 918): 179–93; Rauchhaupt (no. 905, 1971 edition only); Rufer 1979 (no. 950): 226–29; Berg (no. 68): 205–20. In German.

English translation: "Why Is Schönberg's Music So Hard to Understand?," translated by Anton Swarowsky and Joseph H. Lederer, MR 13 (1952): 187–96; Reich 1965 (no. 918): 189–204; Rauchhaupt (no. 905, English edition, 1971 only); *Twentieth-Century Music*, 15–24, Garland Library of the History of Western Music, volume 10 (New York and London: Garland, 1985).

French translations: "Pourquoi la musique de Schoenberg est-elle si difficile à comprendre?," in Pousseur (no. 64): 69–92; in Rauchhaupt (no. 905, French edition, 1971 only).

Analysis of phrasing and harmony in the first ten measures of Schoenberg's String Quartet no. 1. See Rosemary Hilmar (no. 784) for information on assistance that Berg may have received from Erwin Stein in writing this essay.

39. "Alban Bergs Kammerkonzert für Geige und Klavier mit Begleitung von dreizehn Bläsern." *Pult und Taktstock* 2 (1925): 23–28. Reprinted in MEL 6 (1927): 261–64; Reich 1937 (no. 919): 86–91; Reich 1963 (no. 918): 135–40; Berg (no. 68): 228–35.

English translations: "Chamber Concerto for Piano and Violin with Thirteen Wind Instruments," in Reich 1965 (no. 918): 143–48; (untitled) in *The Berg-Schoenberg Correspondence* (no. 704): 334–37.

French translation: "Lettre ouverte à Schoenberg, à l'occasion de la dédicace du 'Concerto de chambre'," in Pousseur (no. 64): 101–108.

Italian translations: "Lettera apperta ad Arnold Schönberg," in Rognoni 1954 (no. 944): 277–82 and Rognoni 1966 (no. 944): 433–37; "Lettera a Schönberg, in occasione della dedica del concerto da camera—1925," in Mancini (no. 837): 79–84.

Contains Berg's "open letter" to Schoenberg (dated 9 February 1925) with the dedication of the Chamber Concerto to Schoenberg and Berg's explanation of aspects of the symbolism and structure of the work.

40.   "Bei Alban Berg: Aus einem Gespräch mit dem Komponisten des *Wozzeck*." *Das kleine Journal* (Berlin), 25 January 1926. Reprinted (excerpts) in Hilmar and Brosche (no. 1060): 115. In German.

An interview with Berg concerning *Wozzeck* in which the composer praises the open-mindedness of Berliners compared to the Viennese. Berg disclaims any attempt in this work at creating a new style of opera. "I understand by opera only drama reinforced through the medium of music. This was my sole objective in *Wozzeck*."

41.   "Unterhaltung mit Alban Berg," by Oskar Baum. *Prager Presse*, 12 November 1926. Excerpts reprinted in Hilmar and Brosche (no. 1060): 118–19. In German.

Baum's interview took place immediately before the stormy Prague premiere of *Wozzeck* in November 1926. The composer had high praise for the sound of the work when sung in Czech, and he was optimistic for a good performance.

42.   "Verbindliche Antwort auf eine unverbindliche Rundfrage." In *25 Jahre neue Musik: Jahrbuch 1926 der Universal Edition*, 220–25. Edited by Hans Heinsheimer and Paul Stefan. Vienna, Leipzig, New York: Universal Edition, n.d. (1926). Reprinted in Reich 1937 (no. 919): 156–60; Rufer 1956 (no. 950):

210–12 (excerpt); Rufer 1979 (no. 950): 229–31 (excerpt); Berg (no. 68): 221–26. In German.

Dutch translation: "Toekomstmuziek," *De muziek* 5 (1930–31): 23–27.

Berg's "obliging response to a nonobligatory survey" concerns predictions as to how music will unfold during the next fifty years. He reiterates his belief that the works of Schoenberg will be central to the future of music.

43. "Gespräch mit Alban Berg: Eindrücke von einer *Wozzeck*-Aufführung in Leningrad." *Neues Wiener Journal*, 23 June 1927. Excerpts reprinted in Hilmar and Brosche (no. 1060): 119–20. In German.

Berg reports positively about the recent performance of *Wozzeck* in Leningrad, noting the stylized mise-en-scène and public enthusiasm.

44. "Das 'Opernproblem'." *Neue Musik-Zeitung* (Stuttgart) 49/9 (1928): 285–87. Reprinted in Reich 1937 (no. 919): 174–77; Rufer 1956 (no. 950): 212–14; Reich 1963 (no. 918): 59–61; Rufer 1979 (no. 950): 232–54; Berg (no. 68): 257–60; Csampai and Holland (no. 103): 153–56. In German.

Selected English translations: "The 'Problem of Opera'," in Reich 1965 (no. 918): 63–66; "Problem of the Opera," translated by Henry J. Schmidt in Schmidt, editor, *Georg Büchner: The Complete Collected Works*, 392–94 (New York: Avon Books, 1977).

French translations: "Le 'problème de l'opéra'" in Pousseur (no. 64); 123–27; *L'avant-scène opéra* (no. 81): 14–15.

Italian translations: "Il 'problema dell'opera'" in Rognoni 1954 (no. 944): 283–86, and Rognoni 1966 (no. 944): 438–40; Mancini (no. 837): 85–88.

Spanish translation: "El problema de la opéra," *Pauta* 4/15 (1985): 33–34.

Partial versions: "A Word About *Wozzeck*," *Modern Music* 5/1 (1927–28): 22–24; reprinted in Jarman, *Alban Berg: Wozzeck* (no. 155): 152–53; "Postscript by Alban Berg," in Reich 1952 (no. 237): 1–21; "The Composer Speaks," in David Ewen, ed. *The Book of*

Modern Composers, 341–42 (New York: Alfred A. Knopf, 1943); "The Musical Form in *Wozzeck*," translated by Erwin Stein, in *Opera* 3 (1952): 23–24. German versions of this part are found in *Der Scheinwerfer: Blätter der städtischen Bühnen* (Essen) 3/4 (1929): 3; "*Wozzek*" [sic], in *Neues Wiener Tageblatt*, 25 December 1929, reprinted in Pass (no. 211): 119–21; *Die Musik* 22 (1930): 319; "*Wozzeck*: Bermerkungen von Alban Berg," MBA 12 (1930): 52–53; "*Wozzeck*: Bemerkungen von Alban Berg," in Fritz Mahler (no. 187): 8–9; "Über den *Wozzeck*," in *Die neue Musik: Dokumente zu ihrem Verständnis*, 25–26, edited by Eugen Proebst, Texte, volume 9 (Bamberg: C. C. Buchners Verlag, 1961); "Der Komponist als Regisseur," *Opernwelt* 12/1(1971): 21. A Dutch translation ("Pro domo") is in *De muziek* 5 (1930–31): 1–3.

> This often reprinted essay has a complex history, suggesting that it originated as several separate articles. Its first version was published in English in *Modern Music* in fall 1927 under the title "A Word About *Wozzeck*." Here Berg attempted to refute the belief, widespread among journalists, that the opera established a new direction in the genre by its use of forms from instrumental music. Their appearance, he contended, was solely a response to the nature of the text. The article reappeared in German, somewhat enlarged, in the fall of 1928. Berg then added an introduction commenting upon an idea, also widespread in the German musical press at this time, that opera was in a state of crisis, its future unclear. It is unnecessary to ponder the future of opera, he says, which will be shaped by the appearance of isolated musical masterpieces. These should not be confused with the shallow modernity of *Zeitoper*. The body of the article, essentially synonymous with the original English version, is then put forward as Berg's solution to the "problem" seen in the operatic genre.

45. "Alban Berg zeneszerző két napig Budapesten volt" [Composer Alban Berg in Budapest for Two Days]. *Pesti napló*, 24 February 1928. Reprinted in Breuer (no. 706): 3. In Hungarian.

Berg was in Budapest to attend a performance of the Lyric Suite. In this interview in the *Pesti napló* he dismisses the importance of the demonstrations against *Wozzeck* in Prague in 1926, which he does not believe were directed against the music itself. His current work, he says, is another opera, a setting of a play by Gerhart Hauptmann (*Und Pippa tanzt!*).

46. "Operntheater." MBA 10 (1928): 305. Reprinted in Reich 1937 (no. 919): 173; Reich 1959 (no. 917): 56–57; Reich 1971 (no. 239): 19; Berg (no. 68): 255–56. In German.

French translation: "Théâtre d'opéra," in Pousseur (no. 64): 132.

Berg responds to editors of the Moscow journal *Music and Revolution* on several questions concerning opera and the stage. What do I demand of modern opera theaters? That they perform classic operas as though they were modern, and vice-versa. How do I conceive of the reciprocal relation among music, text, and stage? $A^2 + B^2 = C^2$. Music in this triangular equation need not always be the hypotenuse. Berg's letter is dated 12 September 1928.

47. "Zu Franz Schuberts 100. Todestag." *Vossische Zeitung* (Berlin), 18 November 1928. Reprinted in Reich 1937 (no. 919): 194; Berg (no. 68): 309. In German.

A tribute to Schubert, bitingly ironic in tone, commemorating the hundredth anniversary of his death. Berg does not agree with a common view held in Vienna that tends to equate Schubert and Johann Strauss. But failing to see the distinction between them is only to be expected at a time when people cannot distinguish between a "threepenny opera" and a "thousand dollar symphony."

48. "Die Stimme in der Oper." In *Gesang: Jahrbuch 1929* [of Universal Edition], 349–50. Edited by Hans Heinsheimer and Paul Stephan. Special issue of MBA 10 (1928). Reprinted in Reich 1937 (no. 919): 164–65; Berg (no. 68): 261–63; Csampai and Holland (no. 103): 157–59; and Hanselmann (no. 134): 177–78.

French translation: "La voix dans l'opéra," in Pousseur (no. 64): 138–40.

Italian translation: "La voce nell'opera," in Rognoni 1954 (no. 944): 287–89, and Rognoni 1966 (no. 944): 441–42.

> Berg recommends the greatest diversity for the voice in modern opera, including speaking, rhythmic declamation, recitative, parlando, cantilena, and coloratura. The spirit of the bel canto should not be lost, as it often is in modern operas that are merely "symphonies for large orchestra with accompaniment by voice."

49.   "Alban Berg über seine Oper."   *Aachener Anzeiger*, 20 February 1930. Excerpt reprinted in Hilmar and Brosche (no. 1060): 122–23. In German.

> Prior to a performance of *Wozzeck* in Aachen in March, 1930, Berg discussed the reduced orchestration prepared by Erwin Stein. Berg writes: "The relation of the winds to the strings is easily imperiled when—as in orchestras that are not very large—too few strings are available. The score of *Wozzeck* relies heavily on the sound of the winds and would suffer in a performance if the strings were too weak. So in this new orchestration the number of winds is reduced from fours in the woodwinds and brass to threes."

50.   [Conversation with Oskar Jancke].   *Aachener Anzeiger*, 20 February 1930. Excerpt reprinted in Ernst Hilmar (no. 145): 60–61, and in Hilmar and Brosche (no. 1060): 60. In German.

> The interview concerned *Wozzeck*, prior to its performance in Aachen. "There was for me probably a natural affinity with the text. Let me emphasize also that *Wozzeck* is no simple play about poverty. It can happen to a poor person, as it did to Wozzeck, in whatever mode of dress he may find himself. It can happen to anyone who is oppressed by others and cannot defend himself."

51.   "Credo."   DM 22 (1930): 264–65.   Reprinted in Reich 1937 (no. 919): 161; Berg (no. 68): 227. In German.
French translation: "Credo," in Pousseur (no. 64): 165–66.

Quotes Riemann on Bach's pivotal position between modal and tonal composition and between the ages of counterpoint and homophony, then rewrites passages placing Schoenberg in the same position of importance between diatonic and chromatic composition and between the ages of homophony and the new counterpoint.

52. **"Doppel-Akrostische Distichen für den zehnten Dezember."** *Adolf Loos: Zum 60. Geburtstag am 10. Dezember 1930.* Vienna: Richard Lanyi, 1930. Entire volume reprinted (*Für Adolf Loos*), Vienna: Locker, 1985; Berg's contribution reprinted in Reich 1937 (no. 919): 202; Berg (no. 68): 312. In German.

An acrostic poem on the names Adolf Loos and Alban Berg in honor of the artist.

53. "Kritik der Kritik: Gespräch mit Alban Berg und Clemens Krauß." *Neues Wiener Journal*, 2 April 1930. Reprinted in Pass (no. 211): 121–24. In German.

The interview followed the Viennese premiere of *Wozzeck*. Berg expresses satisfaction with the performance. He adds that a forthcoming edition with smaller orchestration is not at all a simplified version of the work. (This edition was never published and the reduced orchestration is now apparently lost.) He rejects the idea that the opera is devoid of melody and expresses eagerness to compose his new opera, *Lulu*.

54. **"An Karl Kraus."** *Stimmen über Karl Kraus zum 60. Geburtstage.* Vienna: Richard Lanyi, 1934. Reprinted in Reich 1937 (no. 919): 203; Reich 1959 (no. 917): 74; Reich 1963 (no. 918): 32; Berg (no. 68): 320. In German.
English translation: (untitled) in Reich 1965 (no. 918): 32.

Brief tribute to Kraus on his sixtieth birthday. Berg quotes a passage from *Lulu*, Act 2, scene 1 (Alwa's "Eine Seele, die sich im Jenseits den Schlaf aus den Augen reibt"), whose text had been central to Kraus's speech on *Lulu* in 1905.

55. ["Glaube, Hoffnung und Liebe"]. *Arnold Schönberg zum 60. Geburtstag: 13. September 1934*, 61. Vienna: Universal Edition, 1934. Reprinted in Reich 1937 (no. 919): 162–63; Berg (no. 68): 321; E. Randol Schoenberg (no. 1062): 250. In German.

Acrostic poem in Schoenberg's honor.

56. ["Händel und Bach"]. *23: Eine Wiener Musikzeitschrift* 20–21 (1935): 4. Untitled. Reprinted ("Händel und Bach") in Reich 1937 (no. 919): 193; Berg (no. 68): 321; facsimile in Berg's hand in Reich 1952 (no. 433): 341. In German.

"It is fortunate that Handel and Bach were born in 1685 and not 200 years later. Otherwise, their accomplishments would be questioned, just as the music of others is now deemed cultural bolshevism."

57. "Was ist atonal?" *23: Eine Wiener Zeitschrift*, 26–27 (8 June 1936): 1–11. Reprinted in Rufer 1956 (no. 950): 196–206; *Kontrapunkte* 2 (1958): 17–27; *Die Stimme der Komponisten* (1958): 17–27; Reich 1959 (no. 917): 32–44; Rufer 1979 (no. 950): 214–26; Berg (no. 68): 298–307. Preliminary version in SMZ 85 (1945): 47–48. In German.

English translations: "What is Atonality?," in Nicolas Slonimsky, *Music since 1900*, 1027–29, 5th edition (New York: Schirmer Books, 1994); preliminary version in Willi Reich, *Schoenberg: A Critical Biography* (New York: Praeger, 1974): 32–34.

Italian translation: "Che cosa significa atonale?," in Rognoni 1954 (no. 944): 290–303, and Rognoni 1966 (no. 944): 443–51.

Swedish translation: "Vad är atonal? Intervju med Alban Berg," translated by Helma Skans, *Nutida musik* 22/3 (1978–79): 24–29.

Dutch translation: "Wat is atonaal?," in Schönberger (no. 969): 37–45.

Talk given on Vienna Radio on 23 April 1930, arranged by Webern and prompted by the performance in Vienna of *Wozzeck* on 30 March 1930. The talk had the form of an interview (with Julius Bistron) and contained a discussion of stylistic aspects of atonal music, finding them rooted in a long historical development.

58. "Zu Mahlers Neunter Symphonie." 23: *Eine Wiener Musikzeitschrift* 26–27 (1936): 12. Reprinted in Berg (no. 68): 308.

Taken from a letter of 1912 by Berg to his wife in which the first movement of Mahler's Symphony no. 9 is praised as Mahler's greatest work, filled with love for the earth and yearning for peace prior to death.

59. "Gedenkrede auf Emil Hertzka." In Reich 1937 (no. 919): 197–201. Reprinted in Reich 1963 (no. 918): 78–82; Berg (no. 68): 314–19. In German.

English translation: "Commemorative Address for Emil Hertzka," in Reich 1965 (no. 918): 84–89.

Text of a speech given by Berg at a memorial concert for Emil Hertzka, director of Universal Edition, shortly after his death in 1932. Hertzka is praised as the business man who supported unpopular modern music, sustained only by the power of his ideas.

60. [*Lulu*, selected libretti]. *Lulu: Oper nach den Tragödien "Erdgeist" und "Büchse der Pandora" von Frank Wedekind* (Vienna: Universal Edition [10746], 1937, Acts 1–2 only). *Lulu: Oper in drei Akten nach den Tragödien "Erdgeist" und "Büchse der Pandora" von Frank Wedekind* (Vienna: Universal Edition, 1977, Acts 1–3); reprinted in Csampai and Holland (no. 333). In German.

English translation: *Lulu: Alban Berg*, translated by Arthur Jacobs (n.p.: Universal Edition [16746eNJ], 1977, Acts 1–2 only). *Lulu: Opera in 3 Acts (7 Scenes)*, translated by Arthur Jacobs (n.p.: Universal Edition [16991NJ], 1978).

French translation: *Lulu: Opéra en trois actes, livret bilingue*, translated by Isabelle and Hans Hildenbrand, in *Alban Berg: Lulu* (no. 309, volume 1, Acts 1–3).

Italian translation: *Lulu*, translated by M. T. Mandelari, in Petazzi (no. 884).

61. *Praktische Anweisungen zur Einstudierung des "Wozzeck."* In Reich 1937 (no. 919): 166–72. Reprinted in Berg (no. 68): 291–97. In German.

English translation: "The Preparation and Staging of *Wozzeck*," translated by George Perle, MT 109 (1968): 518–21. Reprinted in Perle (no. 416): 203–206.

French translation: "Indications pratiques pour l'étude de *Wozzeck*," in Pousseur (no. 64): 146–55.

Italian translation: "Istruzioni pratiche per l'esecuzione del *Wozzeck*," in Rognoni 1966 (no. 944): 455–60.

> Berg's guidelines, written in 1930 to be distributed with performance materials, concern tempo, instrumentation, vocal production, and staging. Berg recommends a leisurely and relatively quiet performance style with a generally realistic staging.

62. "Vorstellung Ernst Kreneks."   In Reich 1937 (no. 919): 195–96. Reprinted in Berg (no. 68): 310–11. In German.

> Text of a short talk given by Berg in Vienna on 3 January 1928 prior to a concert sponsored by the Österreichischer Kulturbund and the Verein für Neue Musik (the latter being the Viennese chapter of the International Society for Contemporary Music). Krenek is praised as belonging to the new movement begun by Mahler, Reger, Debussy, and Schoenberg.

63. "Wiener Musikkritik."   Opening passage printed as an appendix to Willi Reich, "Elementarschule für Musikkritiker," MEL 20 (1953): 217–19 (there given the title "Erziehung des Zeitungslesers tut not"). The entire essay published under the title "Zwei Feuilletons: Ein Beitrag zum Kapitel 'Schönberg und die Kritik'" in Reich 1963 (no. 918): 207–14. Reprinted in Reich 1959 (no. 917): 32–44 (excerpt); Berg (no. 68): 182–90. In German.

English translation: "Two Feuilletons: A Contribution to the Topic 'Schönberg and Music Criticism'," in Reich 1965 (no. 918): 219–26.

> Written by Berg in 1920 as a response to feuilletons by Elsa Bienenfeld and Julius Korngold critical of Schoenberg. Berg had no success in finding a publisher for his essay, which he sent in September 1921 to Schoenberg as a birthday greeting. See Berg's letter to Schoenberg of 9 September 1921 in *The*

Berg-Schoenberg Correspondence (no. 704). The essay was later turned over to Reich for use in the journal 23.

64. *Écrits*. Edited by Henri Pousseur. Monaco: Editions du Rocher, 1957. 182 p. ML60.B4665. In French.

Second edition, enlarged: *Écrits*. Edited by Dominique Jameux. Musique/passé/présent. Paris: Christian Bourgois, 1985. 216 p.

French translation of Berg's principal writings with commentary by Pousseur.

65. [*Wozzeck-Vortrag*]. In Redlich (no. 908), 311–27. Reprinted in Berg (no. 68): 268–90; Csampai and Holland (no. 102): 159–77; Hanselmann (no. 134): 159–76. In German.

English translations: "Berg's Lecture on *Wozzeck*," in Redlich (no. 908, English version): 261–85; "A Lecture on *Wozzeck*," in Jarman, *Alban Berg: Wozzeck* (no. 155), 154–170.

Italian translation: "Analisi di *Wozzeck*: Conferenza," in Rognoni 1966 (no. 944): 461–78.

French translation: "Conférence sur *Wozzeck*," translated by Dennis Collins, *Musique en jeu* 14 (1974): 77–94; reprinted in *L'avant-scène opéra* (no. 81), 88–95.

Berg's lecture was first given prior to a performance of *Wozzeck* in Oldenburg in March 1929, and it was later repeated elsewhere. Berg sketches ways in which the opera reveals both variety as well as integration of materials. The need for variety led him to dispense with Wagnerian through composition in favor of a succession of forms drawn from instrumental music. These are described with considerable detail. See Willi Reich's review of the book by Ploebsch (no. 227) for Reich's assertion that Berg did not wish the lecture in this form to be published since some of its parts were disproportionately emphasized. A version of the lecture is given in Reich 1937 (no. 919) and Reich 1963 (no. 918) which, according to Reich, had Berg's approval.

66. [**Neun Blätter zur Lyrischen Suite für Streichquartett: Skizzen einer thematischen Analyse**]. In Reich 1959 (no. 917):

45–54 (also in facsimile). Reprinted in Reich 1963 (no. 918): 141–43 (abridged); Rauchhaupt (no. 905): 136–65; Berg (no. 68): 236–54. In German.

English translations: "Lyric Suite for String Quartet," in Reich 1965 (no. 918): 149–52; "Nine Pages on the Lyric Suite for String Quartet," in Rauchhaupt (no. 905): 287–95.

> Nine pages of analytic sketches and notes on the Lyric Suite prepared for the use of Rudolf Kolisch (undated, probably written before the premier performance in January 1927). The analysis focusses on formal divisions in the work and twelve-tone materials and their use.

67. *Briefe an seine Frau.* Edited by Helene Berg. Munich and Vienna: Albert Langen, Georg Müller, 1965. 656 p. ML410.B47 A47. Excerpts in MEL 32 (1965): 438–42. In German. Reviewed by Kurt Honolka, *Musica* 20/2 (1966): 92–93; Harry Mayer, *Mens en melodie* 22 (1967): 50–53; Hans F. Redlich, ÖMZ 21 (1966): 338–42; Willi Reich, SMZ 106 (1966): 58; Gerhard Schumann, BMW 10 (1968): 220–24; G. A. Trumpff, NZM 127 (1966): 121–22; Konrad Vogelsang, MF 21 (1968): 120–21.

English translation: Alban Berg, *Letters to His Wife.* Translated, edited, and annotated by Bernard Grun. New York: St. Martin's Press; London: Faber and Faber, 1971. 456 p. ISBN 0571083951. ML410.B47 A473 1971 (1971b for American edition). Reviewed by Mosco Carner, ML 52 (1971): 306–11, and MT 112 (1971): 442–43; Max Harrison, *Composer* 43 (1972): 29–30; George Perle, *Saturday Review* 54 (28 August 1971): 38–39, 51.

Italian translation: Alban Berg, *Lettere alla moglie.* Translated by Silvia Bortoli Cappelleto. Milan: Feltrinelli, 1976. Reviewed by Massimo Mila, *Nuova rivista musicale italiana* 10 (1976): 507–11.

> Texts of 569 letters (488 in the English edition) from Berg to his wife, Helene Nahowski Berg, from 1907 to 1935. Concerning an abortive earlier edition of this volume, see Redlich (no. 909), and Helene Berg (no. 694). Additional early letters are found in Rosemary Hilmar (no. 783).

68. *Glaube, Hoffnung und Liebe: Schriften zur Musik.* Edited by Frank Schneider. Leipzig: Verlag Philipp Reclam jun., 1981. 383

p. In German. Reviewed by Udo Clement, *Musik und Gesellschaft* 33 (1983): 439–40; F. Streller, BMW 23 (1981): 300–301.

Berg's writings on music with introduction and commentary by the editor.

(69. ["Aphorisms"]. In Floros 1992 [no. 741]: 359–60.) In German.

Nine aphorisms entered by Berg into an early *Zitatensammlung*. Floros leaves the impression that Berg is the author, although the notebook was used primarily to record passages from works by other writers.

4

Writings on Wozzeck

This chapter contains citations of writings that are primarily concerned with Berg's opera *Wozzeck*, arranged alphabetically by author, or title if an author's name is lacking. Since information on *Wozzeck* is also contained in writings cited in other chapters of this book, the reader is urged to consult the Index under "Berg, Alban: works—*Wozzeck*" for a complete list of sources.

70. **Aber, Adolf.** "Die Wiederbelebung alter Formen in der zeitgenössischen Musik." MBA 7 (1926): 262–64. In German.

Aber's survey of contemporary uses of old musical forms touches briefly on Berg's *Wozzeck*.

71. **Adorno, Theodor W.** "Alban Berg: Oper und Moderne." AGS 18 (1984): 650–72. In German.

A lengthy radio broadcast (1969), primarily concerning *Wozzeck*, in which Adorno focuses on ways in which Berg's operatic style, on one hand conventional in conception, still partakes of modernism.

72. ———. "Alban Berg: Zur Uraufführung des *Wozzeck*." MBA 7 (1925): 531–37. Reprinted in AGS 18 (1984): 456–64. In German.

A philosophical discussion of the interrelatedness of all of Berg's music (*Wozzeck* is mentioned only in passing) and its origins within the spirit of Schoenberg's artistic outlook.

73. ————. "Die Oper *Wozzeck.*" *Der Scheinwerfer: Blätter der städtischen Bühnen* (Essen) 3/4 (1929): 5–11. Reprinted in ABS 18 (1984): 472–79. In German.

Many familiar themes in Adorno's understanding of *Wozzeck* are introduced here, especially that the opera resembles psychoanalysis in that dream images rise up from the inner mind to be given construction by the music.

74. ————. "*Wozzeck* in Partitur." *Frankfurter allgemeine Zeitung* (18 April 1956): 10. Reprinted in AGS 18 (1984): 480–82. In German.

Praises Universal Edition for publishing the opera (1955) in full score, in which can be studied Berg's refined and spartan instrumentation. Orchestral color is used solely to clarify thematic ideas and compositional structures.

75. ————. "Zum *Wozzeck.*" *Bühnen der Stadt Köln* 1 (1958–59): 4, 6–8. In German.

Reused in expanded form in Adorno's book on Berg (no. 667).

76. **Andréani, Eveline, and Jean-Paul Olive.** "La tradition comme invention: Le *Wozzeck* de Berg." *Revue d'esthétique* 4 (1982): 63–76. In French.

Analysis of *Wozzeck* (mainly Act 3) seeking primarily to define its element of spatiality.

77. **Andrews, Hilda.** "Berg's *Wozzeck.*" *Monthly Musical Record* 60 (1930): 331–32. In English.

Wozzeck is still unknown in England despite its status as a landmark in the history of opera. The work is described in both text and music.

78. **Antesberger, Günther.** "Die Passacaglia in der Wiener Schule: Analytische Studien zu einem barocken Formtypus in Werken von Arnold Schönberg, Alban Berg und Anton Webern." In *Festschrift für Franz Koschier: Beiträge zur Volkskunde,*

Naturkunde und Kulturgeschichte, 121–38. Kärtner Museumsschriften, volume 57. Klagenfurt: Verlag des Landesmuseums für Kärnten, 1974. In German.

> Discussion and analysis of the passacaglia from Berg's *Wozzeck*, Act 1, scene 4. Schoenberg's "Nacht" from *Pierrot lunaire* and Webern's Passacaglia for orchestra, Op. 1, are also addressed.

79. Apter, T. E. "Tragedy in Berg's *Wozzeck.*" *Musical Opinion* 99 (1975): 20–22. In English.

> Finds the tragic dimension of the opera in Berg's ability to disconnect the orchestral music from the declamation of text, the former expressing sympathy, the latter lacking in humanity.

80. Ardoin, John. "Apropos *Wozzeck.*" *Opera Quarterly* 3/3 (1985): 68–74. In English.

> General survey of the opera for the nonspecialist reader.

81. *L'avant-scène opéra* 36 (1981): Berg "*Wozzeck,*" *Dossier Pierre Boulez*. In French. 210 p. Section on *Wozzeck* reprinted Paris: Editions premières loges, 1991, 145 p.

> Contains a French translation of the text, writings by Berg on *Wozzeck*, essays on the text and music, and bibliography. The "Dossier Pierre Boulez" does not concern *Wozzeck*.

82. Bach, David Josef. "Die Oper *Wozzeck.*" *Kunst und Volk* 5/3 (1931): 71–72. In German.

> This article was not been examined by the author of this guide. Its contents are probably related to Bach's review of the Vienna premiere of *Wozzeck* that appeared in the socialist *Arbeiterzeitung* (Vienna) on 6 April 1930. The review is excerpted in Pass (no. 211): 105–107.

83. Barraud, Henry. "*Wozzeck.*" In Barraud, *Les cinq grands opéras*, 267–302. Paris: Editions du Seuil, 1972. In French.

General survey of the opera.

84. **Beck, Joachim.** "Bergs *Wozzeck.*" *Die Weltbühne: Wochenschrift für Politik, Kunst, Wirtschaft* 25 (1929): 528–31. In German.

An interpretation of the opera for the nonspecialist reader, finding it a pure example of musical and operatic expressivity rather than a work that aims for beauty per se. The author holds that the future of opera will tend more toward works that combine both expressivity and beauty.

85. **Berio, Luciano.** "Invito a *Wozzeck.*" *Il diapason* 3/3–4 (1952): 14–20. In Italian.

Published on the occasion of the stormy Milan premiere of *Wozzeck* in 1952, Berio interprets the opera as a summary of the entire turbulent period from 1925.

86. **Berra, Donata Schwendimann.** "Interesse di Büchner e Berg per i Volkslieder." *Nuova rivista musicale italiana* 7 (1973): 402–16. In Italian.

Discussion of folk songs in the text and music of *Wozzeck*, suggesting models in German folk song for Berg's folklike melodies.

87. **Blackall, Eric A.** "Büchner and Alban Berg: Some Thoughts on *Wozzeck.*" *German Quarterly* 34 (1961): 431–38. In English.

Finds that Berg's version of Büchner emphasizes pathetic elements susceptible to musical treatment.

88. **Blaukopf, Kurt.** "New Light on *Wozzeck.*" *Saturday Review* 36 (26 September 1953): 62, 76. In English. German version ("Autobiographische Elemente in Alban Bergs *Wozzeck*") in ÖMZ 9 (1954): 155–58.

Report on the content of Berg's correspondence (1913–29) with Gottfried Kassowitz, emphasizing Berg's military service during World War I and its relevance to *Wozzeck*. Also see Kassowitz (no. 808).

89. Boulez, Pierre. "Situation et interprétation de *Wozzeck*."
Sleeve notes to Boulez's recording of the work, CBS set 3221
0001/0002 (ca. 1963). In French, English, and German. French
text reprinted in *Points de repère*, 403–409 (Paris: Christian
Bourgois, Editions du Seuil, 1981). English translation ("*Wozzeck*
and Its Interpretation") in Boulez, *Orientations*, 374–79, translated
by Martin Cooper, edited by Jean-Jacques Nattiez (Cambridge:
Harvard University Press, London: Faber and Faber, 1986).
German translation ("*Wozzeck*: Anlage und Interpretation") in
Boulez, *Anhaltspunkte: Essays*, 325–34, translated by Josef Häusler
(Kassel: Bärenreiter, Munich: Deutscher Taschenbuch Verlag,
1979). Italian translation in Boulez, *Punti di riferimento* (Turin:
Einaudi, 1984).

> Objectives that a conductor and other performers of *Wozzeck*
> must strive toward to faithfully convey the organization of
> the music, which will subsequently convey the organization
> of the drama.

90. ———. "*Wozzeck*: Ein Meilenstein der Musikgeschichte."
Musik + Medezin 1/12 (1975): 49–52. In German.

> This article was not available to the author of this
> bibliography nor is it cited in any bibliography of the
> writings of Boulez. It may be a version of Boulez's
> "Situation et interprétation de *Wozzeck*" (no. 89).

91. Brasch, Alfred. "Alban Bergs *Wozzeck*: Werk der Wende."
Theater und Zeit 3 (1955): 14–15. In German.

> Brief survey of the opera.

92. Breuer, János. "Száz éve született Alban Berg. Tóth Aladár
két Berg-elemzése." *Muzsika* 28/2 (1985): 18–20. In Hungarian.

> Reports from the Prague press in 1928 and 1930 concerning
> *Wozzeck*.

93. Brisk, Barry. "Leopold Stokowski and *Wozzeck*: An
American Premiere in 1931." *Opera Quarterly* 5/1 (1987): 71–82.
In English.

Information about the American premiere of *Wozzeck* in Philadelphia in 1931 and the contributions of Stokowski, Robert Edmond Jones, and other collaborators. The recollections of Stowkowski's assistant conductor, Sylvan Levin, are cited.

94. Bruhn, Siglind. *Die musikalische Darstellung psychologischer Wirklichkeit in Alban Bergs "Wozzeck."* Dissertation, Hochschule für Musik und Darstellende Kunst, Vienna, 1985. Europäische Hochschulschriften, series 36, volume 22. Frankfurt, Bern, and New York: Peter Lang, 1986. 392 p. ISBN 3820489517. ML410.B47 B7 1986. In German.

A broad study of the music and text of *Wozzeck* concentrating on psychological aspects of the drama and its musical interpretation.

95. Budde, Elmar. "Musik, Zeit und Szene in Alban Bergs Oper *Wozzeck.*" ABS 2 (1981): 69–79. In German.

Proposes an explanation of the connection between music and time in Act 1, scenes 1–2, of *Wozzeck*, viewed in terms of compositional problems and materials. Begins by surveying Berg's tempo indications. A detailed analysis of the two scenes leads to conclusions concerning the close connection among form, elapse of time, and dramaturgy.

96. Carapezza, Paolo Emilio. *Scritti e documenti per il "Wozzeck" di Alban Berg.* Palermo: Edizioni dell' E. A. Teatro Massimo, 1965. 65, xxvii p., plates. In Italian.

Booklet accompanying the first Palermo performance of *Wozzeck*, containing the text (translated into Italian), a chronology of Berg, pictures, and a selection of Berg's writings drawn from Rognoni (no. 944).

97. Chittum, Donald. "The Triple Fugue in Berg's *Wozzeck.*" MR 28 (1967): 52–62. In English. German translation ("Die Tripelfuge in Bergs *Wozzeck*") in *Zur musikalischen Analyse,* 508–22, edited by Gerhard Schuhmacher (Darmstadt: Wissenschaftliche Buchgesellschaft, 1974).

Analysis of the fugue in *Wozzeck*, Act 2, scene 2, and its relation to dramatic action.

98. Chop, Max. *"Wozzeck."* Signale für die musikalische Welt 51–52 (1925): 1954. In German.

A cautious, skeptical review of *Wozzeck* after hearing the first performance in Berlin in 1925.

99. Collins, Dennis. "L'avant-dernier opéra." *Musique en jeu* 14 (1974): 73–76. In French. Spanish translation ("La penúltima ópera") in *Pauta* 4/15 (1985): 61–65.

Preface to the author's translation of Berg's *Wozzeck-Vortrag*. See also Berg (no. 65).

100. Connor, Herbert. "Alban Bergs *Wozzeck* (Die Wiedergeburt des naturlichen Dramas)." *Signale für die musikalische Welt* 84 (1926): 1131–33. In German.

Sees the opera as neoromantic rather than in the more contemporary objectivist style of Ernst Krenek or Igor Stravinsky. *Wozzeck* is found to be a synthesis of several late-romantic trends: the *Tristan*like emotionality of German Expressionism and coloristic aspects of Impressionism.

101. Crankshaw, Edward. "Alban Berg's *Wozzeck*." *Bookman* 86 (1934): 103. In English.

Reviews a concert performance of the work by the BBC, finding Berg lacking in an effective use of the atonal idiom. The libretto is far more interesting than the music.

102. Cronheim, Paul. "De taak der Wagnervereeniging." *De muziek* 5 (1930–31): 29–30. In Dutch.

Describes activities of the Wagner Society in Amsterdam, of which the author was director, and its sponsorship of a performance of *Wozzeck* in 1930. Also see Op de Coul (no. 208).

103. Csampai, Attila, and Dietmar Holland, editors. *Alban Berg* *"Wozzeck": Texte, Materialien, Kommentare.* Rororo Opernbücher. Reinbek bei Hamburg: Rowohlt; Munich: G. Ricordi, 1985. 284 p.   ISBN 3499179296. ML50.B491 W6 1985.   In German. Reviewed by Volker Scherliess, NZM 147/2 (1986): 65.

Articles on the opera and play, writings by Berg, early reviews, text of the opera, and reprinted materials.

104.   Cserépy, Zoltán.   "Zur visionären Klangwelt der Passacaglia in Alban Bergs *Wozzeck."   Schweizer Jahrbuch für Musikwissenschaft,* new series 8–9 (1988–89): 81–93. In German.

Analysis of compositional devices in the passacaglia from *Wozzeck* (Act 1, scene 4) that create a sense of psychological drama.

105. David, K. H. *"Wozzeck* in Zürich." SMZ 71 (1931): 745–49. In German.

A description of the opera following its Zurich premiere in October 1931. The interpretation emphasizes the work's expressive power: "Opinionated disputes and prattle about art fall silent in the face of this work. Since *Tristan* it stands forth as one of the works of significance and greatness that the new epoch has produced."

106. DeVoto, Mark. *"Wozzeck* in Context." In John (no. 156): 7–14. In English.

A general sketch of the historical background to the work.

107.   Dibelius, Ulrich.   "Einheitlichkeit der Architektur— Mannigfaltigkeit der Gestalten: Formtendenzen und Sprachduktus in Alban Bergs *Wozzeck."* In Csampai and Holland (no. 103): 9–33. In German.

General appraisal of the play emphasizing its influence upon the operatic structure.

108.   Duvignaud, Jean.   "Büchner, Berg: Une continuité." *L'avant-scène opéra* (no. 81): 6–9. In French.

Concerns Berg's experiences with Büchner's play and his revisions of it as an operatic libretto.

109. Einstein, Alfred. "Alban Bergs *Wozzeck*." In Einstein, *Von Schütz bis Hindemith: Essays über Musik und Musiker*, 142–46. Zurich and Stuttgart: Pan-Verlag, 1957. In German.

General appraisal of the opera, reprinted from an earlier review.

110. ———. "Alban Berg's *Wozzeck*." *Monthly Musical Record* 64/issue 755 (1934): 142–44. In English.

A general interpretation of the opera in connection with a concert performance (14 March 1934) for the London British Broadcasting Corporation. Einstein finds that the work represents both the spirit of Impressionism and Expressionism.

111. Fanning, David. "Berg's Sketches for *Wozzeck*: A Commentary and Inventory." RMA 112 (1987): 280–322. In English.

Detailed discussion of the contents and dating of selected manuscripts for *Wozzeck*. A comprehensive list of such sources is given as an appendix.

112. Fano, Michel. "Quatre notes sur le 'temps' dans *Wozzeck*." *L'avant-scène opéra* (no. 81): 96–99. In French.

The author finds in *Wozzeck* four categories of time: circular, simultaneous, logical, and apparent.

113. Ferlan, Françoise. "Le symbolisme du sang." *L'avant-scène opéra* (no. 81): 117–21. In French.

Interprets *Wozzeck* as a spectacle of blood and death and traces recurrences of a blood motif.

114. Fiechtner, Helmut A. "Neues aus Wien. Zur Premiere von Alban Bergs Oper: *Wozzeck* und die Wiener." MEL 19 (1952): 192–94. In German.

Compares reviews of the premier peformance of *Wozzeck* in 1925 to those of a Viennese performance in 1952.

115. Floros, Constantin. "Alban Bergs *Wozzeck* als Botschaft an die Menschheit." In *Der kulturpädagogische Auftrag der Musik im 20. Jahrhundert: Bericht über das Symposion vom 14.-15. Juli 1989 in der Hochschule für Musik München*, 25–42. Edited by Ute Jung-Kaiser. Musik im Diskurs, volume 9. Regensburg: Gustav Bosse Verlag, 1991. In German.

Argues for an interpretation of *Wozzeck* as a work of social concern and commitment. Evidence for this viewpoint is found especially in the music of the final interlude of Act 3.

116. Forneberg, Erich. "Alban Bergs Passacaglia aus der Oper *Wozzeck*." *Musik im Unterricht* 53 (1962): 100–102. In German.

117. ———. "Das Volkslied als expressionistisches Symbol in Alban Bergs *Wozzeck*." NZM 120 (1959): 261–65. In German.

Discussion of the folklike songs of *Wozzeck* and their dramaturgical significance as expressionistic symbols by which characters allude to a better world outside of their own. Berg's folk-song allusions help to create an expressionistic tone in the opera.

118. ———. *"Wozzeck" von Alban Berg*. Die Oper: Schriftenreihe über musikalische Bühnenwerke. 2 volumes. Third edition. Berlin-Lichterfelde: Robert Lienau, 1963. 87 p. MT100.B57 F67. In German.

Information on Büchner, the play *Woyzeck*, the form of the opera, with a scene-by-scene analysis.

119. Forte, Allen. "The Mask of Tonality: Alban Berg's Symphonic Epilogue to *Wozzeck*." In *Alban Berg: Historical and Analytical Perspectives* (no. 746): 151–200. In English.

A detailed analysis of pitch structures of the final interlude in *Wozzeck* (Act 3, mm. 320–71), comparing a tonal reading in the key of D to an atonal reading using the author's method of linear analysis. The author concludes that tonality in the interlude is "arbitrary," sporadic, and superficial.

120. ———. "Tonality, Symbol, and Structural Levels in Berg's *Wozzeck.*" MQ 71 (1985): 474–99. In English.

Analysis of the theme and fifth variation in *Wozzeck*, Act 3, scene 1, alternately as tonal and nontonal music, with emphasis upon the use of pitch-class sets as dramatic symbols.

121. **Franzi, Johannes.** "*Wozzeck* de Alban Berg: Emoción humana en la ópera 'atonal': En ocasión del iminente estreno sudamericano de la obra en el Teatro Colón." *Lyra* (Buenos Aires), 10 (September 1952): 106–109. In Spanish.

122. **Freeman, John W.** "The Man Who Feels: In *Wozzeck*, Alban Berg Made Intellect Serve Emotion." *Opera News* 33/24 (1968–69): 24–26. In English.

General appraisal of the text and aesthetic of *Wozzeck*, seeing the work as based on a nineteenth-century subject but put through a twentieth-century, expressionistic process of distortion.

123. **Friedland, Martin.** "Zur Aesthetik des *Wozzeck.*" *Allgemeine Musikzeitung* 53 (1926): 61–63. In German.

Wozzeck appears to attempt a new aesthetic in musical theater. It strives toward a total work of art in which music cannot exist independently.

124. **Friedrich, Rudolf, editor.** *Alban Bergs "Wozzeck" und die Musikkritik.* Musik der Gegenwart: Eine Flugblätterfolge, no. 9. Vienna: Universal Edition, n.d. (1926). 31 p. ML94.B48 no. 11. Reprinted in *Pult und Taktstock* 3 (1926): 16–48 with added commentary. In German.

Excerpts from the critical appraisal of *Wozzeck* in the German press.

125. Gerhard, Roberto. *"Wozzeck." Foyer: A Survey of Music, Opera and Ballet Past, Present and Future* 2 (1951–52): 16–20. In English.

A general account of the opera.

126. Gerhartz, Leo Karl. "Der Glücksfall einer Oper für das 20. Jahrhundert: Alban Bergs *Wozzeck*." In Gerhartz, *Opera: Aspekte einer Gattung*, 114–29. Laaber: Laaber-Verlag, 1983. Reprinted in Csampai and Holland (no. 103): 260–73. In German.

Surveys the opera, pointing to musical details that express dramatic ideas.

127. Gervais, Françoise. "Étude sur *Wozzeck* d'Alban Berg." *L'éducation musicale* 27 (1971–72): 88–91, 134–37, 173–77, 218–20, 260–65. In French.

Broad, general study of *Wozzeck* outlining its place in the history of opera, leitmotifs, structure of interludes, and all of Act 3.

128. Goertz, Harald. "*Wozzeck* als Lehrstoff und Lehrstück." In *50 Jahre Wozzeck* (no. 173): 84–91. In German.

Discusses the opera from a pedagogical standpoint, asserting the practicality and necessity of considering *Wozzeck* as an object of study for workshops and aspiring operatic singers.

129. Goldet, Stéphane. [Untitled commentary on *Wozzeck*]. *L'avant-scène opéra* (no. 81): 19–87. In French.

Running commentary to the French-German libretto of the opera explaining and interpreting elements of musical expression, especially as regards formal and thematic practices.

130. Goléa, Antoine. "A propos du *Wozzeck* de Alban Berg." *Vie musicale* 1 (1951): 10–12. In French.

131. Greene, Susan. "Wozzeck and Marie: Outcasts in Search of an Honest Morality." *Opera Quarterly* 3/3 (1985): 75–86. In English.

General account of the dramatic content of the opera and of the moralistic aspects of the two central characters.

132. Gruber, Gernot. "Natur, Tod und Unendlichkeit in *Woyzeck* und *Wozzeck*." In *50 Jahre Wozzeck* (no. 173): 68–77. In German.

Büchner's play still evokes among its audiences conflicting interpretations as both social criticism and existential tragedy. This ambivalence of meaning is also captured by Berg, whose opera fluctuates between constructive clarity and open forms. Such important themes in the play as nature, death, and eternity receive distinctive musical treatment in the opera. Nature, for example, which Berg wished to interpret as lifeless, threatening, and overwhelming, is depicted by music that is iridescent, rhythmically vibrating, and unstable in sonorous texture.

133. Hamilton, Iain. "*Wozzeck* and the Use of Musical Imagery." *Listener* 63 (1960): 44. In English.

Points to the great and varied "imagery" in *Wozzeck*, suggesting a profoundly impressionistic use of sound.

134. Hanselmann, Beat, editor. *Alban Berg "Wozzeck": Libretto mit musikalischer Analyse, Dokumentation zur Entstehung, Kommentare, Diskographie, Aufführungstabellen, Bibliographie, Zeittafeln.* Munich: PremOp Verlag, 1992. 248 p. ISBN 3927724076. ML50.B491 W6 1992. In German. Reviewed by Michael Arndt, NZM 154/4 (1993): 71–72; Peter Petersen, *Musica* 47 (1993): 176–77.

Libretto, articles, discography, and bibliography concerning *Wozzeck*. The articles include several by Berg, others reprinted from earlier sources, and some appearing for the first time in this book.

135. ———. "Die vielen Leiden des armen W." In Hanselmann (no. 134): 9–29. In German.

General historical background to the opera *Wozzeck* including information on Johann Woyzeck, Büchner, and the creation of the opera.

136. Harding, James Martin. "Integrating Atomization: Adorno Reading Berg Reading Büchner." *Theatre Journal* 44 (1992): 1–13. In English.

Application of methods located in Adorno's critical study of Berg's *Wozzeck* toward a materialistic interpretation of Büchner's play. "The relation between particular and universal is reversed, the latter being subordinated to the evolution of the former."

137. Heckroth, Hein. "Das Bühnenbild zum *Wozzeck.*" *Die Theaterwelt* 5/10 (1930): 170. In German.

138. Heinsheimer, Hans W. Chapter 6 (untitled). In Heinsheimer, *Best Regards to Aida: The Defeats and Victories of a Music Man on Two Continents,* 46–66. New York: Alfred A. Knopf, 1968. In English. Excerpt in German translation ("Begegnung mit einem Riesen: Alban Berg") in MEL 36 (1969): 462–68.

139. ———. "*Wozzeck*: One Hundred Rehearsals." *Musical Digest* (London) 10 (1949): 57–60. Extracted from Heinsheimer, *Menagerie in F Sharp* (Garden City: Doubleday, 1947). In English.

Heinsheimer's lively books recount his recollections of Berg, especially as regards the publication and early performances of *Wozzeck,* while he was the head of the opera department of Universal Edition (1924–38).

140. Hermand, Jost. "Tiefstes Elend—höchste Kunst: Alban Bergs *Wozzeck.*" In Hermand, *Beredte Töne: Musik im historischen Prozeß,* 119–36. European University Studies, series 36 (musicology), volume 51. Frankfurt: Peter Lang, 1991. In German.

Surveys the literature on *Wozzeck*, finding that it attaches value to the work on the basis of its ingenious closed forms but ignores the implications of Büchner's "proletariat" drama. The author concludes that the genre of opera itself is ill-suited to deal with social issues.

141. **Heyer, Hermann.** "Inventionen über Alban Bergs *Wozzeck*." *Die Weltbühne* 11 (Berlin 1956): 527–33. In German.

General account of the opera, comparing its controversial reception in 1925 to its bland acceptance in the 1950s.

142. **Hijman, Julius.** "Berg en Webern." In Hijman, *Nieuwe oostenrijkse muziek: (Schönberg, Berg, Webern)*, 83–123. Caecilia reeks, volume 5. Amsterdam: Bigot en Van Rossum, n.d. (1938). In Dutch.

General account of Berg's life and music, emphasizing *Wozzeck*.

143. **Hiller, Charlotte.** "*Wozzeck*: A Short Guide to Alban Berg's Music Drama." *Musical Courier* 143/7 (1951): 6–7. In English.

A general account of the opera.

144. **Hilmar, Ernst.** "Die verschiedenen Entwicklungsstadien in den Kompositionsskizzen." In *50 Jahre Wozzeck* (no. 173): 22–26. In German.

Longstanding questions concerning the sketches and chronology of composition for *Wozzeck* still remain unanswered. The lack of extensive sketches to Act 1, for example, still finds no conclusive explanation. All the same, a rough outline of the chronology of composition is presented, beginning with sketches for Act 2, scene 2 (1914) and continuing until composing of the opera was completed in 1921 and instrumentation begun. The extant sketches provide clear information about Berg's working methods, which are outlined.

145. ————. *"Wozzeck" von Alban Berg: Entstehung—erste Erfolge—Repressionen (1914–35).* Vienna: Universal-Edition, 1974. 106 p. ISBN 3702401148. MT100.B57 H54. Excerpts reprinted in Csampai and Holland (no. 103): 105–46, and in Hanselmann ("Nach der Uraufführung: Die weitere Stationen der Oper zu Lebzeiten Alban Bergs") (no. 134): 179–90. In German. Reviewed by Douglas Jarman, ML 58 (1977): 82–83; Rudolf Klein, ÖMZ 31 (1976): 250; Rudolf Stephan, MEL/NZM 4 (1978): 265; Konrad Vogelsang, MF 31 (1978): 495–96.

Documentary study of the historical background and early stagings of *Wozzeck*.

146. Hilmar, Rosemary. "Die von Berg in der Textvorlage festgelegten musikalischen Formen." In *50 Jahre Wozzeck* (no. 173): 27–31. In German.

As stated by Ernst Hilmar in no. 145, Berg's working source of Büchner's play was the Insel Verlag edition (Leipzig 1913) of *Wozzeck* and *Lenz*. Although Berg owned a copy of the Karl Emil Franzos edition, it was not used by him in conceiving the text of his opera. Probably between 1917 and 1919, as he reworked Büchner's text, he entered annotations concerning musical forms. These fall into two groups: those concerning Act 1 (scenes 2–3), Act 2 (scene 4), and Act 3 (scene 3) and those scenes that Berg conceived as variations forms. The composer's annotations of the text are discussed.

147. ————. "'. . . nach den hinterlassenen endgültigen Korrekturen des Komponisten revidiert': Eine Studie zur Drucklegung von Musikalien im 20. Jahrhundert, dargestellt am Beispiel der Oper *Wozzeck* von Alban Berg." *Gutenberg-Jahrbuch* 58 (1983): 112–30. In German.

Traces the stages through which the Hans E. Apostel edition of *Wozzeck* (1955) came into being, beginning in 1925 with Berg's own manuscript score, the error-filled score of 1926 by Universal Edition, and Berg's *Handexemplar* of this score. Apostel is shown to have used Berg's own autograph materials. An appendix compares the readings contained in these documents.

148.　Hirsbrunner, Theo. "Musical Form and Dramatic Expression in Alban Berg's *Wozzeck.*" In John (no. 156): 25–36. In English.

A brief thematic guide to the opera.

149.　Hirschberg, Walther. "Alban Bergs *Wozzeck.*" *Signale für die musikalische Welt* 9 (1932): 981–82. In German.

A review of Erich Kleiber's second staging of *Wozzeck* at the Berlin Staatsoper in 1932. The author found moments of great power alternating with stretches of boredom. "Gifted intuition and sterility balance out to a remarkable degree."

150.　Hiß, Guido. *Korrespondenzen: Zeichenzusammenhänge im Sprech- und Musiktheater: Mit einer Analyse des "Wozzeck" von Alban Berg.* Dissertation, University of Tübingen, 1988. Medien Forschung + Unterricht, series A, volume 24. Tübingen: M. Niemeyer, 1988. 176 p. ISBN 348434024X. ML1705.H58 1988. In German. Reviewed by Klaus Angermann, NZM 150/6 (1989): 49; Peter Petersen, *Musiktheorie* 4 (1989): 182–84, and *Musica,* 43 (1989): 260–62.

Asserts that theatrical and operatic signs function as a "tertiary code" in that the primary verbal element mixes with several secondary semiotic systems from other art forms to create a theatric speech system. *Wozzeck* is used as an analytic example.

151. Holland, Dietmar. "'Linienkreise—Figuren—Wer das lesen könnte!': Zur Funktion der Musik im *Wozzeck.*" In *Wozzeck-Programmheft der Bayerischen Staatsoper,* 1982. Reprinted in Csampai and Holland (no. 103): 252–59. In German.

Studies the relation of text to musical form: "The 'Application of Music in Drama,' about which Wagner spoke in his famous essay, is changed by Berg into the question of how autonomous musical shapes—including those of entire scenes, acts, and even the entire opera—can be drawn from the text. In other words, the operatic composer Berg read the dramaturgy of the text with musical eyes, without any sacrifice of scenic directness."

152. Holmberg, Arthur. "Core of Loneliness." *Opera News* 44/15 (1980): 20–23. In English.

Interpretation of Büchner's play *Woyzeck*.

153. Jameux, Dominique. "La croisée des chemins." *L'avant-scène opéra* (no. 81): 11–13. In French.

General discussion of the characters of *Wozzeck*.

154. ———. "Le nouvel opéra." *Diapason-Harmonie* 322 (1986): 52–53. In French.

Information concerning the premiere of *Wozzeck* in 1925.

155. Jarman, Douglas. *Alban Berg: "Wozzeck."* Cambridge Opera Handbooks. Cambridge: Cambridge University Press, 1989. xi, 181 p. ISBN 0521241510 (hardback), 0521284813 (paperback). ML410.B47 J3 1989. In English. Reviewed by Jon Alan Conrad, *Opera Quarterly* 7/4 (1990–91): 151–53; David Fanning, ML 71 (1990): 427–29; Dave Headlam, *Notes* 47 (1990–91): 1139–42; Alan Street, MT 131 (1990): 262; Rudolf Stephan, MF 43 (1990): 387.

Similar to no. 370. Contains chapters on the historical background to the play and the opera, a synopsis, the formal design, interpretive theories, staging history, and a detailed analysis of Act 3, scene 4. Among translated and reprinted "Documents" are articles on Büchner's play by Karl Emil Franzos and Hugo Beiber and early writings on Berg and the opera by Erwin Stein, Fritz Klein (no. 169), Ernst Viebig (no. 292), and Emil Petschnig (no. 223). There are also three essays by Berg concerning the opera (nos. 37, 44, and 65).

156. John, Nicholas, series editor. *"Wozzeck": Alban Berg.* Opera Guide Series. London: John Calder; New York: Riverrun Press, 1990. Published in association with English National Opera. 116 p. ISBN 0714542016. ML50.B491 W62 1990. In English. Reviewed by Catherine Dale, MR 52 (1991): 316–21.

Essays on the opera, a thematic guide, text translation (by Eric Blackall and Vida Harford).

157. Jones, Kimberley Mercedes. "Aesthetic Distance: An Artistic Principle Manifested in August Strindberg's *The Ghost Sonata* and Alban Berg's *Wozzeck*." Dissertation, Ohio University, 1991. UMI order no. 9121265. 277 p. In English.

Primarily a literary analysis comparing the two works by August Strindberg and Berg by the idea of "aesthetic distance" as set forth in literary criticism of expressionist writing.

158. Jouve, Pierre-Jean. "Forme et invention dans *Wozzeck*." *La table ronde* 54 (1952): 86–91. In French.

Extract from no. 162 by Jouve and Fano, dealing primarily with the leitmotivic content of *Wozzeck*.

159. ⸻. "Matière musicale de *Wozzeck*." *Preuves* 2/issue 15 ("L'oeuvre du vingtième siècle") (1952): 3–6. In French.

Impressions of the opera for the nonspecialist written at the time of the Paris premiere. The author emphasizes the work's eclecticism and liberty, all aimed at a heightened expressivity. The article is derived from the study by Jouve and Fano (no. 162).

160. ⸻. "*Wozzeck*: Argument d'après le drame de Georg Büchner dans l'opéra d'Alban Berg." RM 213 (1952): 6–29. In French.

Extracted from Jouve and Fano, no. 162, a summary of the text of the opera.

161. Jouve, Pierre-Jean, and Michel Fano. "*Wozzeck* d'Alban Berg (Act III, scène iv)." RM 212 (1952): 87–98.

Extracted from Jouve and Fano (no. 162), a description of the musical and dramatic language of Act 3, scene 4 from *Wozzeck*.

162. ————. *"Wozzeck" ou le novel opéra.* Paris: Librairie Plon, 1953. 242 p. MT100.B4 J7.

Reissued in a slightly expanded form as *"Wozzeck" d'Alban Berg,* Paris: Union Générale d'Editions, 1964.   Second edition. Paris: Christian Bourgois, 1985. 311 p. In French.

A widely distributed description of *Wozzeck* among French readers.   Contains the text, translated into French, a chronological description of the drama and music, and a brief discussion of forms.

163. Karbusicky, Vladimir. *"Der Kreuzweg* Otakar Ostrčils: Ein soziologischer Beleg zur *Wozzeck*-Rezeption?"   HJM 4 (1980): 225–58. In German.

Analysis of Ostrčil's orchestral variations, *The Way of the Cross* (1927–28), emphasizing structure and social symbolism and the relation to similar elements in Berg's *Wozzeck.*

164. Keldysch, J. "Alban Bergs *Wozzeck* und der musikalische Expressionismus." *Sowjetwissenschaft: Kunst und Literatur* 13 (1965): 746–60. In German.

The author finds in *Wozzeck* "one of the most typical and important examples of Expressionism in the postwar period." The constructive principles in the opera conform exactly to the aesthetic of the text. A Russian-language version of this article appeared in *Sovetskaya Muzyka* 29 (1965): 103–12.

165. Keller, Hans. "First Performances: The Eclecticism of *Wozzeck.*" MR 12 (1951): 309–15; 13 (1952): 133–37. In English.

Finds the stylistic eclecticism of *Wozzeck* basic to its musical thought and locates many thematic resemblances between this work and those of Schoenberg, whose music is the model of which *Wozzeck* is an inferior copy.   Regarding Keller's interpretation of the triadic sonority in *Wozzeck,* Act 2, scene 1 (mm. 116 and following), also see the letter by Hans F. Redlich, MR 13 (1952): 252, and Keller's response, MR 13 (1952): 332.

166.   Kelterborn, Rudolf.   "*Wozzeck*: Wie Oper heute noch möglich ist."   *Oper 1985* (yearbook of the journal *Opernwelt*): 44. In German.

Kelterborn finds *Wozzeck* "the classical example of opera that is still possible in the twentieth century": it is literary, rigorous in structure, and it has action that is plausible but not tied to the mundane world.

167.   Kerman, Joseph.   "Terror and Self-Pity: Alban Berg's *Wozzeck*."   *Hudson Review* 5 (1952–53): 409–19.   In English. German translation ("Naturalismus, Psychose und Sentimentalität: Alban Bergs *Wozzeck*. Analyse einer modernen Oper"), *Perspektiven* 10 (1955): 72–86.

Dismisses the relevance to criticism of Reich's analytic emphasis on the formal aspects of the opera.   More relevant are Berg's naturalistic musical usages and musical constructions that suggest psychotic states and sentimentality.

168.   ———.   Chapter 8 ("*Wozzeck* and *The Rake's Progress*").   In Kerman, *Opera and Drama*, 219–49.   New York: Vintage Books, 1956.   In English.

An interpretation of the dramaturgy of *Wozzeck*, placing it in the context of operas by Debussy, Wagner, Schoenberg, and Strauss.

169.   Klein, Fritz Heinrich.   "Alban Bergs *Wozzeck*."   MBA 5 (1923): 216–19.   In German.   English translation ("Alban Berg's *Wozzeck*") in Jarman, *Alban Berg: Wozzeck* (no. 155): 135–39.

Praises the structure of *Wozzeck* as unprecedented in its use of sections cast into the forms of absolute music.   These forms are enumerated.

170.   Klein, John W.   "Some Reflections on *Wozzeck*."   *Musical Opinion* 75/issue 896 (1952): 465–66.   In English.

Wozzeck is described as "the greatest tragic opera since Verdi's *Otello*," especially notable for its humanitarian content. Brief comparison with Benjamin Britten's *Peter Grimes.*

171. ———. *"Wozzeck:* A Summing-Up." ML 44 (1963): 132–39. In English.

A personal assessment, finding *Wozzeck* uneven (*Lulu* even more so).

172. **Klein, Rudolf.** "Zur Frage der Tonalität in Alban Bergs Oper *Wozzeck."* In *50 Jahre Wozzeck* (no. 173): 32–45. In German.

The author outlines a system of tonal relations that is applicable to traditional as well as modern works. He applies the system to Marie's Lullaby from *Wozzeck,* Act 1, scene 3: Beneath the melody he places a hypothetical line made from fundamental tones extracted from each chord. These tones suggest, by motion from tonic to dominant, the existence of the key of B♭. Quickly, however, this key meets opposition from unrelated fundamental tones, creating a sense of bitonality, which the author finds frequently throughout the opera.

173. **Kolleritsch, Otto, editor.** *50 Jahre "Wozzeck" von Alban Berg: Vorgeschichte und Auswirkungen in der Opernästhetik.* Studien zur Wertungsforschung, volume 10. Graz: Universal Edition für Institut für Wertungsforschung, 1978. 146 p. ISBN 370240130X. ML55.S92 Bd. 10. In German. Reviewed by Mosco Carner, MT 120 (1979): 654–55; Douglas Jarman, ML 61 (1980): 73–74; Volker Scherliess, MF 34 (1981): 85–87.

A collection of eleven articles concerning *Wozzeck,* originating as papers read in November 1975 at a conference on the opera in Graz, sponsored by the Institut für Wertungsforschung of the Hochschule für Musik und Darstellende Kunst of that city. The mailing address of each of the eleven authors is given as an appendix. The eleven articles are enumerated elsewhere in this bibliography.

174. ———. *"Wozzeck* und die Steiermark." In *50 Jahre Wozzeck* (no. 173): 125–41. In German.

Recounts the importance of the district of Styria for Berg personally and artistically. Many of his most outstanding pieces, including *Wozzeck,* were composed there, making it all the more painful for Berg that the Styrians were slow to accept his music. The first performance of a work by Berg in Styria (Three Fragments from *Wozzeck,* conducted by Karl Rankl in Graz) did not take place until November, 1935. Reviews of this concert show the lack of understanding at the time for Berg's music. A letter from Berg to Rankl following the concert is reproduced, in which the composer states that *Wozzeck* is "truly a product of Styria" since the "entire work" was composed in Trahütten from 1914 to 1919.

175.   König, Werner. *Tonalitätsstrukturen in Alban Bergs Oper "Wozzeck."* Dissertation, University of Heidelberg, 1974. Tutzing: Hans Schneider, 1974. 118 p. ISBN 3795201314. ML410.B47 K6. In German.

Argues that *Wozzeck* should be considered essentially a tonal work in which keys, expressed primarily in cadential formations, are systematically linked to dramatic entities.

176.   Krämer, Ulrich. "Die Suite als Charakterstudie des Hauptmanns in Alban Bergs *Wozzeck.*" HJM 10 (1988): 46–75. In German.

Analysis of the suite in Act 1, scene 1, of *Wozzeck,* suggesting parallels in rhythmic and melodic character with Bach's French Suites.

177.   Krause, Ernst. "Der Komponist des *Wozzeck*: Zum 80. Geburtstag von Alban Berg." *Musik und Gesellschaft* 15 (1965): 98–100. In German.

A general appreciation of the composer, focusing on *Wozzeck.* "To speak of Alban Berg is by itself to speak of *Wozzeck.*"

178.   La main gauche. "On the Other Hand." *Musical Opinion* 59 (1936): 393–95. In English.

Sympathetic note concerning Berg and *Wozzeck* following the composer's death.

179. Landau. Alexander. "Die Musik und das soziale Problem." MBA 8 (1926): 273–76. In German.

A socialist interpretation of *Wozzeck*, notable since it is the only interpretive study of the opera ever to receive Berg's explicit approval (see Volkov, no. 1033). The opera "serves as an especially fortunate example of the interdependence of sociological and musical-artistic forces." The play itself is essentially a social drama, but Berg's formalistic treatment has lifted it above the specific and temporal level at which it was left by Büchner to the higher level of universals and collective perceptions. Thus the individuals in the play are reduced in importance beneath the events that they enact. The real primary roles in the opera are poverty, hunger, mistreatment, illness, death.

180. Lang, Patrick. "Mahler, mein lebendes Ideal: Zum Einfluß Gustav Mahlers auf Berg und *Wozzeck.*" In Hanselmann, *Alban Berg Wozzeck* (no. 134): 191–208. In German.

Detailed analysis comparing *Wozzeck* to works by Mahler. Similarities are found in instrumentation, compositional procedure, counterpoint, rhythm, thematic-motivic processes, and expressive content.

181. Lang, Paul Henry. Chapter 15 ("Berg"). In Lang, *Critic at the Opera,* 264–68. New York: W. W. Norton and Company, 1971. In English.

This book is a collection of reviews and articles written by Lang for the *New York Herald Tribune* between 1954 and 1963. The chapter on Berg deals with *Wozzeck* ("undoubtedly the outstanding opera of the last half-century") following its first performance at the Metropolitan Opera in New York in 1959.

182. Läuchli, Alex. [Untitled commentary on *Wozzeck*]. In Hanselmann (no. 134): 51–153. In German.

Running commentary to the German libretto of the opera
explaining and interpreting elements of musical expression,
especially as regards formal and thematic practices.

183. Lederer, Josef-Horst. "Zu Alban Bergs Invention über den
Ton H." In *50 Jahre Wozzeck* (no. 173): 57–67. In German.

Explores the background to and the symbolic meaning of
Berg's use of the tone B to symbolize Wozzeck's murderous
obsession.   The key of B (especially B minor) has a long
history of negative, even grotesque, symbolism.   Berg's
orchestrational interpretation of the continuous tone suggests,
however, no deadly paralyzation, but instead life in both a
naturalistic and psychoanalytic sense.   It is crucial to note
that the tone B finds its release and resolution in the tone C,
symbolic of Marie's release from her miserable earthly
existence.

184. Leister, Hans. "Alban Bergs *Wozzeck* im Musikunterricht
der Studienstufe." *Music und Bildung* 2 (1970): 10–13. In German.

Strategies for teaching about *Wozzeck*.

185.   Liebestöckl, Hans. "Die häßliche Oper: Alban Bergs
Wozzeck in der Wiener Oper." *Sonn- und Montagszeitung*
(Vienna), 31 March 1930. Reprinted in *Der Auftakt* 10 (1930): 118.
In German.

A critique notable for its vitriolic language. Hearing *Wozzeck*
is compared to a trip to the dentist. The reviewer is forced
to admit that the audience was enthusiastic.

186.   Lobanov, Arkadij. *"Voccek" A. Berga.   Sproba kiritcnogo
analizy* [Alban Berg's *Wozzeck*: Essay in Critical Analysis]. Kiev:
Muzicna Ukraina, 1977. In Ukranian, summary in Russian. 87
p.

187.   Mahler, Fritz. *Zu Alban Bergs Oper "Wozzeck": Szenische
und musikalische Übersicht.* Vienna: Universal Edition, 1957. 9 p.
MT100.M14. In German.

English translation: *Concerning Alban Berg's Opera "Wozzeck"*: *Scenic and Musical Analysis*. Vienna: Universal Edition, 1965. 9 p.

Chartlike summary of scenic and musical components of *Wozzeck*.

188. Malipiero, Riccardo. "La lezione di Alban Berg: *Wozzeck*." *Il diapason* 3/5–6 (1952). In Italian.

189. Mann, Carol Finn. "A Comparison of Musical Settings of Georg Büchner's *Woyzeck* by Alban Berg and Manfred Gurlitt." Dissertation, University of Cincinnati, 1986. UMI order no. 8708128. 235 p. In English.

General description and comparison of the two settings of *Wozzeck*.

190. Mann, Monika. "Anläßlich einer Aufführung des *Wozzeck*." *Musik der Zeit* 6 ("Oper im XX. Jahrhundert") (1954): 34. In German.

Brief interpretive reflection upon *Wozzeck* and its relation to the genre of opera.

191. Markus, Wim. "*Wozzeck* en het uitbeelden van de verblinding: Een gevoel voor het weggeworpene." *Mens en melodie* 49 (1994): 82–89. In Dutch.

Interprets *Wozzeck* as an existentialist work.

192. Matkey, Isolde. "Alban Bergs *Wozzeck* in Leningrad." *Oper heute* 8 (1985): 214–28. In German.

Discussion of the historical background to and performances of *Wozzeck* in Leningrad (1927), their political ramifications, and selections from press reviews. Reprints the text of Berg's letter (5 August 1929) to Boris Asaf'ev (also given in Volkov, no. 1032).

193. Mauser, Siegfried. "Arnold Schönbergs *Erwartung* und Alban Bergs *Wozzeck*: Studie zur Entwicklungsgeschichte des expressionistischen Musiktheaters." ABS 2 (1980): 91–96.   In German.

> Compares and contrasts *Wozzeck* and *Erwartung* as representing two stages in the development of expressionist musical theater. Schoenberg's monodrama relates closely to expressionist drama prior to World War I in its brevity and reductive elements; *Wozzeck*, on the other hand, is similar to expressionist drama after the war in its use of closed dramatic forms and longer overall form. (See no. 194 by the same author, which contains many of the same conclusions.)

194. ————. *Das expressionistische Musiktheater der Wiener Schule: Stilistische und entwicklungsgeschichtliche Untersuchungen zu Arnold Schoenbergs "Erwartung," op. 17, "Die glückliche Hand," op. 18 und Alban Bergs "Wozzeck," op. 7.* Dissertation, University of Salzburg, 1981. Regensburg: Gustav Bosse Verlag, 1982. 168 p. ISBN 3764922648. ML1723.M38 1982. In German. Reviewed by Martin Elste, NZM 144/7–8 (1983): 67–68; Rudolf Stephan, MF 39 (1986): 68–69; Sigrid Wiesmann, ÖMZ 39 (1984): 343.

> Attempts to establish an expressionistic musical and dramaturgical style in modern opera by comparison with accepted precepts in literary criticism. The formal differences between *Erwartung* and *Wozzeck* reflect the evolution of literary form in expressionist dramas written during the same period as the operas.

195. McCredie, Andrew D. "A Half Centennial New Look at Alban Berg's *Wozzeck*: Its Antecedents and Influence on German Expressionist Music Theatre." *Miscellanea musicologica: Adelaide Studies in Musicology* 9 (1977): 156–205. In English.

> Broad study of *Wozzeck*, especially its textual and musical antecedents, comparisons with Manfred Gurlitt's *Wozzeck*, aspects of large and detailed structure, and impact on later composers.

196. Mellers, Wilfrid. "*Wozzeck* after Twenty-Five Years." *Listener* 46 (1951–52): 238. In English.

General appraisal of the opera and its aesthetic, holding that Berg's creativity renewed the decay implicit in the genre in the late romantic period.

197. Melo, Juan Vicente. *"Wozzeck en México."* *Siempre*, 21 September 1966. Reprinted in *Pauta* 4/15 (1985): 57–60. In Spanish.

Brief account of the history of *Wozzeck* in Mexico.

198. Mimoso-Ruiz, Duarte. *"Wozzeck et le mythe du pauvre soldat."* *L'avant-scène opéra* (no. 81): 100–103. In French.

Comparison of soldier figures in *Wozzeck*, Charles Ramuz's *L'histoire du soldat*, and Jaroslav Hašek's *The Good Soldier Schweik*.

199. Mistler, Jean. *"Woyzeck, Wozzeck."* *La revue de Paris* 71/1 (1964): 114–18. In French.

General account of *Wozzeck*, the Büchner play, and the opera's structure and aesthetics on the occasion of the first Paris staging.

200. Mooser, R.-Aloys. *"Wozzeck d'Alban Berg."* *Dissonances* 15/3 (1934): 67–69. In French.

201. Müller, Gerhard. *"Georg Büchner als Musikdramatiker: Anmerkungen zu einer Aporie."* *Theater der Zeit* 39/2 (1984): 10–14. In German.

Analysis of Büchner's appeal for modern opera composers.

202. Müller, Ingvelde. *"Wozzeck* in 90 Minuten: Eine Untersuchung der Inszenierungsprinzipien von Alban Bergs *Wozzeck* in der Ostberliner Staatsoper."* *Bühnentechnische Rundschau* 47/2 (1957): 5–9. In German.

Detailed description of the decor designed by Werner Kelch and Hainer Hill for the 1955 staging of *Wozzeck* at the Staatsoper in East Berlin. The production was spare, in keeping with the "astounding concentration of musical thoughts," and aimed for a "magical realism."

203. *De muziek.* 5/1 (1930-31). Alban Berg number. In Dutch.

Published to coincide with a performance of *Wozzeck* in Amsterdam in 1930, the volume contains articles by Berg, Paul Pisk, Paul Sanders, Willem Pijper, and Paul Cronheim.

204. **Neef, Sigrid.** "Von der Ungleichheit des Ähnlichen: *Wozzeck* von Alban Berg und *Die Nase* von Dmitri Schostakowitsch." *Musik und Gesellschaft* 35 (1985): 85–89. In German.

Compares and contrasts the two works, finding Berg's opera to be a decisive point from which Shostakovich pushed off toward "new shores."

205. **Nejedlý, Zdeněk.** "Zur Erstaufführung des *Wozzeck* von Alban Berg in Prag 1926: Aufsätze und Zeitungsartikel." BMW 25 (1983): 272–87. In German.

Reprint of the author's articles and reviews in the journal *Var* and the communist newspaper *Rudé právo* of Berg's *Wozzeck* following its tumultuous premiere in Prague in 1926. Nejedlý and other left-wing intellectuals tended to be supportive of the work.

206. **Neuwirth, Gösta.** "*Wozzeck*—I, i: Formdisposition und musikalisches Material." In *50 Jahre Wozzeck* (no. 173): 46–56. In German.

The suite in Act 1, scene 1, consists of nine sections, organized symmetrically about the central gigue. Each section is discussed in terms of its distinguishing features, which include motives, temporal-metric relations, and instrumentation.

207. **Noske, Frits.** "The Captain and the Doctor in *Wozzeck*." In *Analytica: Studies in the Description and Analysis of Music*, 269–75. Edited by Anders Lönn and Erik Kjellberg. Stockholm: Almqvist

& Wiksell, 1985. Reprinted in *La musique et le rite sacré et profane*, volume 2: 689–701, Actes du XIIIe Congrès de la Société Internationale de Musicologie (Strasbourg: University of Strasbourg), 1986. In English.

Finds the two characters presented as "inverted stereotypes," the irony of which is also captured in Berg's depiction of them. Like Wozzeck and Marie, they too are victims of society.

208. Op de Coul, Paul. "*Wozzeck,* Amsterdam 1930: Alban Berg und die 'Wagnervereeniging'." In *Neue Musik und Tradition: Festschrift Rudolf Stephan zum 65. Geburtstag*, 473–83. Edited by Josef Kuckertz, et al. Laaber: Laaber-Verlag, 1990. In German.

Outlines the history of the first performances of *Wozzeck* in Holland in 1930, sponsored by the Amsterdam Wagner Society and its leader, Paul Cronheim. Four letters from 1930 from Berg to Cronheim are transcribed (dated 25 April, 31 July, 9 September, 14 October).

209. Oppens, Kurt. "Alban Bergs *Wozzeck*." *Merkur* 21 (1967): 1154–69. In German.

Discussion of aesthetic issues regarding *Wozzeck*, especially the capacity of atonal music to express a realistic image of nature and character. Although atonality gives the music a subjective character that is difficult to project upon a realistic drama, Berg succeeded in making his musical idiom effective.

210. Paap, Wouter. "Twee moderne opera's: *Wozzeck* en *De droom.*" *Mens en melodie* 26 (1971): 143–44. In Dutch.

Reviews and compares *Wozzeck* and Ton de Leeuw's opera *De droom*.

211. Pass, Walter. "Für und Wider im Streit um die Wiener Erstaufführung des *Wozzeck*." In *50 Jahre Wozzeck* (no. 173): 92–124. In German.

Discussion of the factors—artistic and political—that were at play leading to and following the Viennese premiere of *Wozzeck* on 30 March 1930. The discussion relies primarily on journalistic reporting regarding the 1930 performances. Berg's article "Wozzek" (sic) (no. 44) and an interview ("Kritik der Kritik," no. 53) by Otto König with Berg and Clemens Krauss are reprinted.

212. Pazdro, Michel. "Les échos de la presse française." *L'avant-scène opéra* (no. 81): 158–59. In French.

Excerpts from French journalistic writing on *Wozzeck* from the 1960s.

213. ———. "L'oeuvre à l'affiche." *L'avant-scène opéra* (no. 81): 142–57. In French.

Summary of stagings of *Wozzeck* in major cities from 1925 until the 1980s.

214. Perle, George. "The Musical Language of *Wozzeck*." *Music Forum* 1 (1967): 204–59. In English.

An exploration of "those elements of pitch organization [in *Wozzeck*] that generate the context within which themes and motives operate." The analysis deals specifically with tone centers (in both atonal and pseudo-tonal passages), vertical sets, series of chords, basic cells, segments of whole-tone, semitonal, and diatonic scales, symmetrical formations, and ostinati. This article is largely incorporated in Chapter 5 of no. 215.

215. ———. *The Operas of Alban Berg.* Volume 1: *"Wozzeck."* Berkeley, Los Angeles, and London: University of California Press, 1980. xvii, 231 p. ISBN 0520034406. ML 410.B47 P48. In English. Reviewed by Robert Craft, *New York Review of Books,* 27/18 (1980): 37–39; Mark DeVoto, *Notes,* 37 (1980-81): 851–52; Douglass M. Green, *Journal of Music Theory* 26 (1982): 145–55; Paul Griffiths, MT 122 (1981): 604; Hanns-Werner Heister, NZM 143/2 (1982): 68; Martha Maclean Hyde, JAMS 34 (1981): 573–87; Douglas Jarman, ML 62 (1981): 409–12; Rudolf Klein, ÖMZ 40

(1985): 61–62; George Martin, *Opera Quarterly* 3/3 (1985): 158–63; Paul A. Pisk, *American Music Teacher* 31/5 (1981–82): 50; Patrick J. Smith, *High Fidelity/Musical America*, 31/3 (1981): MA 19; Michael Taylor, MA 2 (1983): 294–97; Glenn Watkins, *In Theory Only* 5/3 (1979): 40-42; Arnold Whittall, MR 42 (1981): 149–51.

An analytic study incorporating and expanding upon several earlier essays by the same author. The first chapter surveys Berg's music prior to *Wozzeck*; elsewhere the discussion deals with the composer's revision of text fragments, large-scale formal design, elements of musical symbolism, and specific aspects of musical style and compositional material. As an appendix, the German text of the play is given in its entirety, from the edition by Paul Landau (from Büchner, *Gesammelte Schriften*, Berlin: Paul Cassirer, 1909).

216. ———. "Representation and Symbol in the Music of *Wozzeck*." MR 32 (1971): 281–308. In English.

Surveys the leitmotifs and recurrent sections of *Wozzeck* in addition to other musical elements that convey dramatic symbolism. Much of this article returns in Chapter 1 of Perle's book, no. 215.

217. ———. "*Woyzeck* and *Wozzeck*." MQ 53 (1967): 206–19. In English.

History of Büchner's play, its early editions (especially those by Karl Emil Franzos and Paul Landau), and their use by Berg. (Also see Petersen, no. 219.) Much of the material from this article is reused in Perle's book, no. 215, Chapter 2.

218. ———. "*Wozzeck*: Ein zweiter Blick auf das Libretto." NZM 129 (1968): 218–21. In German.

Further information (with some updating) is added to Perle's 1967 article, no. 214, such as the use of Georg Witkowski's edition of *Wozzeck* as a text source for Berg in the late stages of composition.

219. Petersen, Peter. *Alban Berg. "Wozzeck": Eine semantische Analyse unter Einbeziehung der Skizzen und Dokumente aus dem Nachlaß Berg.* Dissertation, University of Hamburg, 1980. MK Sonderband. Munich: Edition text + kritik, 1985. 306 p. ISBN 3883772143. MT100.B57 P5 1985. In German.

An attempt to attach semantic functions to elements of *Wozzeck* that will be more precise than the meaning ascribed heretofore to these component parts. An appendix deals analytically with *Lulu*, Act 1, scene 3.

220. ———. "Büchner aus zweiter Hand: Neue Thesen über Bergs *Wozzeck*-Libretto." ABS 2 (1981): 80–90. In German.

It has been assumed (see Ernst Hilmar, no. 145) that Berg constructed the libretto of Wozzeck from the 1913 Insel Verlag edition (*Wozzeck-Lenz: Zwei Fragmente*), which was based on the wording used in the first edition of the play by Karl Franzos. But, nearing the final stages of composing the opera, Berg also used the 1920 edition of Georg Witkowski. Witkowski went back to the original manuscripts and showed that Franzos had often been free, even careless, with his source. Berg presumably acquired the Witkowski edition in summer 1921: he then copied into the Insel edition several of Witkowski's more authoritative readings.

221. ———. "Leitmotive und andere Semanteme in Bergs *Wozzeck.*" *Musik und Bildung* 17 (1985): 853–61. In German.

A semantic analysis of the music of *Wozzeck*, focusing upon leitmotifs as referential symbols as well as "semantemes" (musical elements imbued historically with referential significance).

222. ———. "Wozzecks persönliche Leitmotive: Ein Beitrag zur Deutung des Sinngehalts der Musik in Alban Bergs *Wozzeck.*" HJM 4 (1980): 33–83. In German.

Detailed account and interpretation of five motifs in the music of *Wozzeck* that are associated with aspects of the title character: Wozzeck as proletariat; as man, father, and individual; as paranoid; as murderer; and as soldier (the last interpreted as a rhythmic motif).

223. Petschnig, Emil. "Atonales Opernschaffen." *Die Musik* 16 (1924): 340-45. In German. English translation in Jarman, *Alban Berg: Wozzeck* (no. 155): 143–49.

Provoked by the article concerning *Wozzeck* by Ernst Viebig (no. 292), Petschnig gives his impression of Berg's still unperformed opera. He rejects the atonal language of the work and the "unnatural" vocal style, neither capable of reversing the decline into which modern operatic composition has fallen. He also finds the use of forms from absolute music to be unsuccessful since they do not do justice to the prototypes that they copy and are generally inaudible as to their type. Also see Berg's response to Petschnig (no. 37).

224. Pijper, Willem. "Alban Berg's *Wozzeck*-muziek." *De muziek* 5 (1930-31): 15–21. In Dutch.

Sketch of the structure and aesthetic of the opera.

225. Pirro, Carlo de. "Forma e auto-memoria: Montaggio delle ripetizioni nel *Wozzeck* di Berg." *Musica/realtà* 43 (1994): 173–95. In Italian.

Study of recurrent elements in *Wozzeck*, including rhythmic figures, harmonic units, leitmotifs, and ostinati.

226. Pisk, Paul A. "Eine neuartige Oper: Bemerkungen zu Alban Bergs *Wozzeck*." *Der Auftakt* 4 (1924): 10-13. In German.

Sees *Wozzeck* as a pathbreaking work, prepared only by operas by Arnold Schoenberg and Franz Schreker. The use of symphonic form in Act 2 of Schreker's *Der ferne Klang* is held to be a direct antecedent of Berg's formalistic practices.

227. Ploebsch, Gerd. *Alban Bergs "Wozzeck": Dramaturgie und musikalischer Aufbau. Nebst einer Bibliographie der Schriften und Briefe Bergs sowie der Literatur.* Dissertation, University of

Hamburg, 1968. Sammlung musikwissenschaftlicher Abhandlungen, volume 48. Strasbourg: P. H. Heitz; Baden-Baden: Verlag Heitz, 1968. 97 pp. with unpaginated bibliography. ML100.B57 P6. In German. Reviewed by Carl Dahlhaus, MF 23 (1970): 482–83; Rudolf Klein, ÖMZ 24 (1969): 342; Massimo Mila, *Nuova rivista musicale italiana* 4 (1970): 162–63; Willi Reich, MEL 36 (1969): 426, and *Musica* 23 (1969): 506; Klaus Schweizer, NZM 130 (1969): 534.

General study of *Wozzeck*, covering literary sources, musical forms, style. Extensive bibliography.

228. ———. "'Die Stimme in der Oper': Zu Alban Bergs *Wozzeck*." NZM 126 (1965): 416–17. In German.

General discussion of singing in *Wozzeck* based on Berg's essay (no. 48).

229. Radice, Mark A. "The Anatomy of a Libretto: The Music Inherent in Büchner's *Woyzeck*." MR 41 (1980): 223–33. In English.

A study of the musical elements and imagery inherent in Büchner's *Woyzeck* and Berg's faithful adaptation of them. Folk songs are especially important.

230. Rawlins, Joseph T. *"Moses und Aron and Wozzeck*: Monumental Music." *Opera Journal* 18/1 (1985): 11–18. In English.

Compares and contrasts the two works.

231. Redlich, Hans F. "Die Opern des sozialen Mitleids." ÖMZ 15 (1960): 233–36. In German.

Extracted from Redlich's book (no. 908).

232. Reich, Willi. "Alban Berg: *Wozzeck*." *Musik der Zeit* 6 ("Oper im XX. Jahrhundert") (1954): 27–34. In German.

General account of the opera. The structure of the various scenes and acts is described.

233. ———. "Alban Berg *Wozzeck* im Zürcher Stadttheater." SMZ 96 (1956): 132–33. In German.

Discusses performance problems in *Wozzeck* and the 1956 performances in Zurich.

234. ———. "Alban Bergs Oper *Wozzeck.*" SMZ 70 (1930): 173–77. In German. Dutch version ("Alban Berg's *Wozzeck*") in *De muziek* 3 (1928–29): 457–59.

Overview of the opera, its historical background, and its forms.

235. ———. "Das Schicksal einer modernen Oper." MBA 17 (1935): 24–25. In German.

Recounts the success of *Wozzeck*, from its uncertain beginnings in January 1923, when Berg published the piano score at his own expense, to later triumph. Also see no. 240.

236. ———. "Vertauschte Dimensionen: (Ein Beitrag zur Morphologie der 'atonalen Oper')." MBA 14 (1932): 15–17. In German.

Using *Wozzeck* as an example, the author explores ways in which musical elements in the atonal language exchange functions, for example, a rhythm developed as a chord, or line becoming a rhythm.

237. ———. *"Wozzeck": A Guide to the Words and Music of the Opera by Alban Berg.* Modern Music Monographs. New York: League of Composers, 1931. 24, ii p. Reprinted in MQ 38 (1952): 1–21 with a "Postscript by Alban Berg."
Second edition, New York: G. Schirmer, 1952. MT100.B4 R4 1952. In English.

Covers Berg in general, his organization of Büchner's text fragments, overall musical structure, forms present in the individual scenes and interludes, and a history of the opera.

238. ———. *"Wozzeck*—heute." ÖMZ 6 (1951): 176–77. In German.

Reflections upon *Wozzeck* following a performance in Bern in 1951.

239. ———. *"Wozzeck* Miszellen." *Opernwelt* 12/1 (1971): 18–19. In German.

Documents concerning *Wozzeck*: Berg's wartime service; letter from Berg to Webern of 19 August 1918 regarding the opera; Berg's "Operntheater" (no. 46).

240. ———. [Untitled essay, "Dies war die erste Nachricht"]. *Europäische Rundschau* 22 ("Musikfest Wien") (1948): 1017. In German.

A shortened version of Reich, no. 235.

241. ———. *"Wozzeck:* Reminiszenzen aus seiner Urzeit." *Musik und Szene* 7/10 (1962–63): 1–6. In German.

242. Réti, Rudolf. *"Wozzeck* in der Staatsoper." *Der Abend,* 31 March 1930. Excerpts reprinted in Pass (no. 211): 104–105. In German.

Réti's commentary upon the opera followed its Vienna premiere. "Even today a light dust falls on this *Wozzeck,* ultramodern at its time of origin."

243. Richter, Christoph. "Die Wirtshausszene aus Alban Bergs *Wozzeck.* Unterrichtsmodell: Verhältnis von Musik und Sprache in der Oper." *Musik und Bildung* 14 (1982): 553–63. In German.

Analysis of music and dramaturgy in *Wozzeck,* Act 2, scene 4, concerning didactic approaches.

244. Roman, Zoltan. "The Orchestral Interlude in *Wozzeck,* III, 4/5: Berg's 'Homage' to Mahler and *Das Lied von der Erde."* In *Atti del XIV congresso della Società Internazionale di Musicologia,* volume 3: 361–68. Turin: Edizioni di Torino, 1990. In English.

A passage from Berg's interlude (mm. 320–71) is interpreted as containing an allusion to a parallel passage (mm. 303–74) in "Der Abschied" from Mahler's *Das Lied von der Erde,* a tribute by Berg to Mahler. The similarities include melodic and contextual elements.

245. Rosenfeld, Gerhard, Siegfried Matthus, and Pavel Eckstein. "Der epochale *Wozzeck*: Zum 100. Geburtstag von Alban Berg." *Oper heute* 7 (1984): 110–45. In German.

Eckstein's contribution ("Der 'Fall *Wozzeck*' in Prag") reproduces and discusses press notices of the 1926 Prague premiere of *Wozzeck*.

246. Rosenfeld, Paul. "Alban Berg's *Wozzeck*." *New Republic* 66 (1931): 100–101. In English.

Regrets the absence of *Wozzeck* from the Metropolitan Opera, although "Berg's inspiration certainly is even less thorough than Schoenberg's, occasionally lapsing into mediocrity."

247. Rösing, Helmut. "Zu einem Ausdrucksmodell in Beethovens *Fidelio* und Bergs *Wozzeck*." MF 23 (1970): 303–10. In German.

Analysis of Act 3, scene 1 (mm. 109–21) of *Wozzeck* using information theory, finding similarities with a passage from Beethoven's *Fidelio*, Act 2, scene 1.

248. Rostand, Claude. "*Wozzeck* d'Alban Berg." *Musique contemporaine: revue internationale* 2–3 (1952): 104–107. In French.

General report on *Wozzeck* following its performance at the Salzburg Festival in 1951. The author interviewed Helene Berg as to Berg's wishes regarding objectivity in the performance of his music. She asserted that the work was itself highly objective and should be performed as such.

249. Ruppel, Karl Heinz. "Alban Berg und der musikalische Expressionismus." *Deutsche Zeitung und Wirtschaftszeitung* 11/2 (7 January 1956): 18. In German.

Interprets Berg's *Wozzeck* as having kinship with German expressionist painting and literature. Like Schoenberg's *Erwartung*, Berg's opera is characterized by "ecstatic-confessional,   self-exposing,   screaming   and exalted-yearning,   stammering   and   feverish-visionary qualities."

250. Russell, John. Chapter 8 ("Berlin: *Wozzeck* Triumphant"). In Russell, *Erich Kleiber: A Memoir*, 84–102. London: André Deutsch, 1957. Reprint, New York: Da Capo Press, 1981. In English.

Chapter 8 of Russell's study contains information on Erich Kleiber's preparations for the first performance of *Wozzeck* in Berlin in 1925. Passages from Berg's correspondence with the conductor are liberally quoted, and Berg's later contact with Kleiber (especially concerning preparations for staging *Lulu*) is sketched elsewhere in the book.

251. Sabin, Robert. "*Wozzeck*: No Music of Our Time Is More Subtly Organized Than This Score." *Musical America* 71/5 (1951): 6–7, 34. In English.

"A complete analysis of the score," prior to a concert performance of the opera in April 1951 by the New York Philharmonic (under Dimitri Mitropoulos).

252. Sanders, Paul F. "Het *Wozzeck*-drama en zijn dichter." *De muziek* 5 (1930–31): 8–14. In Dutch.

Discussion of the dramatic element of Büchner's play and Berg's opera.

253. Sargeant, Winthrop. "Musical Events: Dear Alban." *New Yorker* (14 March 1959): 91–94. In English.

Apropos of the staging of *Wozzeck* at the Metropolitan Opera in 1959, Sargeant finds the work to project "an adolescent view of life and art" with music that creates merely "a period piece."

254. Schäfke, Rudolf. "Alban Bergs Oper *Wozzeck*." MEL 5 (1925–26): 267–83. Reprinted in Csampai and Holland (no. 103): 183–99. In German.

Pioneering analysis of *Wozzeck,* appearing shortly after the premier performance. The author emphasizes the relation of the work to formal prototypes in instrumental music.

255. *Der Scheinwerfer: Blätter der städtischen Bühnen* (Essen) 3/4 (1929).

Special *Wozzeck* issue appearing at the time of the work's first performance in Essen.

256. **Scherber, Ferdinand.** *"Wozzeck* in Wien." *Signale für die musikalische Welt* 16 (1930): 514. In German.

A review and interpretation of *Wozzeck* following the first Viennese performance in 1930. The author laments the absence of singable melodies, speculating also that the opera may be more attuned to 1950 than to 1930.

257. **Scherliess, Volker.** "Weitere Dokumente zum Prager *Wozzeck* 1926." MF 27 (1974): 465–71. In German.

Excerpts from reviews in Prague following the tumultuous premiere of *Wozzeck* there in 1926, concluding that the work was the object of political antipathies more than artistic ones.

258. **Schilling, O. E.** "Wir arme Leut: Zum 70. Geburtstag von Alban Berg." *Das Musikleben* 8 (1955): 112–13. In German.

Brief appreciation, mainly concerning *Wozzeck.* Reprinted from the *Stuttgarter Zeitung.*

259. **Schmalfeldt, Janet.** *Berg's "Wozzeck": Harmonic Language and Dramatic Design.* New Haven, London: Yale University Press, 1983. xii, 281 p. ISBN 0300027109. MT100.B57S35 1983. In English. Reviewed by Juliane Brand, *Opera Quarterly* 3/3 (1985): 163–65; Peter Cahn, NZM 145/4 (1984): 45–46; Douglass M. Green and Stefan Kostka, *Journal of Music Theory* 29 (1985): 177–86; David Headlam, *In Theory Only* 8/4–5 (1985): 65–77; David Hush, JAMS 37 (1984): 424–28; Douglas Jarman, ML 65 (1984): 294–96; Jan Maegaard, *Dansk musiktidsskrift* 58 (1983–84): 188–89;

Anthony Pople, MA 5 (1986): 265–70; Rudolf Stephan, ÖMZ 39 (1984): 343–44.

> Analysis of pitch-class sets in passages from *Wozzeck*. The pitch configurations associated with Marie and Wozzeck are of primary concern. The analytic method is also applied to Act 1, scene 1, and conclusions are drawn concerning relations among the many pitch-class sets that are adduced. An explanatory discussion of set theory is provided.

260. ———. "Berg's *Wozzeck*: Pitch-Class Set Structures and the Dramatic Design." Dissertation, Yale University, 1979. UMI order no. 8121410. 363 p. In English.

> Related in content to no. 259.

261. Schmidgall, Gary. Chapter 9 ("Alban Berg: *Wozzeck*"). In Schmidgall, *Literature as Opera*, 287–319. New York: Oxford University Press, 1977. In English.

> A general survey of the opera emphasizing the literary element. The relation of Büchner's text to early twentieth-century Expressionism is outlined. Also contains a "postscript" on *Lulu*, again dealing mainly with issues arising in the text.

262. Schmidt, Henry J. "Alban Berg's *Wozzeck* (1921)." In *Georg Büchner: The Complete Collected Works*, 388–92. Edited and translated by Henry J. Schmidt. New York: Avon Books, 1977. In English.

> A general description of Berg's musical language in *Wozzeck* and its appropriateness to Büchner's disordered text. Also a comparison with Manfred Gurlitt's *Wozzeck*.

263. Schnebel, Dieter. "*Wozzeck*, ein Gesamtkunstwerk? Notizen zu einer Frage." In *50 Jahre Wozzeck* (no. 173): 78–83. In German.

> Compares the setting, lighting requirements, and actions of the cast for each scene of *Wozzeck* to judge whether the work is a "total work of art" in the Wagnerian sense. In general,

it is not an example of a *Gesamtkunstwerk* in which multimedia factors are developed, but only (as Berg himself claimed) an opera whose subject is Wozzeck himself.

264. Schroeder, David P. "Berg's *Wozzeck* and Strindberg's Musical Models." *Opera Journal* 21 (1988): 2–12. In English.

Argues that Berg's formal approach to Büchner's play was suggested by the writings of Strindberg, especially the play *There Are Crimes and Crimes*.

265. ————. "Opera, Apocalypse and the Dance of Death: Berg's Indebtedness to Kraus." *Mosaic: A Journal for the Interdisciplinary Study of Literature* 25/1 (1992): 91–105. In English.

A study of the influence exerted by the writings of Karl Kraus upon Berg's *Wozzeck*. In Kraus, Berg found a model for a new operatic conception by which issues such as the apocalypse, despair, and redemption could be expressed.

266. Schuh, Willi. "*Wozzeck*-Studienpartitur." SMZ 96 (1956): 133–34. In German.

Review of and commentary upon Hans E. Apostel's edition of the opera.

267. Schüler, Johannes. "Das Märchen von den unüberwindlichen Schwierigkeiten des *Wozzeck*." *Pult und Taktstock* 6 (1929): 32–34. In German.

Gives Schüler's rehearsal schedule for his recent production of *Wozzeck* in Oldenburg, showing that the work can be mastered in a reasonable period of time.

268. Schulz, Reinhard. "Bergs Ausweg aus einem Dilemma." In *Wozzeck-Programmheft der Bayerischen Staatsoper*, 1982. Reprinted in Csampai and Holland (no. 103): 246–51. In German.

The "dilemma" seen by the author is the problem of applying the atonal language to an entire opera, which by World War I seemed in a state of crisis. Berg solved the dilemma by his nondoctrinaire eclecticism.

269. Siegmund-Schultze, Walther. "Janáček und Berg." In *Colloquium Leoš Janáček et musica europaea*, 213–17. Edited by Rudolf Pečman. Colloquia on the History and Theory of Music at the International Musical Festival in Brno, volume 3. Brno: International Musical Festival, 1970. In German.

Finds common ground between the operas of Leoš Janáček and Berg in their use of texts dealing with social issues, tragic conclusions, and intensely psychological insights. Musical similarities include the common use of symmetrical forms, variational procedures, and concertante media. A specific comparison of *Wozzeck* and *Katya Kabanova* is made.

270. Simon, Eric. "A Chance Discovery." BSN 10 (1981): 11. In English.

Suggests a possible folk-song model for Marie's cradle song (*Wozzeck*, Act 1, scene 3); lists other folk song texts adopted by Berg from Büchner.

271. Simon, John. "Meeting of Minds." *Opera News* 49/9 (1985): 14–16, 46. In English.

Emphasizes the differences of the opera *Wozzeck* from the play.

272. Smith, Patrick J. "Order from Disorder: Berg Employs Formal Devices to Record Modern Man's Disintegration." *Opera News* 54/8 (1990): 14–15, 45. In English.

Sees *Wozzeck* as embodying a central paradox of order existing within disorder.

273. Stefan, Paul. "*Wozzeck*." MBA 8 (1926): 4. In German.

Brief praise for the work.

274. ——. "*Wozzeck*: an Atonal Opera." *Modern Music* 3/3 (1925–26): 38–40. In English.

A report on the work and its first performance.

275. ——. "*Wozzeck* und Wien." MBA 12 (1930): 176. In German.

Laments the slowness with which Vienna accepts new repertory and calls for the performance of *Wozzeck*.

276. Stefan, Paul, and Hans H. Heinsheimer. "*Wozzeck* in Prag." MBA 8 (1926): 416–18. In German.

Stefan reports on the scandal and banning of *Wozzeck* in Prague, which he attributes in part to the disruption in the work's atmosphere resulting from its translation into Czech. Heinsheimer cites writings in Prague in support of the opera and demands to have the ban lifted.

277. Stein, Erwin. "Berg's *Wozzeck*." *Ballet and Opera* 7/5 (1949): 29–33. In English.

General discussion of the opera and its forms. Stein dismisses the notion that the opera is atonal.

278. ——. "*Wozzeck*." *Opera* 3 (1952): 17–22. Reprinted in Stein, *Orpheus in New Guises*, 103–107 (London: Rockliff, 1953). In English.

Historical background of the opera, information about early performances and revivals following World War II, and a general description of the musical language.

279. Stein, Jack M. "From *Woyzeck* to *Wozzeck*: Alban Berg's Adaptation of Büchner." *Germanic Review* 47 (1972): 168–80. In English.

Discusses Berg's adaptation of Büchner's fragmentary drama into a powerful and coherent operatic text.

280. Steinhard, Erich. "Alban Berg: Nach der *Wozzeck*-Uraufführung an der Berliner Staatsoper." *Der Auftakt* 6 (1926): 10–12. In German.

Praise for the work and for the performers. The opera is summarized as "the end of a phase of development in the genre of opera."

281. Stephan, Rudolf. "Anmerkungen zu Bergs *Wozzeck*." In *Opern und Opernfiguren: Festschrift für Joachim Herz*, 387–97. Wort und Musik: Salzburger Akademische Beiträge, volume 2. Anif/Salzburg: Ursula Müller-Speiser, 1989. In German.

General survey of Berg's experiences leading toward the composing of *Wozzeck*.

282. ———. "Aspekte der *Wozzeck*-Musik." In *50 Jahre Wozzeck* (no. 173): 9–21. Reprinted in Stephan, *Vom musikalischen Denken: gesammelte Vorträge*, 199–206, edited by Rainer Damm and Andreas Traub (Mainz: Schott, 1985). In German.

Deals primarily with the Captain's motif, questioning the assumption that its first occurrence is the basis for later variants. Also finds a quotation in *Wozzeck* (m. 338) from Schoenberg's *Gurrelieder*.

283. Strobel, Heinrich. "Nach dreißig Jahren." MEL 23 (1956): 97–99. In German.

General appreciation of *Wozzeck* and its persistence in the standard opera repertory, which is attributable to Berg's *Klangphantasie*.

284. Stuckenschmidt, H[ans] H[einz]. "Ausbreitung und Konsolidierung: Bergs *Wozzeck*." In Stuckenschmidt, *Neue Musik*, volume 2 (*Zwischen den beiden Kriegen*), 245–51. Berlin: Suhrkamp Verlag, 1951. In German.

General discussion of European music between the world wars with brief references to Berg and *Wozzeck*.

285. ———. "Bergs *Wozzeck* und die Berliner Aufführung." *Pult und Taktstock* 3 (1926): 1–5. Reprinted in Stuckenschmidt, *Die Musik eines halben Jahrhunderts, 1925–1975*, 24–27 (Munich and Zurich: R. Piper, 1976). In German.

Performance problems of *Wozzeck,* which were admirably solved by Erich Kleiber and his musicians in the first performances. The opera is deemed "one of the most important works of our time."

286. ———. "Totgesagt, aber jung wie gestern: Alban Bergs *Wozzeck* nach fünfzig Jahren." *Frankfurter allgemeine Zeitung,* 13 December 1975. Reprinted in Stuckenschmidt, *Die Musik eines halben Jahrhunderts, 1925–1975,* 333–38 (Munich and Zurich: R. Piper, 1976). In German.

Surveys the history and original reception of the opera, the history of its composition, details of the premier performance, and critics' viewpoints.

287. Taylor, Deems. "Ein Meisterwerk: *Wozzeck.*" ÖMZ 1 (1946): 50–52. In German.

General account of the opera, filled with praise.

288. Treitler, Leo. "*Wozzeck* and the Apocalypse: An Essay in Historical Criticism." *Critical Inquiry* 3 (1976): 251–70. Reprinted in Treitler, *Music and the Historical Imagination,* 242–63 (Cambridge, Mass., London: Harvard University Press, 1989), and in *Opera. II: Mozart and After,* 307–26, edited by Ellen Rosand, Garland Library of the History of Western Music, volume 12 (New York and London: Garland, 1985). In English. French translation ("*Wozzeck* et l'apocalypse") in SMZ 116 (1976): 249–62. Italian translation ("*Wozzeck* e l'apocalisse: saggio di esegesi storica"), in *La drammaturgia musicale,* 309–32 edited by Lorenzo Bianconi (Bologna: Mulino, 1986).

Büchner's imagery drawn from the Apocalypse and applied throughout *Wozzeck* suggests the hand of fate that controls the characters and creates "an atmosphere of foreboding and doom that hangs like a pall over the drama." Berg's treatment of motifs contributes to the same sense of control beyond the powers of the will. Motifs from the second scene of Act 1 are shown to spawn a complex of related configurations that recurs later in the opera and creates a sense of powerful links in the dramatic chain of events culminating in the deaths of Wozzeck and Marie.

289. Ullman, Bo. "Die Oper *Wozzeck*: Alban Berg und der Büchner-Text." In Ullman, *Die sozialkritische Thematik im Werk Georg Büchners und ihre Entfaltung im "Woyzeck."* Mit einigen Bermerkungen zu der Oper Alban Bergs, 140-53. Acta Universitatis Stockholmiensis, Stockholmer Germanistische Forschungen, volume 10. Stockholm: Almqvist & Wiksell, 1972. In German.

Concerns Berg's version of the play, its dramaturgy, and elements of social criticism.

290. ———. "Produktive Rezeption ohne Mißverständnis: Zur Büchner-Deutung Alban Bergs im *Wozzeck*." In *Zeitgenosse Büchner*, 9–39. Edited by Ludwig Fischer. Literaturwissenschaft-Gesellschaftwissenschaft, volume 39. Stuttgart: Verlag Klett-Cotta, 1977. Reprinted in Csampai and Holland (no. 103): 221–46. In German.

Studies Berg's response to the stylistic and structural issues in Büchner's play, comparing the composer to a dramaturge and regisseur.

291. Velten, Klaus. "Wozzeck und der Doktor: Ein Beitrag zur Deutung der Szene I, 4 aus Alban Bergs Oper." *Musik und Bildung* 17 (1985): 164–67. In German.

A dramaturgical interpretation of *Wozzeck*, Act 1, scene 4, finding Wozzeck as an effective opponent of the Doctor's theories.

292. Viebig, Ernst. "Alban Bergs *Wozzeck*: Ein Beitrag zum Opernproblem." *Die Musik* 15 (1923): 506–10. Reprinted in Csampai and Holland (no. 103): 178–82. In German. English translation ("Alban Berg's *Wozzeck*: A Contribution to the Problem of Opera") in Jarman, *Alban Berg: Wozzeck* (no. 155): 139–43.

The author praises Berg's apparent courage in a new direction in opera represented by *Wozzeck*. By adopting forms from instrumental music to the various sections of the work, the composer has made an important innovation, suggesting a path to a truly "musical" opera that would bypass the older Wagnerian formula. The musical style is said to stem directly from Franz Schreker's *Der ferne Klang*. See the reply by Petschnig (no. 223) and Berg's own response (no. 37).

293. **Vieuille, Marie-Françoise.** "Le meurtre de Marie ou Requiem pour une pute?" *L'avant-scène opéra* (no. 81): 104–11. In French.

Study of the character of Marie in *Wozzeck* and of her musical interpretation by Berg.

294. **Voermans, Erik.** "*Wozzeck* en het einde van de opera: de mens is een afgrond." *Mens en melodie* 49 (1994): 74–81. In Dutch.

General account of *Wozzeck* apropos of a performance in 1994 by the Netherlands Opera.

295. **Vogelsang, Konrad.** "Alban Bergs *Wozzeck* in Prag 1926 und in Leningrad 1927." MF 26 (1973): 352–64. In German.

History of the premier performances of *Wozzeck* in Prague and Leningrad and their critical receptions.

296. ———. "Alban Bergs *Wozzeck* in Rom 1942." MF 42 (1989): 150–54. In German.

Information concerning a wartime performance of *Wozzeck* in Rome (3 November 1942) and the positive journalistic reviews that followed. An appendix contains a list of performances of *Wozzeck* in Italy from 1942 to 1971.

297. ———. *Dokumentation zur Opera "Wozzeck" von Alban Berg: Die Jahre des Durchbruchs, 1925–1932*. Dissertation, University of Frankfurt, 1977. Laaber: Laaber-Verlag, 1977. 129 p. ISBN 3921518040. ML410.B47 D6. In German. Reviewed by Bruce Archibald, *Fontes artis musicae* 26 (1979): 69–70; Douglas Jarman,

ML 59 (1978): 361–62; Volker Scherliess, MF 33 (1980): 392–93; Rudolf Stephan, MEL/NZM 4 (1978): 73–74; Walter Szmolyan, ÖMZ 33 (1978): 99.

Survey of performances of *Wozzeck* (1925–32), reprinting programs and reviews.

298. ———. "Fünfzig Jahre *Wozzeck*: Ein Beitrag zur Rezeptionsgeschichte." *Zeitschrift für Musikpädagogik* 2/3 (1977): 8–14. In German.

Survey of early performances of *Wozzeck* and an assessment of the opera as an expressionistic work. Reviews by Paul Zschorlich (from the *Deutsche Zeitung*) and H. H. Stuckenschmidt (*Thüringer allgemeine Zeitung*) of the 1925 premier performance are appended.

299. ———. "Umstrittener *Wozzeck*: visionäre Schau? Endstation? Wie die Kritik vor 50 Jahren auf Alban Bergs Oper reagierte." *Musik + Medezin* 1/12 (1975): 41–47. In German.

300. Weill, Kurt. "Alban Berg: *Wozzeck*." *Der deutsche Rundfunk* 3 (1925): 3422. Reprinted in Weill, *Ausgewählte Schriften*, 153–54, edited by David Drew (Frankfurt: Suhrkamp, 1975). In German.

An icy review of the premier performance of *Wozzeck*, which is found to be "a completely negative art" forming the end point of an operatic development passing from *Tristan* through *Pelléas et Mélisande* and *Elektra*.

301. Werner, Theodor W. "Alban Bergs *Wozzeck* in Oldenburg." MBA 11 (1929): 164–65. In German.

Reflections on the work and a review of its performance in Oldenburg.

302. Westermeyer, Karl. "Nochmals: *Wozzeck*." *Signale für die musikalische Welt* 85 (1927): 107–109. In German.

Discussion of the text of the opera (a forerunner of Naturalism), for which Berg's music is fittingly grotesque.

303. Wilhelm, Sandro. "Diskographie." In Hanselmann, *Alban Berg Wozzeck* (no. 134): 215-23. In German.

An extensive review, comparison, and analysis of recordings of *Wozzeck*.

304. Wörner, Karl H. "Die musikalischen Formen im *Wozzeck*: ein Streit um des Kaisers Bart." NZM 117 (1956): 539–40. In German.

Dismisses the critique of *Wozzeck* made by Emil Petschnig (see no. 223) as "an argument over the king's beard." The work is a masterpiece, especially evident in light of Hans E. Apostel's new edition.

305. Youngren, William H. "Expressive Atonality." *Atlantic* 251/6 (1983): 97–102. In English.

Discussion of recordings of and books about *Wozzeck* and the work's expressivity.

5

Writings on Lulu

This chapter contains citations of writings that are primarily concerned with Berg's opera *Lulu* and the Symphonic Pieces from *Lulu*, arranged alphabetically by author, or title if an author's name is lacking. Since information on *Lulu* is also contained in writings cited in other chapters of this book, the reader is urged to consult the Index under "Berg, Alban: works—*Lulu*" for a complete list of sources.

306.   Adorno, Theodor W. "Rede über Alban Bergs *Lulu*." *Frankfurter allgemeine Zeitung* (19 January 1960): 12. Reprinted in AGS 18 (1984): 645–49; Csampai and Holland (no. 333): 265–70. In German.

> Primarily an interpretation of Wedekind's characters as adapted by Berg. Adorno quotes approvingly from Karl Kraus's 1905 lecture on *Die Büchse der Pandora*, ultimately finding the characters surreal.

307. ———— [Hektor Rottweiler]. "Zur *Lulu*-Symphonie." *23: Eine Wiener Musikzeitschrift* 24–25 (1936): 5–11. Reprinted ("Bergs *Lulu*-Symphonie") in MEL 27 (1960): 43–46. In German.

> Miscellaneous remarks, said to have been reviewed by Berg shortly before his death, concerning the Symphonic Pieces from *Lulu*. The article returns in revised form in Adorno's book on Berg (no. 667).

308. Agea, Francesco. "Piezas sinfónicas de *Lulu.*" *Pauta* 4/15 (1985): 38–42. In Spanish.

General descriptive account of the Symphonic Pieces from *Lulu.*

309. *Alban Berg: "Lulu.*" 2 volumes. Paris: Théatre National de l'Opéra de Paris, Jean-Claude Lattès, 1979. 269, 167 p. In French.

Volume 1 contains a French translation of the text of *Lulu* by Isabelle and Hans Hildenbrand; volume 2 contains essays concerning the Paris performance of the complete *Lulu* in 1979 by Pierre Boulez, Patrice Chéreau, Friedrich Cerha, and François Regnault.

310. "Alban Bergs nachgelassene Oper." MBA 19 (1937): 174–75. In German.

Notice on *Lulu* and its premier performance in Zurich.

311. Åstrand, Hans. "Operan *Lulu*: Trippelmordet lyckligt fullbordat." *Nutida musik* 24/3 (1980–81): 34. In Swedish.

Reviews the historical background to and recent performances and editions of the complete *Lulu.*

312. Bachmann, Claus-Henning. "*Lulu* bisher: '. . . ein Anschlag auf den Dramatiker Berg.' Herstellung des dritten Aktes—Gespräch mit Friedrich Cerha." NZM 140 (1979): 264–66. In German.

Interview outlining Cerha's work on Act 3 of *Lulu*, its historical background, the concerns of Helene Berg, and related issues.

313. ———. "Unschuld jenseits der Moralbegriffe: Alban Bergs Oper *Lulu*—von Friedrich Cerha komplettiert—in Paris." *Musik + Medezin* 4 (1979): 43–45. In German.

314. Bartosch, Alex Hans. "Durfte der dritte Akt von *Lulu* ergänzt werden? Erwägungen aus rechtlicher Sicht." ÖMZ 34 (1979): 142–44. In German.

Discussion of the legal issues concerning the completion of
Lulu vis-à-vis the will of Helene Berg and the role of the
Alban Berg-Stiftung, which Bartosch represented. Also see
Szmolyan (no. 461) and Bartosch (no. 315).

315. ————. "Prozeßbeendigung in Sachen *Lulu*: Einigung über
Beachtung der Interessensphären." ÖMZ 35 (1980): 300–301. In
German.

A report on the legal settlement between the Alban
Berg-Stiftung and Universal Edition concerning its
publication of Act 3 of *Lulu*. Also see the author's no. 314.

316. **Bennett, Clive.** "Maschinist Hopkins: A Father for Lulu?"
MT 127 (1986): 481–84. In English.

An overview of Max Brand's opera *Maschinist Hopkins*, the
score of which was examined by Berg in 1928. This opera is
similar to *Lulu* in its recapitulation of musical materials
toward its end and in aspects of its plot.

317. **Bitter, Christof.** "Notizen zu Mozarts *Don Giovanni* und
Bergs *Lulu*." In *Festschrift für einen Verleger: Ludwig Strecker zum
90. Geburtstag*, 123–34. Edited by Carl Dahlhaus. Mainz: Schott,
1973. In German.

Although Berg and Mozart enunciated opposing views on
the relation of music to poetry in opera, *Lulu* and *Don
Giovanni* still share common ground, as in the seminal
importance of emotion and in the unchanging dramaturgical
roles played by the title characters of both works.

318. **Blaukopf, Kurt.** "Darf man Alban Bergs Oper *Lulu*
vollenden?" *HiFi Stereophonie* 18/2 (1979): 136. In German.

A brief notice concerning the legal proceedings of the Alban
Berg-Stiftung against Universal Edition regarding the
publication of *Lulu*, Act 3. Also see Bartosch, nos. 314 and
315.

319. Bohm, Jerome D. "Berg, Poet of the Atonal, Tells of His New Opera *Lulu.*" *Musical America* 51/18 (1931): 10. In English.

The author reports on an interview with Berg at the Berghof. Berg noted that *Lulu* will have more character development than *Wozzeck.*

320. Boulez, Pierre. *"Lulu*: Court post-scriptum sur la fidélité." In *Alban Berg: Lulu* (no. 309), volume 2: 161–66. Reprinted in Boulez, *Points de repère*, 452–58 (Paris: Christian Bourgois, Éditions du Seuil, 1981); *Ricerchi musicali* 6 (1982): 56–60. In French. English translation (*"Lulu*: A Short Postscript on Fidelity") in Boulez, *Orientations*, 398–403, translated by Martin Cooper, edited by Jean-Jacques Nattiez (Cambridge: Harvard University Press; London: Faber and Faber, 1986). Italian translation in Boulez, *Punti di riferimento* (Turin: Einaudi, 1984).

A defense of Patrice Chéreau's production of *Lulu* in 1979, which Boulez conducted. "Literalness kills invention and anaesthetizes intelligence," Boulez protests. The close connection between music and staging was only a "fashion" maintained by the Schoenbergian school. The mere reproduction of a musical structure on stage is thus "an embarrassing redundancy."

321. ———. *"Lulu*: Questions d'interprétation." Sleeve notes to Boulez's recording of the opera, DGG 2711024, (1979), pp. 78–79. In French, English, German, and Italian. French text reprinted in Boulez, *Points de repère*, 449–51 (Paris: Christian Bourgois, Éditions du Seuil, 1981). English translation (*"Lulu*: Questions of Interpretation") in Boulez, *Orientations*, 395–97, translated by Martin Cooper, edited by Jean-Jacques Nattiez (Cambridge: Harvard University Press; London: Faber and Faber, 1986). Italian translation in Boulez, *Punti di riferimento* (Turin: Einaudi, 1984).

Considerations regarding the score of Berg's *Lulu* that a conductor must bear in mind.

322. ———. *"Lulu*: le second opéra." Sleeve notes to Boulez's recording of the opera, DGG 2711 024 (1979). In French, English,

German, and Italian. French text reprinted in *Alban Berg: Lulu* (no. 309), volume 2: 13–37. Reprinted (abbreviated) in Boulez, *Points de repère*, 293–311, edited by Jean-Jacques Nattiez (Paris: Christian Bourgois, Éditions du Seuil, 1981). English translation ("*Lulu*: The Second Opera") in Boulez, *Orientations*, 380–97, translated by Martin Cooper, edited by Jean-Jacques Nattiez (Cambridge: Harvard University Press; London: Faber and Faber, 1986).

> A general appraisal of the music and text of the opera. Finds Wedekind's texts to constitute a "morality play" (see Treitler's response to this assessment, no. 463). The music represents a merger of the form of older number opera with a more modern Wagnerian conception. The twelve-tone element is described as mere "lip-service" to the Schoenbergian principle.

323. Briner, Andreas. "Ist Bergs Oper eine Tautologie?" In *Werk und Wiedergabe: Musiktheater exemplarisch interpretiert,* 283–94. Edited by Sigrid Wiesmann. Thurnauer Schriften zum Musiktheater, volume 5. Bayreuth: Mühl'scher Universitätsverlag, 1980. In German.

> Critique of Patrice Chéreau's 1979 staging of *Lulu*, especially the attempt to invoke National Socialism in order to recreate the element of shock that the play and opera originally had but which had been lost by 1979.

324. Burgartz, Alfred. "Alban Bergs *Lulu*-Musik: Uraufführung im Berliner Staatsopernkonzert." *Die Musik* 27 (1935): 262. In German.

> Review of the first performance of the Symphonic Pieces from *Lulu*, followed by a selection of journalistic notices concerning Berg. Burgartz's negative tone reflects the accepted political view of Berg in Germany in 1935.

325. Carner, Mosco. "Berg and the Reconsideration of *Lulu*." MT 124 (1983): 477–79. In English. Italian translation ("Berg e il riesame di *Lulu*"), *Nuova rivista musicale italiana* 18 (1984): 434–40.

Despite admitting *Lulu* as a masterpiece, the author enumerates aspects of the dramaturgy and musical treatment that he finds problematic, including the large amount of spoken dialogue and the film sequence in Act 2.

326. ———. "Berg's *Lulu*." *Time and Tide* 34 (1953): 1098. In English.

Commentary on the opera following a radio broadcast from the Holland Festival.

327. Carpentier, Alejo. "*Lulu*, gran tragedia." *Pauta* 4/15 (1985): 66–69. In Spanish.

General interpretation of *Lulu* reprinted from a 1979 article.

328. Cerha, Friedrich. *Arbeitsbericht zur Herstellung des 3. Akts der Oper "Lulu" von Alban Berg*. Vienna: Universal Edition, 1979. 51 p. ISBN 371240080X. ML410.B47 C5. Abstract in ÖMZ 34 (1979): 130–41. In German. Reviewed by Sieghart Döhring, NZM 141 (1980): 163–64; Douglas Jarman, ML 61 (1980): 348–49; Rudolf Klein, ÖMZ 34 (1979): 130–41; Anthony Pople, RMA 114 (1989): 251–73; Joan Smith, *Notes* 36 (1979–80): 881–83; Claudio Spies, *Notes* 38 (1981–82): 410–16.
French translation: "La réalisation du troisième acte de *Lulu*." Translated by Patrice Decorte. In *Alban Berg: Lulu* (no. 309): volume 2: 107–60. Italian translation ("Sulla realizzazione del III atto di *Lulu*"), *Ricerche musicali* 6 (1982): 12–55.

Survey of the historical background of *Lulu*, the state of its manuscript materials, and problems which the author encountered in completing the last act.

329. ———. "Some Further Notes on My Realization of Act III of *Lulu*." In *The Berg Companion* (no. 803): 261–68. In English.

A report on additional improvements to Cerha's version of *Lulu* made after the first full-length performance in 1979. These are minor but nevertheless important details concerning both music and text. The author reasserts that the *Particell* of the opera is Berg's "final version," the product of numerous revisions and retouchings.

330. ———. "Zum III. Akt der Oper *Lulu*." ÖMZ 36 (1981): 541–50. In German.

Report on Cerha's work (1962–74) on Act 3 of *Lulu* and his hypotheses concerning the attitude of Helene Berg about the performability of this music.

331. Chéreau, Patrice. "Si tant est que l'opéra soit du théâtre." In *Alban Berg: Lulu* (no. 309), volume 2: 49–106. Reprinted (*Si tant est que l'opéra soit du théâtre: Notes sur la mise-en-scène de la création mondiale d'oeuvre intégral d'Alban Berg "Lulu"*), Petite bibliothèques Ombres, volume 10 (Toulouse: Ombres, 1992). In French.

Chéreau's interpretation of the libretto and music of *Lulu*, which guided him in creating the mise-en-scène for the first production of the complete work at the Paris Opéra in 1979. "The great virulence of the work has been changed in the same measure as *Lulu*'s erotic provocativeness has changed from what it was in 1900."

332. Collaer, P[aul], and J. Weterings. "Une nouvelle oeuvre d'Alban Berg: *Loulou*." RM 16 (1935): 169–74. Reprinted in RM 416–417 (1989): 117–22. In French.

Description of the Symphonic Pieces from *Lulu*.

333. Csampai, Attila, and Dietmar Holland, editors. *Alban Berg "Lulu": Texte, Materialien, Kommentare.* Rororo Opernbücher. Reinbek bei Hamburg: Rowohlt; Munich: G. Ricordi, 1985. 316 p. ISBN 3499173409. ML50.B491 L8 1985. In German.

The guide to *Lulu* assembled by Csampai and Holland contains articles on the operas and plays, writings by Berg, early reviews, texts of the operas, and reprinted materials.

334. Dahlhaus, Carl. "Berg und Wedekind: Zur Dramaturgie der *Lulu*." ABS 2 (1981): 12–19. Reprinted in Dahlhaus, *Vom*

Musikdrama zur Literaturoper: Aufsätze zur neueren Operngeschichte,
165–73 (Munich and Salzburg: Musikverlag Emil Katzbichler,
1983), and in Csampai and Holland (no. 333): 291–300. In
German.

> Compares *Lulu* to the Wagnerian model of literary opera, to
> which it adheres except for the use of musical numbers.

335. David, K. H. "Zürcher Juni-Festspiele: *Lulu* von Alban
Berg." SMZ 77 (1937): 397–99. In German.

> A review of the premier performance of *Lulu*, positive in
> tone. Finds the work "a final extension of late romantic
> opera, a final eruption of the play psychologically
> underscored with music whose special characteristic is that
> the means are applied with scrupulous naturalism, although
> they are constructed in a subtle way."

336. Decroupet, Pascal. "Une approche de *Lulu* d'Alban Berg:
Entre héritage et prospection." *Bulletin de la Société liègeoise de
musicologie* 54 (1986): 20–32. In French.

337. Döhring, Sieghart. "Illusionismus und Verfremdung:
Anmerkungen zu Chéreaus Inszenierungskonzept." In *Werk und
Wiedergabe: Musiktheater exemplarisch interpretiert,* 295–306. Edited
by Sigrid Wiesmann. Thurnauer Schriften zum Musiktheater,
volume 5. Bayreuth: Mühl'scher Universitätsverlag, 1980. In
German.

> An analysis and interpretation of Patrice Chéreau's 1979
> staging of *Lulu*, holding that Chéreau worked on the level
> both of illusion and alienated social interpretation to create
> a "staged commentary upon the work." The article
> (originally a spoken paper) is concluded by a summary of a
> discussion; photographs of the Chéreau decor are also
> appended.

338. Dümling, Albrecht. "Symbol des Fortschritts, der
Dekadenz und der Unterdrückung: Zum Bedeutungswandel des
Jazz in den zwanziger Jahren." In *Angewandte Musik, 20er Jahre,*

81–100. Edited by Dietrich Stern. Argument-Sonderbände, volume 24. Berlin: Argument-Verlag, 1977. In German.

Finds two general intentions among composers of the 1920s in their use of jazz idioms: as a protest against an older social and artistic order and as a symbol of the decadence of modern culture. Berg's use of ragtime in *Lulu* is an example of the latter.

339. Ekbom, Torsten. "Tillvarons grymma menageri." *Nutida musik* 5/2 (1961–62): 1–3. In Swedish.

Brief account of *Lulu* and the Symphonic Pieces from *Lulu*.

340. Elsendoorn, Jo. "De wereld rond Alban Berg: *Lulu*." *Opera journaal: Nederlandse operastichting*, no volume number (1977–78, issue no. 5): 2–5. In Dutch.

Sketch of Berg's Viennese intellectual and artistic milieu and background information on Frank Wedekind and *Lulu*.

341. Ertelt, Thomas F. *Alban Bergs "Lulu": Quellenstudium und Beiträge zur Analyse*. Dissertation, Freie Universität Berlin. ABS 3. Vienna: Universal Edition, 1993. 220 p. ISBN 370240208X. ML410.B47 E7 1993. In German.

Analytic study of *Lulu* based on compositional manuscripts with emphasis on Dr. Schön's music, the interlude between Act 3, scenes 1–2, and the beginning of the work.

342. ———. "'Hereinspaziert. . .'": Ein früher Entwurf des Prologs zu Alban Bergs *Lulu*." ÖMZ 41 (1986): 15–25. In German.

Describes Berg's first version of the opening scene of *Lulu*, as contained in an early "piano sketch" in the Austrian National Library. Also see Green (no. 347).

343. Foldi, Andrew. "The Enigma of Schigolch: A Character Analysis." BSN 9 (1980): 4–7. In English.

A discussion of the uncertainties in Wedekind's characterization of Schigolch and of ways in which Berg

underscored these ambiguities in motivic material assigned
to this character. The author is well known for his operatic
interpretations of the role of Schigolch.

344. ———. "Who Is This Man?" *Opera News* 49 (13 April
1985): 14–18, 44. In English.

Discussion of the character of Schigolch in *Lulu*.

345. Ganz, Arthur. "Transformations of the Child Temptress:
Mélisande, Salomé, Lulu." *Opera Quarterly* 5/4 (1987): 12–20. In
English.

Draws comparisons among the operas by Debussy, Strauss,
and Berg as expressions of intimate biographical details in
musical form. All three are "dramatized myths of a sexuality
projected finally through music."

346. Giannone, Roberto. "Musica e crisi: Crisi e musica?"
Rassegna musicale Curci 34/2–3 (1981): 15–19. In Italian.

Concerns *Lulu*.

347. Green, Douglass M. "A False Start for *Lulu*: An Early
Version of the Prologue." In *Alban Berg: Historical and Analytical
Perspectives* (no. 746): 203–13. In English.

Discussion of the dramatic and musical implications of Berg's
first version of the Prologue to *Lulu*, based on a two-page
sketch in the Austrian National Library (F21 Berg 80/VII),
dated 23 June 1928. See also Ertelt (no. 341).

348. Green, London. "Lulu Wakens." *Opera Quarterly* 3/3
(1985): 112–21. In English.

General interpretation of the character Lulu.

349. Grim, William E. "Das Ewig-weibliche zieht uns zurück:
Berg's *Lulu* as Anti-Faust." *Opera Journal* 22 (1989): 21–28. In
German.

Interprets the text of *Lulu* as having a reverse relationship with Goethe's *Faust*.

350. **Gruhn, Wilfried.** "Alban Berg. *Lulu*. Mythos und Allegorie bei Wedekind und Berg. Gedanken zum dritten Akt der Oper." In *Musiktheater heute: Sechs Kongreßbeiträge*, 34–62. Edited by Hellmut Kühn. Veröffentlichungen des Instituts für Neue Musik und Musikerziehung, volume 22. Mainz: Schott, 1982. In German.

Uses the third act of *Lulu* to draw conclusions about the entire work, especially its textual dimension as social criticism and mythic tragedy.

351. **Gysi, Fritz.** "Alban Bergs *Lulu*." *Allgemeine Musikzeitung* 64 (1937): 394–95. In German.

352. **Hall, Patricia.** "The Progress of a Method: Berg's Tone Rows for *Lulu*." MQ 71 (1985): 500–19. In English.

Berg, in collaboration with Willi Reich, discovered that new rows could be generated from a basic series by selecting every fifth or seventh tone. This and related means of row transformation were used extensively in *Lulu*.

353. ———. "Role and Form in Berg's Sketches for *Lulu*." In *Alban Berg: Historical and Analytical Perspectives* (no. 746): 235–59. In English.

A study of Berg's sketches for *Lulu* as regards the composer's dramatic intentions, especially his changing conception of correspondences among roles.

354. ———. "The Sketches for *Lulu*." In *The Berg Companion* (no. 803): 235–59. In English.

A study of the *Lulu* sketches from the Berg Collection at the Austrian National Library, drawing conclusions concerning chronology, compositional process, and dramatic intentions.

355. ———. *A View of Berg's Lulu Through the Autograph Sources.* Dissertation, Yale University, 1989. Berkeley: University of California Press, forthcoming 1996. In English.

356. Headlam, David. "The Derivation of Rows in *Lulu.*" PNM 24 (1985): 198–233. In English.

> Seeks to define precisely the procedures by which Berg derives rows from a single basic row in his opera. An analysis of the ostinato film music (Act 2) aims to reveal the musical significance of these procedures.

357. ———. "The Musical Language of the Symphonic Pieces from *Lulu.*" Dissertation, University of Michigan, 1985. UMI order no. 8600454. 340 p. In English.

> An analysis of the Symphonic Pieces from *Lulu* that aims at clarifying systematic compositional procedures, twelve-tone and non-twelve-tone materials, the harmonic language of the pieces, and their small and large forms.

358. Heller, Erich. "From Love to Love: Goethe's Pandora and Wedekind-Alban Berg's *Pandora-Lulu.*" *Salmagundi: A Quarterly of the Humanities and Social Sciences* 84 (1989): 94–108. In English.

> Relates Wedekind's character Lulu to prototypes in Goethe, primarily Pandora from the fragmentary play *Pandora's Return* (1808) and the Earth Spirit from *Faust I.*

359. Helms, Hans G. "Voraussetzungen eines neuen Musiktheaters." MEL 34 (1967): 118–30. In German.

> Broad discussion of models for new directions in opera. *Lulu* could be one such alternative, given the absurdity and illogic of its text.

360. Herschkowitz, Filip. "Some Thoughts on *Lulu.*" BSN 7 (1978): 11. In English.

> Brief reflections on formal innovations in *Lulu*. The author was a student of Berg's from 1928.

361. Hilmar, Ernst. "Alban Bergs Selbstzeugnisse zur Entstehung und Aufführbarkeit der Oper *Lulu*." In Berg, *Lied der Lulu* (no. 19b): 12–23. In German.

An extensive collection of excerpts from Berg's letters concerning the composing of *Lulu*, 1928–35. The letters are addressed to Berg's wife, Erich Kleiber, Josef Polnauer, Universal Edition, Anton Webern, Franz Schreker, Heinz Tietjen, and Arnold Schoenberg.

362. Hilmar, Rosemary. "Die Bedeutung der Textvorlagen für die Komposition der Oper *Lulu* von Alban Berg." In *Festschrift Othmar Wessely zum 60. Geburtstag*, 265–93. Edited by Manfred Angerer, et al. Tutzing: Hans Schneider, 1982. In German.

Using Berg's text sources, drafts, and marginal notes for *Lulu*, the author summarizes Berg's changes in Wedekind's plays and dramatic intentions.

363. Hirsbrunner, Theo. "Bergs *Lulu*: Dramentext und Opernlibretto. Die Bearbeitung von Frank Wedekinds *Erdgeist* und *Die Büchse der Pandora* durch Alban Berg." *Neue Zürcher Zeitung* 195 (24 March 1974): 53. In German.

Analysis of pseudomusical elements of Wedekind's *Lulu* texts (including rhyme, form, and symmetry) and their use in Berg's libretto.

364. Holland, Dietmar. "'. . .über die ließe sich freilich eine interessante Oper schreiben. . .': Wedekinds *Lulu* auf der Opernbühne." In Csampai and Holland (no. 333): 9–29. In German.

Reviews Berg's change in Wedekind's text and dramatic conception, finding in Berg's version "nothing less than a reinterpretation" of Wedekind. The character Lulu is explored and the dramaturgical content of Berg's music studied.

365. Holloway, Robin. "The Complete *Lulu*." *Tempo* 129 (1979): 36–39. In English.

Finds Acts 1 and 2 of *Lulu* to be more compelling emotionally than Act 3, which, especially in the chorale variations, seems confusing and impenetrable.

366. Holmberg, Arthur. "Opening Pandora's Box." *Opera News* 45/8 (1980): 14–22. In English.

Interpretation of Wedekind's Lulu plays and the character Lulu.

367. Jacquot, Jean. "Les musiciens et l'expressionnisme." In *L'expressionnisme dans le théâtre européen*, 245–75. Edited by Denis Bablet and Jean Jacquot. Paris: Centre National de la Recherche Scientifique, 1971. In French.

An attempt to relate the music of Schoenberg (especially *Erwartung*) and Berg's *Lulu* to the spirit of Expressionism. Wedekind's plays and Berg's music reveal an affinity with Expressionism in their "climate of anguish and anti-bourgeois revolt," their rejection of Naturalism, and their use of the grotesque as an instrument both of social satire and ridicule of the tragic spirit.

368. Jalowetz, Heinrich. "Alban Berg." *Der Auftakt* 15 (1935): 117–21. Excerpt reprinted in Reich 1959 (no. 917): 62–65. In German.

Brief appreciation, especially concerning *Lulu*.

369. Jameux, Dominique. "Form und Erzählung in Alban Bergs Oper *Lulu*." ABS 2 (1981): 40–45. In German.

Discusses the nature of narrative in *Lulu* and how it is presented. *Lulu* is an example of a mythic libretto, whose narrative focuses on the life of a protagonist whose destiny is already known to the audience. The author defines and discusses three ways in which the music relates to the narrative: analogy, symbol, and linearity.

370. Jarman, Douglas. *Alban Berg: "Lulu."* Cambridge Opera Handbooks. Cambridge: Cambridge University Press, 1991. xiii,

146 p. ISBN 0521241502 (hardback), 0521284805 (paperback). ML410.B47 J28 1991. In English. Reviewed by Nick Chadwick, MT 132 (1991): 516–17; Peter A. Hoyt, *Notes* 49 (1992–93): 577–78.

Written for the general reader in addition to the specialist, the work contains a synopsis of the libretto, an analysis of Act 3, scene 2, and information on the historical background to the opera, the Wedekind plays and their adaptation, and aspects of musical form, melody, harmony, and rhythm. An English translation (by Celia Skrine) of Karl Kraus's lecture on *Die Büchse der Pandora*, read in 1905 before a Vienna performance of Wedekind's play (attended by Berg), is included, as are documents concerning Wedekind's trial in 1905 on charges of obscenity following the publication of *Die Büchse der Pandora*. Articles by George Perle (no. 415) and Douglas Jarman (no. 377) are reprinted.

371. ———. "Berg's Surrealist Opera." MR 31 (1970): 232–40. In English.

Finds a recurrent sense of the incongruous and unreal in Wedekind's Lulu plays, a sense that is reinforced in Berg's doubling of roles among which there is "no real relationship." The resulting opera is puppetlike, "an absurd and dream-like dance of death." (Regarding Berg's rationale for role doubling, see the article by Hall, no. 353.)

372. ———. "The Completed *Lulu*." MT 122 (1981): 106–107. In English.

A positive review of Friedrich Cerha's work on Act 3 of *Lulu*.

373. ———. "Countess Geschwitz's Series: A Controversy Resolved?" RMA 107 (1980–81): 111–18. In English.

Analysis of pitch materials associated with Countess Geschwitz in Act 3 of *Lulu* and their derivation from Basic Cell I and the interval of a perfect fifth.

374. ———. "Dr. Schön's Five-Strophe Aria: Some Notes on Tonality and Pitch Association in Berg's *Lulu*." PNM 8 (1970):

23–48. Reprinted in *Die Wiener Schule*, 225–55, edited by Rudolf
Stephan (Darmstadt: Wissenschaftliche Buchgesellschaft, 1989).
In English.

> Dr. Schön's aria (Act 2, scene 1) recapitulates harmonic and
> thematic material associated throughout the opera with this
> character. The aria involves a sense of pitch centricity in
> which C# and F# are "tonics."

375. ———. "The 'Erdgeist Fourths': Some Structural and
Theoretical Consequences of the Basic Cells of *Lulu*." In *Bericht
über den 2. Kongreß der internationalen Schönberg-Gesellschaft: Die
Wiener Schule in der Musikgeschichte des 20. Jahrhunderts*, 180–87.
Edited by Rudolf Stephan and Sigrid Wiesmann. Vienna: Verlag
Elisabeth Lafite, 1986. In English.

> Analysis of the motivic applications of basic cells in *Lulu*,
> materials which function "as a means of establishing a
> hierarchy of harmonic and transpositional relationships."
> The analysis mainly concerns the ostinato film music of Act
> 2.

376. ———. "Friedrich's *Lulu*." BSN 10 (1981): 13–14. Also in
Contact 22 (1981): unpaginated. In English.

> The Covent Garden production of *Lulu* by Götz Friedrich
> (1981) "displayed a shocking ignorance of the most
> elementary principles of Berg's musico-dramatic
> organization."

377. ———. "The 'Lost' Score of the Symphonic Pieces from
Lulu." BSN 12 (1982): 14–16. Reprinted in Jarman, *Alban Berg:
Lulu* (no. 370), 125–32. In English.

> The autograph score of the Symphonic Pieces is not lost, as
> some have assumed (see Cerha, *Arbeitsbericht*, no. 328), but
> was simply returned by Berg back to the full score of the
> opera after the manuscript had been detached for use by
> Universal Edition in summer 1934.

378. ———. *"Lulu*: The Sketches." BSN 6 (1978): 4–8. In English.

A brief survey of the contents of musical sketches for *Lulu*, giving examples of the composer's sketches concerning pitch and rhythmic organization, role doublings, and a list (transcribed) showing Berg's final thoughts on the dramatis personae.

379. ———. "Some Observations on Rhythm, Metre and Tempo in *Lulu*." ABS 2 (1981): 20–30. In English, synopsis in German.

An analytic survey of *Lulu* as to rhythm, meter, and tempo. Rhythmic procedures of local significance include the use of ostinati (examples drawn from Act 2, scene 1) and rhythmic figures derived from the row (as in the film music interlude in Act 2). Temporal devices with large-scale significance include the use of certain meters to characterize roles, the use of a rhythmic motif associated with Countess Geschwitz, the application of a *Hauptrhythmus*, associated with fate, and the structuring of large sections of music through the use of interrelated tempi. After examining sketches for Acts 1 and 3, the author finds errors in metronomic calculation which the composer evidently corrected in the final version.

380. ———. "Some Rhythmic and Metric Techniques in Alban Berg's *Lulu*." MQ 56 (1970): 349–66. In English.

Deals with a central rhythmic figure (the *Hauptrhythmus*) having large-scale motivic significance throughout the opera, the use of mathematically related metronome markings to create large musical-dramatic sections, and the use of rhythmic and metric patterns as dramatic leitmotifs.

381. ———. "Weill and Berg: *Lulu* as Epic Opera." In *A New Orpheus: Essays on Kurt Weill*, 147–56. Edited by Kim Kowalke. New Haven and London: Yale University Press, 1986. In English.

Finds Berg to be personally and artistically sympathetic to the direction in opera represented by Kurt Weill in the late 1920s. Although *Wozzeck* is related to post-Wagnerian developments in opera, *Lulu* bridges the gap between this trend and the emerging *Zeitoper* and Epic Opera, with which Weill was associated.

382. Jones, Gaynor. "Food for Thought." *Opera Canada* 21/4 (1980): 52. In English.

Describes the completion of *Lulu* by Friedrich Cerha and Helene Berg's opposition.

383. Keller, Hans. "Holland Festival: *Lulu.*" MR 14 (1953): 302–303. In English.

Finds that the music of *Lulu* does not conform to the drama and that the derivation of all row forms from one central row is specious. Still, *Lulu* is superior to *Wozzeck*.

384. Klein, Rudolf. "Das Geheimnisvolle in *Lulu*: Gespräch mit Hans Hollmann zu seiner Grazer Inszenierung." ÖMZ 36 (1981): 539–41. In German.

Interview concerning the 1981 staging of *Lulu* in Graz. Hollmann enunciates a fascination for the secretive element in Berg's music, "which must be interpreted as subtly in staging as it is in the music."

385. ———. "Pariser Premiere löste nicht alle Probleme." ÖMZ 34 (1979): 144–48. In German.

A negative evaluation of Patrice Chéreau's production of *Lulu* in Paris in 1979, finding that it obscured Berg's intentions as to the opera in general.

386. Krenek, Ernst. "Alban Bergs *Lulu.*" *Wiener Zeitung*, 6 June, 1937. Reprinted in Krenek, *Zur Sprache gebracht*, 241–50 (Munich: Albert Langen, Georg Müller, 1958), and in Krenek, *Im Zweifelsfälle: Aufsätze über Musik*, 115–24 (Vienna, Munich, and Zurich: Europa Verlag, 1984). In German. English translation ("Alban Berg's *Lulu*") in Krenek, *Exploring Music*, 113–22, translated by Margaret Shenfield and Geoffrey Skelton (London: Calder and Boyars, 1966).

An interpretive study of the general musical content of *Lulu* and its aptness to the Wedekind plays and to the character Lulu. Berg's musical personality represented a conflation of the emotional element—"absorbed in the mystery of Woman"—and the intellectual, tending toward strict constructions. The author explores parallels between Berg's opera and Mozart's *Don Giovanni*: the musical world of tonality proved an apposite background for Mozart's dramatic material, "dominated by the father-idea." Berg's drama of disintegration aptly uses the post-tonal language, preserved constructively by the twelve-tone method. For Berg the dodecaphonic language was a means to memorialize the decaying beauty of a lost age of the emotions. "The lost country of tonality, of the beauty of that masculine-ordered world, is reconstructed in *Lulu* with the means of a new unknown order which was both the cause and the result of its decay."

387. ———. "Die Begegnung Alban Berg—Frank Wedekind in der Oper *Lulu*." In Berg, *Lied der Lulu* (no. 19b): 9–11. In German.

Krenek elaborates upon the weaknesses of the play, about which he spoke in no. 388, and its negative impact upon the opera, although this work remains for him "passionately conceived and lovingly worked out."

388. ———. "Marginal Remarks to *Lulu*." BSN 9 (1980): 9–10. Reprinted in ABS 2 (1981): 8–11. In English. German translation ("Randbemerkungen zu *Lulu*") in *Das Orchester* 29 (1981): 1013–1016.

Reflections upon the "flaws" of the completed *Lulu*, most of which stem from Wedekind's plays. These often lack tragic grandeur, sometimes even approaching the ridiculous.

389. ———. "Zur Vollendung von Alban Bergs *Lulu*-Fragment." *Musica* 31 (1977): 401–403. In German.

Argues in favor of completing *Lulu*.

390.   Le Rider, Jacques.   *"Lulu* de Wedekind à Berg: Métamorphoses d'un mythe."   *Critique* 36 (1980): 962–74.   In French.

An article-review prompted by the appearance of the French edition of Carner's *Alban Berg* (no. 714) and *Alban Berg: Lulu* (no. 309). Addresses ambiguities in Wedekind's Lulu plays, ultimately finding the opera dramatically more successful than the plays. "Karl Kraus, Peter Altenberg, Fritz Wittels, Otto Weininger were the ones who blazed the trail that led from Wedekind to Berg."

391.   List, Kurt. *"Lulu,* after the Premiere."   *Modern Music* 15 (1937–38): 8–12.   In English.

Reports on the Zurich premiere of *Lulu* in 1937, finding Wedekind's plays "flat and ineffectual." The opera is still deemed to be a major work, especially notable for Berg's independent approach to the twelve-tone technique. The performance was found lacking.

392.   Massow, Albrecht von. *Halbwelt, Kultur und Natur in Alban Bergs "Lulu."* Dissertation, University of Freiburg im Breisgau, 1991.   Beihefte zum Archiv für Musikwissenschaft, volume 33. Stuttgart: Franz Steiner, 1992.   281 p.   ISBN 3515060103. ML5.A63 Supp. Bd. 33.   In German.   Reviewed by Sabine Giesbrecht-Schutte, NZM 155/2 (1994): 75–76; Douglas Jarman, ML 75 (1994): 295–96.

Detailed study of the dramatic content of *Lulu* and its musical presentation, emphasizing aspects of the characters' psychology. The author finds a conflict between culture and nature to be at the root of Wedekind's texts, and he explores the dramatic implications of this conflict in Berg's music, which in part reshapes the essential issues of the plays.

393.   Maurer Zenck, Claudia. "Lulu, die Sphinx, und der Traum vom Tropenvogel."   HJM 10 (1988): 77–111.   In German.

A wide-ranging interpretation of the character of Lulu in Wedekind's plays and, by implication, in Berg's opera, invoking stereotyped ideas concerning women among such writers as Otto Weininger and Karl Kraus.

394. Mayer, Otto. *"Lulu* en México." *Pauta* 4/15 (1985): 35–37. In Spanish.

Reprint of an article from 1979, a brief account of the history of the opera in Mexico.

395. Mitchell, Donald. "The Character of *Lulu*: Wedekind's and Berg's Conceptions Compared." MR 15 (1954): 268–74. In English.

Analyzing the dramaturgy and music of the two-act version of the opera, the author is troubled by an "unhappy coalition" between Lulu as an individual with human feelings and also as an abstraction above morality. The conflict between the two conceptions appears to leave the opera flawed. An opposing interpretation is given by Perle, no. 404.

396. Naudé, Janet. "The Neglected Basic Series-Permutation in Alban Berg's *Lulu.*" *South African Journal of Musicology* 5 (1985): 93–98. In English, summary in Afrikaans.

Finds Berg's concern for the theme of fate in *Lulu* to be expressed by his use of a precompositional pattern of row permutations.

397. Neumann, Karl. "Wedekind's and Berg's *Lulu.*" MR 35 (1974): 47–57. In English.

After reviewing historical data on the work and its fragmentary state at the time of Berg's death, the author seeks to justify Wedekind's plays and their characters as coherent and persuasive in dramatic terms. He finds much of the criticism of the opera to be based on misreadings of Wedekind.

398. Newlin, Dika. "Out of Pandora's Box: How a Ziegfeld Girl Starred in a Silent Film of *Lulu.*" *Opera News* 41/21 (1977): 20–22. In English.

Calls attention to the G. W. Pabst film *Die Büchse der Pandora*.

399. Nielsen, Tage. "Alban Bergs *Lulu.*" *Dansk musiktidsskrift* 55 (1980–81): 9–14. In Danish.

Survey of Friedrich Cerha's completion of Act 3 of *Lulu*.

400. Northcott, Bayan. "*Lulu*—langt om laenge." *Dansk musiktidsskrift* 53 (1978–79): 262–64. In Danish.

Brief account of the completion and first complete performance of *Lulu*.

401. Offergeld, Robert. "Some Questions about *Lulu.*" *HiFi/Stereo Review*, 13/4 (1964): 58, 60, 64, 68, 70, 74, 76. In English.

Reflecting the ideas of George Perle, the author finds the continuing fragmentary state of *Lulu* to be a form of "musical censorship." Includes the text of a lengthy communication dated 5 April 1964 from Perle to Alfred Schlee of Universal Edition.

402. Pandolfi, Vito. "Wedekind, Berg et Pabst, tre *Lulu.*" *Cinema*, new series 2/26 (November 1949): 255–58. In Italian.

Describes a performance of *Lulu* in Venice in 1949; also information on G. W. Pabst's silent film *Die Büchse der Pandora*.

403. Perle, George. "The Cerha Edition." BSN 8 (1979): 5–6; PNM 17 (1979): 251–59. In English.

A positive review of Friedrich Cerha's work on Act 3 of *Lulu* and a mordant critique of the 1979 Paris Opéra performances. Perle's commentary on Cerha's edition is continued in nos. 414 and 419.

404. ———. "The Character of *Lulu*: A Sequel." MR 25 (1964): 311–19. In English.

A response to the article by Donald Mitchell (no. 395). The incoherence that Mitchell found in the character of Lulu is resolved by considering the text and music of the entire work.

405. ———. "The Complete *Lulu*." MT 120 (1979): 115–20. In English.

Discussion of the background to the incomplete state of *Lulu* and Perle's involvement in bringing it to completion.

406. ———. "Current Chronicle: Scotland." MQ 53 (1967): 101–108. In English. German translation (abridged; "Auf der Suche nach *Lulu*"), *Der Monat* 222 (March 1967): 63–65.

Review of a performance of *Lulu* at the Edinburgh Festival and a renewed call for the completion of the work.

407. ———. "Erwiderung auf Willi Reichs Aufsatz 'Drei Notizblätter zu Alban Bergs *Lulu*'." SMZ 107 (1967): 163–65. In German.

Response to Willi Reich's article no. 434, rejecting Reich's questions about the advisability of completing *Lulu* and reiterating shortcomings that Perle finds with Reich's analysis of the work (no. 429). A brief response by Reich is also appended.

408. ———. "Das Film-Zwischenspiel in Bergs Oper *Lulu*." ÖMZ 36 (1981): 631–38. In German. English version ("The Film Interlude of *Lulu*"), BSN 11 (1982): 3–8.

Transcription and discussion of two documents by Berg (a scenario and annotations) that clarify the dramatic content of the film music in *Lulu*, Act 2.

409. ———. "The First Four Notes of *Lulu*." In *The Berg Companion* (no. 803): 269–89. In English.

The author reflects upon his own theorizing concerning the first four notes of Lulu (B♭ E♭ E A), which he refers to as Basic Cell I (elsewhere as cell z). Manipulations of this cell are pertinent to the language not only of Berg but also prominent in the works of Bartók. The author suggests that the systematic use of this and other symmetrical collections calls into question his own earlier definition of atonality as a language defying a priori fundamental conditions. The article ends with a further study of pitch collections with symmetrical properties, including cyclic sets and interval cycles.

410. ———. "An Introduction to *Lulu*." *Opera Quarterly* 3/3 (1985): 87–111. In English.

General introduction, based on a lecture of 1981, to the opera.

411. ———. "*Lulu*: The Formal Design." JAMS 17 (1964): 179–92. In English. German translation ("Inhaltliche und formale Strukturen in Alban Bergs Oper *Lulu*"), ÖMZ 32 (1977): 427–41.

Approaches the work as a number opera, listing the various subdivisions and their type. There is also a list of *Leitsektionen*, subsections with referential functions that are recapitulated as the work progresses. Much of the material is reused in Chapter 3 of no. 416.

412. ———. "*Lulu*: Thematic Material and Pitch Organization." MR 26 (1965): 269–302. In English.

Related in content to no. 411. Survey of pitch structures that convey dramatic content, including basic pitch cells, twelve-tone sets (ordered or unordered), leitmotifs, and *Leitsektionen*, with examples of their uses.

413. ———. "The Music of *Lulu*: A New Analysis." JAMS 12 (1959): 185–200. In English.

Criticizes the analysis of *Lulu* by Willi Reich (see no. 429) as irrelevant and speculative. Perle objects to Reich's idea that *Lulu* essentially conforms to Schoenbergian twelve-tone practices. Perle maintains that Berg's treatment of pitch is different from Schoenberg's in that several different rows are used, rows are more closely defined as themes, certain tone rows do not have fixed precompositional order, and the harmonic language is more detached from row considerations of any sort.

414. ———. "Die Neuausgabe von *Lulu.*" ÖMZ 42 (1987): 18–27. In German.

Criticism of Friedrich Cerha's editorial practices as following too closely the 1964 Hans E. Apostel edition of Acts 1 and 2 of *Lulu*, but, in general, "the new edition [1985] is in every respect a notable achievement—the best that one could expect under the present circumstances."

415. ———. "A Note on Act III of *Lulu.*" PNM 2 (1964): 8–13. Reprinted in Jarman, *Alban Berg: Lulu* (no. 370): 118–24. In English.

Reprints a letter from Perle to Alfred A. Kalmus, director of Universal Edition, dated 21 August 1963, in which Perle reports on the feasibility of completing the unpublished portions of Act 3 of *Lulu*. Perle had been allowed to examine the existing manuscripts in the keeping of Universal Edition during that summer. His report stresses that the act was essentially completed by Berg, needing relatively minor fleshing out and straightforward orchestrational realizations. "I would go so far as to say that it is an error to speak of another person 'completing' *Lulu*, for in every essential respect this has already been done by Alban Berg."

416. ———. *The Operas of Alban Berg.* Volume 2: *"Lulu."* Berkeley, Los Angeles, and London: University of California Press, 1985. x, 315 p. ISBN 0520045025. ML410.B47 P48. In English. Reviewed by Andrew Clements, *Opera* 36 (1985): 1365–66; Mark DeVoto, *Notes* 43 (1986–87): 785–88; Douglass M. Green, JAMS 40 (1987): 122–29; Patricia Hall, *Journal of Music Theory* 31 (1987): 140–46; Dave Headlam, *In Theory Only* 9/5–6 (1987): 57–76; Douglas Jarman, MA 4 (1985): 289–92; George

Martin, *Opera Quarterly* 3/3 (1985): 158–63; Anthony Pople, RMA 114 (1989): 251–73; Claudio Spies, MQ 71 (1985): 520–36; Michael Taylor, ML 67 (1986): 404–405.

> Similar to no. 215. An analytic study of *Lulu* dealing with large-scale forms, elements of musical style and compositional material, and the transformation of Wedekind's plays into an operatic text. Aspects of Berg's life and music between *Wozzeck* and *Lulu* and during the composer's last years are surveyed. The historical background to the opera following Berg's death is also related, including information on the suppression of materials by his widow, Perle's own involvement with the fragmentary opera, and its ultimate completion by Friedrich Cerha and premier performance.

417. ———. "Die Personen in Bergs *Lulu*." *Archiv für Musikwissenschaft* 24 (1967): 283–90. In German.

> Discussion of the characters in *Lulu*, emphasizing Berg's role doublings. Also see Jarman (no. 378) concerning additional manuscript sources and Berg's dramatis personae in *Lulu*.

418. ———. "Die Reihe als Symbol in Bergs *Lulu*." ÖMZ 22 (1967): 589–93. In German. English version ("The Tone-Row as Symbol in Berg's *Lulu*") in *Essays on the Music of J. S. Bach and Other Diverse Subjects: A Tribute to Gerhard Herz*, 304–308, edited by Robert L. Weaver (Louisville: University of Louisville, 1981).

> The presence of tone rows in *Lulu* gave Berg new ways to interpret or symbolize ideas from the text in musical form.

419. ———. [Review of the score of *Lulu*]. *Notes* 43 (1986–87): 915–18. In English. Reprinted in *The Right Notes: Twenty-Three Selected Essays by George Perle on Twentieth-Century Music* (Stuyvesant, N.Y.: Pendragon Press, forthcoming ca. 1996).

> Ostensibly a review of the 1985 miniature scores of *Lulu* by Universal Edition, Perle's article summarizes and updates the history of Berg's incomplete work on the score and the problems facing all subsequent editors. Friedrich Cerha's

edition "is the very best that one can hope for, and the best that we are likely to have for a long time."

420. ———. "The Score of *Lulu*." PNM 3 (1964): 127–32. In English.

Commentary upon the 1964 orchestral score of *Lulu*, whose incomplete state and introductory commentary are rejected as "outrageous distortions."

421. ———. "The 'Sketched-in' Vocal Quartet of *Lulu*, Act III." BSN 12 (1982): 12–13. In English.

Measures 976 to 1002 of Act 3 of the *Particell* of *Lulu* were left by Berg in an incomplete sketch. The necessary text to finish these measures is located by Perle in a libretto typescript in the Austrian National Library. The missing music may have been filled in on a manuscript that has yet to be located.

422. ———. "Some Thoughts on an Ideal Production of *Lulu*." *Journal of Musicology* 7 (1989): 244–53. In English.

Notes Berg's meticulous connections between music and staging instructions in *Lulu* and the insensitivity to such matters by many contemporary stage directors.

423. ———. "Der Tod der Geschwitz." ÖMZ 36 (1981): 20–28. In German.

At the end of *Lulu*, Geschwitz speaks for Berg, both in text and music, by covertly addressing Hanna Fuchs. The words that she sings parallel sentiments that Berg directed to Hanna in a letter, and the music is filled with musical letters of their names. Perle decries the addition of the epithet "Verflucht!" as her dying word, which he sees as a "cheap interpolation."

424. Petazzi, Paolo. "Appunti sul III atto di *Lulu*." *Ricerche musicali* 6 (1982): 1–11. In Italian.

Discussion of the musical and dramatic form of Act 3 of *Lulu*, emphasizing the "play of return and symmetry" that the act exhibits.

425. Pople, Anthony. "Serial and Tonal Aspects of Pitch Structure in Act III of Berg's *Lulu.*" *Soundings* 10 (1983): 36–57. In English.

A theoretical evaluation of the relatedness of row forms in *Lulu*, with analytic applications to the chorale variations in Act 3.

426. Porter, Andrew. "Lulu and Helene and Alban and Alwa." *New Yorker* (4 April 1977): 125–31. Reprinted in Porter, *Music of Three Seasons: 1974–1977*, 550–58 (New York: Farrar Straus Giroux, 1978). In English. Spanish translation ("Lulu y Helene y Alban y Alwa") in *Pauta* 4/15 (1985): 43–51.

Apropos of recent performances of *Lulu*, Porter reviews the history of Berg's intrigues with Alma Mahler and Hanna Fuchs-Robettin and their relevance to *Lulu* and the Lyric Suite.

427. Regnault, François. "J'ai longtemps habité sous des vastes portiques." In *Alban Berg: Lulu* (no. 309), volume 2: 39–47. In French.

Commentary upon the decor of Richard Peduzzi for the 1979 Paris premiere of the complete *Lulu*.

428. Reich, Willi. "Alban Berg und seine Musik zu Wedekinds *Lulu*-Tragödie." SMZ 75 (1935): 81–85. In German.

Distinguishes formal principles in *Lulu* from those in *Wozzeck* using the Symphonic Pieces from *Lulu* as examples. Close in content to Reich's no. 432.

429. ———. "Alban Berg's *Lulu.*" MQ 22 (1936): 383–401. In English.

An important early discussion of the opera *Lulu*, touching on aspects of the text, musical structure, comparisons with *Wozzeck*, and compositional techniques. A letter from Berg is quoted in which the composer points to the importance of vocal forms and genres. Reich also uses ideas about the music based on analytic sketches provided in 1934 by the composer (see Reich no. 434), holding that all pitch materials derive from a single tone row. Passages from an article by Heinrich Jalowetz (no. 368) are quoted concerning the aptness of the dramatic material to operatic treatment.

430. ———. "Alban Bergs *Lulu*." *Der Auftakt* 14 (1934): 202–204. In German.

Analysis of the Symphonic Pieces from *Lulu*, emphasizing their structure as a symphonic work. Report on the 1934 Berlin performance under Erich Kleiber.

431. ———. "Alban Bergs *Lulu*: Zur Zürcher Uraufführung der Oper." SMZ 77 (1937): 337–43. In German.

General appraisal of the opera, recounting the story act by act and comparing the music to that of *Wozzeck*. "The completion of the instrumentation should be done by a musician familiar with Berg's way of working and in Berg's own spirit. This will take a good while since it will require the most thorough knowledge of the parts of the score already orchestrated by Berg and their relation to the short score." Compare this conclusion with Reich 1966 (no. 434).

432. ———. "Alban Bergs *Lulu*-Symphonie: Beziehungen zur Oper. Das Berliner Erlebnis." MBA 16 (1934): 190–92. Abbreviated version in the *Neue Zürcher Zeitung* 157 (30 March 1936). In German.

Finds a genuine symphonic form in the Symphonic Pieces from *Lulu*, a form that is reflected in aspects of the text and structure of the music in the opera itself.

433. ———. "Deutsche Premiere nach 15 Jahren: Alban Bergs Oper *Lulu*." MEL 19 (1952): 337–42. In German.

History of the opera and details about its music apropos a performance in Essen.

434. ———. "Drei Notizblätter zu Alban Bergs Oper *Lulu*." SMZ 106 (1966): 336–39. In German.

Finds hasty the "American campaign" led by George Perle to publish and perform *Lulu* in its entirety, given that both Arnold Schoenberg and Anton Webern declined to complete the work. Defends his analysis of the opera (no. 429) as having Berg's approval, also noting that it was based on Berg's own musical examples covering three sheets (one is reproduced in facsimile). See George Perle's response, no. 407, and Rudolf Stephan (no. 1002) for a complete facsimile of all three sheets.

435. ———. *"Lulu*: The Text and Music." *Modern Music* 12/3 (1935): 103–11. In English.

General description of the opera, closely related in content to several other articles by the same author.

436. ———. "Über Lulu." In Reich 1959 (no. 917): 66–73. In German.

Excerpt from a speech given by Reich in 1957 prior to a performance of the opera in Hamburg. He emphasizes the influence upon Berg exerted by Karl Kraus's speech on *Lulu* given in 1905, which is extensively quoted. The problem of musical form posed by the text of *Lulu* is different from that posed by the text of *Wozzeck*. In the latter, forms from absolute music were applied to individual scenes; in *Lulu* they emerge over a broader scale, often intermittently spanning several acts and interwoven by fragments of other forms.

437. ———. "Zur Oper *Lulu.*" ÖMZ 17 (1962): 205–12. In German.

Analysis of *Lulu* that the author says is based on discussions with the composer. Quotes at length from a speech given by Heinrich Jalowetz at Berg's fiftieth birthday celebration concerning the aptness of the Lulu plays for operatic treatment. Here the character Lulu is said to be the female counterpart to Don Giovanni, a comparison that Berg himself found apt. As to the incomplete state of the work, Reich concludes that "only a small part" of Act 3 was orchestrated:

"In light of the imagination and originality of Berg's orchestral language, it has seemed impossible to complete it in his own spirit, even by masters as close to him as Arnold Schoenberg and Anton Webern." Compare this conclusion to Reich's earlier views, as stated in 1937 (no. 431).

438. Reiter, Manfred. *Die Zwölftontechnik in Alban Bergs Oper "Lulu."* Dissertation, University of Cologne, 1973. Kölner Beiträge zur Musikforschung, volume 71. Regensburg: Gustav Bosse Verlag, 1973. 155 p. ISBN 3764920874. In German. Reviewed by Franz Blasl, *Musikerziehung* 32 (1978–79): 141–42.

Analysis of Berg's twelve-tone techniques, finding an "enhancement" of the approach of Schoenberg in the manipulation of elements of stasis and dynamism. Also see Scherliess (no. 442) for other information concerning Berg's row materials in *Lulu*.

439. Rode, Susanne. *Alban Berg und Karl Kraus: Zur geistigen Biographie des Komponisten der "Lulu."* Dissertation, University of Hamburg, 1988. Europäische Hochschulschriften, series 36, volume 36. Frankfurt: Peter Lang, 1988. 489 p. ISBN 3631405057. ML410.B47 R6 1988. In German. Reviewed by Rosemary Hilmar, MF 45 (1992): 202–204; Rudolf Stephan, ÖMZ 46 (1991): 353–54; Hartmut Vinçon, *Musiktheorie* 5 (1990); 278–81.

Study of Berg's connections with Karl Kraus, drawing upon their correspondence and Berg's sketches for *Lulu*.

440. Sandow, Gregory. "Music: What You Didn't Read about *Lulu*." *Village Voice* 26/4 (1981): 64. In English.

Partly an interpretation of aspects of the score, partly a review of a recent performance at the Metropolitan Opera.

441. Schauensee, Max de. "Yesterday's Novelties in Today's Perspective." *Opera News* 14 (1949–50): 15, 26–29. In English.

Report on the performance of *Lulu* at a recent festival of the International Society for Contemporary Music in Venice.

Finds the work a "period piece" that does not compare to *Wozzeck*.

442. **Scherliess, Volker.** "Alban Bergs analytische Tafeln zur *Lulu*-Reihe." MF 30 (1977): 452–64. In German.

Discussion and transcription of the contents of two row tables prepared by Berg early in the composing of *Lulu*.

443. ———. "Briefe Alban Bergs aus der Entstehungszeit der *Lulu*." MEL/NZM 2 (1976): 108–14. In German.

Quotations from and discussion of the contents of letters from 1927 to 1934 concerning *Lulu* from Berg to Arnold Schoenberg, Theodor Adorno, Universal Edition (primarily to Hans Heinsheimer), Heinz Tietjen, and Wilhelm Furtwängler.

444. **Schneider, Frank.** "Bericht: Friedrich Cerha rekonstruierte den 3. Akt der *Lulu*." *Musik und Gesellschaft* 30 (1980): 233–35. In German.

General report on the materials for Act 3 of *Lulu* and Friedrich Cerha's work on them.

445. **Schreiber, Ulrich.** "Hetzjagden bis in den Tod: Spiegelungen von *Don Giovanni* und *Lulu*." *Lulu*-Programmheft, Hamburg Staatsoper, 1978. Reprinted in Csampai and Holland, *Alban Berg Lulu* (no. 333): 282–91. In German.

A study of the character Lulu, finding her to be complementary to Mozart's Don Giovanni and a recrudescence of the recurrent figure of the "child-woman" in modern literature. See also Krenek, no. 386.

446. **Shawe-Taylor, Desmond.** *"Lulu." New Statesman and Nation* 38/964 (1949): 217–18. In English.

Report on a broadcast of the work from the Salzburg Festival. The reviewer was present also at the 1937 premiere, upon which he reflects.

447. Simms, Bryan R. "Berg's *Lulu* and Theatre of the 1920s." *Cambridge Opera Journal* 6 (1994): 147–58. In English.

Berg's dramatic conception of *Lulu* derived several distinctive features from versions of Wedekind's spoken plays given in the 1920s, especially those of Erich Engel and Otto Falckenberg.

448. Simon, John. "And Now, Everywoman." *Opera News* 52/14 (1988): 28–31, 45. In English.

Opines as to the flaws of the opera *Lulu* and its text.

449. Smith, Patrick J. "Tale of Two Women." *Opera News* 45/17 (1981): 18–19. In English.

Compares and contrasts *Lulu* with the figure of Emilia Marty from Janáček's *The Makropoulos Case*.

450. Spies, Claudio. "Some Notes on the Completion of *Lulu*." In *Alban Berg: Historical and Analytical Perspectives* (no. 746): 215–34. In English.

An analysis of mm. 86–199, from the beginning of Act 1, scene 1, of *Lulu*, showing the use of basic harmonic and linear figures. The author speculates that the dramatic function of these measures appears redundant in light of the music of the Prologue, suggesting that Berg may have had a "memory lapse." He ends with an appeal for more scrutiny of Berg's music—"criteria governing compositional choice as regards continuity and syntax"—in place of the current interest in "beguiling but trivial rattle of 'secret' programmes or the itchy sensationalism of disclosures in a life no longer private."

451. Stein, Erwin. "Berg's Opera *Lulu*, in Zurich." *Christian Science Monitor* 29, no. 192 (13 July 1937): 8. Reprinted in Stein, *Orpheus in New Guises*, 108–109 (London: Rockliff, 1953). In English.

A brief review of the premier performance of *Lulu*.

452.   Stein, Jack M.   *"Lulu*: Alban Berg's Adaptation of Wedekind."   *Comparative Literature* 26 (1974): 220–41.   In English.

Surveys aspects of Berg's adaptation of Wedekind, emphasizing multiple casting and its relation to Wedekind's own "Prologue in a Bookshop."

453.   Steiner, Ena.   "Why *Lulu* Stayed Unfinished."   *Music and Musicians* 26/8 (April 1978): 28–29.   In English.

Discussion of Schoenberg's decision to back out on the completion of *Lulu* upon seeing its unflattering caricature of the Jewish banker, Puntschu.   Correspondence which deals with this issue between Schoenberg and Erwin Stein from 1936 is quoted.

454.   Steiner, George.   "Lulu: 'She is the Femme Fatale, the Man-devouring Vamp'."   *Listener* 105 (26 February 1981): 265–68.   In English.

Finds *Lulu* to be "ferociously of our own time":   an uncompromising challenge for the listener equal to the challenge posed by new literature, art, and science.   Repeats the idea that Helene Berg repressed the third act of Lulu out of jealousy over the idea that Lulu represented Hanna Fuchs-Robettin.

455.   Stenzl, Jürg.   "Lulus 'Welt'."   ABS 2 (1981): 31–39.   In German.

Just as Karl Kraus found Wedekind's private world reflected in his play *Die Büchse der Pandora*, so too Berg's world is reflected in the music of *Lulu*.   The characters and other dramatic elements of the opera are projected musically in a strictly hierarchical manner.   The rigid hierarchies and order relations are seen by an analysis of the dodecaphonic aspect of the work, its numerological elements, and its symmetrically closed form.   These are typified in the central "Lied der Lulu."

456. Stephan, Rudolf. "Alban Bergs *Lulu.*" NZM 122 (1961): 269–76. In German.

> General appraisal of the opera in both dramaturgy and music, also with notes on Act 3.

457. ―――. "Zum Verständnis der Diskussion über den dritten Aufzug der Oper *Lulu.*" In *Werk und Wiedergabe: Musiktheater exemplarisch interpretiert*, 265–75 plus discussion, 275–82. Edited by Sigrid Wiesmann. Thurnauer Schriften zum Musiktheater, volume 5. Bayreuth: Mühl'scher Universitätsverlag, 1980. In German.

> A general review of the history of Act 3 of *Lulu*, its documentary status, and Friedrich Cerha's edition, concluding that the work must be performed in its entirety to be coherent. Also commentary on the *Lulu* Symphony and its relation to the opera and on the appropriateness of Geschwitz's final epithet—"Verflucht!"—in both the opera and the Symphony.

458. ―――. "Zur Sprachmelodie in Alban Bergs *Lulu*-Musik." In *Dichtung und Musik: Kaleidoskop ihrer Beziehungen*, 246–64. Edited by Günter Schnitzler. Stuttgart: Klett-Cotta, 1979. Reprinted in Stephan, *Vom musikalischen Denken: Gesammelte Vorträge*, 207–20, edited by Rainer Damm and Andreas Traub (Mainz: Schott, 1985). In German.

> Examination of the types of singing in *Lulu*, which range in twelve gradations from unaccompanied speech to singing "molto cantabile." The declamatory melodies of the work are also elucidated by a consideration of the melodic content of the *Lulu* Symphony.

459. Stevenson, Florence. "Lulu's Last Stand: Jack the Ripper." *Opera News* 41/21 (1977): 36. In English.

> Information on the historical figure of Jack the Ripper and his fictional embodiments.

460.   Szmolyan,   Walter.   "*Lulu*-Diskussion   in   der Nationalbibliothek." ÖMZ 32 (1977): 572–74. In German.

Report on a conference at the Austrian National Library concerning the completion and performance of Act 3 of *Lulu*. Participants included Rosemary Hilmar and Alex Hans Bartosch.

461. ——. "Zum III. Akt von Alban Bergs *Lulu*." ÖMZ 32 (1977): 396–401. In German.

Updates the dispute over the completion and performance of Act 3 of *Lulu*. Prints Schoenberg's letter to Erwin Stein (9 March 1936) telling the true reason why Schoenberg withdrew his offer to complete Act 3 and Stein's reply (30 April 1936). See Ena Steiner, no. 453, for an English translation of these two letters.

462. Tortolano, Martha Kane, and William Tortolano. "An Appreciation of Alban Berg and *Lulu*." *NATS Bulletin* 36 (September–October 1979): 10–15, 36. In English.

General account of the opera.

463. Treitler, Leo. "The Lulu Character and the Character of *Lulu*." In Treitler, *Music and the Historical Imagination*, 264–305. Cambridge, Mass., London: Harvard University Press, 1989. Reprinted in *Alban Berg: Historical and Analytical Perspectives* (no. 746): 261–86. In English.

Observations concerning the ambiguous nature of the character Lulu in Wedekind and Berg. A unifying element of these observations takes its departure from a statement by Pierre Boulez, "Lulu is definitely a morality play," which Treitler interprets as suggesting human, moralistic judgments about Lulu and other figures from the play and opera. The author rejects the possibility of normal ethical judgment since the plays establish an intentional alienation between their characters and the audience and since Lulu herself is largely an abstraction. Her basic ambiguity, created by Wedekind and underscored by Berg, is between her implicit "natural" quality and her essence as a *Rollenträgerin*—a complex of roles projected upon her by the men of the drama. On this last interpretation, also see the articles by Maurer Zenck (no. 393) and Krenek (no. 386).

464. Vedrone, Mario. "Un breve scenario cinematografico di Alban Berg." In *La musica nel film*, 135–38. Edited by Luigi Chiarini. Quaderni della Mostra internazionale d'arte. Rome: Bianco e Nero Editore, 1950. In Italian.

Description and Italian translation of Berg's film scenario for *Lulu*, Act 2.

465. Vermeulen, Ernst. "Muzikale torso's (9): *Lulu* van Alban Berg." *Mens en melodie* 49 (1994): 378–85. In Dutch.

General account of the opera, one of a series of short studies of incomplete musical works.

466. Weiss, Norbert. "Film and *Lulu*." *Opera* 17 (1966): 707–709; reprinted ("Film in Opera") in *Opera Canada* 9/4 (1968): 16–17. In English. German version ("Film in der Oper") SMZ 106 (1966): 208–210.

Brief description of Berg's plan for film in Act 2 of *Lulu* and the problems that his idea raises.

467. Werker, Gerard. "Alban Berg en zijn opera *Lulu*." *Mens en melodie* 8 (1953): 167–72. In Dutch.

General account of *Lulu* following a performance in Essen.

468. Yamaguchi, Masao. "Arrière-plan sémiologique de *Lulu*." In *Approches de l'opéra*, 289–96. Collections "Langages, discours et société." Paris: Didier Erudition, 1986. In French.

Sketches the formation of the Lulu myth in the nineteenth century and the ambiance in which it developed. A brief semiological analysis of the structure of the text is undertaken.

469. Youngren, William H. "Berg's *Lulu.*" *Atlantic* 260/3 (1987): 93–96. In English.

General review of the history of the work, its completion by Friedrich Cerha, and various recordings. The opera is deemed "a modern masterpiece that has come into its own."

6

Writings on Berg's Chamber Music

This chapter contains citations of writings that are primarily concerned with Berg's chamber music (Piano Sonata, Op. 1; String Quartet, Op. 3; Clarinet Pieces, Op. 5; Chamber Concerto; and Lyric Suite). The citations are arranged alphabetically by author, or title if an author's name is lacking. Since information on the chamber works is also contained in writings cited in other chapters of this book, the reader is urged to consult the Index under "Berg, Alban: works" for a complete list of sources.

Piano Sonata, Op. 1

470. Adorno, Theodor W. "Alban Berg: Sonate pour piano." *Revue de musicologie* 69 (1983): 209–16. In French.

Extracted from Adorno's book on Berg (no. 667).

471. "Alban Berg." *Neue Musikzeitung* 42 (1921): 320. In German.

Notice concerning Berg and his Sonata, Op. 1, apropos of a performance of the work at the Donaueschingen Festival (1 August 1921). The analysis (Berg may have been the author) illustrates the main, subsidiary, and closing themes and coda within a sonata-form scheme.

472. Hiller, Lejaren, and Calvert Bean. "Information Theory Analyses of Four Sonata Expositions." *Journal of Music Theory* 10 (1966): 96–137. In English.

Berg's Sonata, Op. l, is among the works analyzed, essentially by counting notes.

473. Scherliess, Volker. "Zur Rezeption der Klaviersonate Op. 1." ABS 2 (1981): 232–44. In German.

The premier performance of the Sonata by Etta Werndorff (Vienna, 24 April 1911) had little response in the press, but later performances drew more attention, typically mixing positive and negative assessments. Following World War I, the work was performed by Erwin Schulhoff in several German cities. It was widely reviewed following a 1919 performance in Berlin by Eduard Erdmann, who later became an important advocate for the work.

474. Schmalfeldt, Janet. "Berg's Path to Atonality: The Piano Sonata, Op. 1." In *Alban Berg: Historical and Analytical Perspectives* (no. 746): 79–109. In English.

An analysis of the Sonata, Op. 1, using the notion of developing variations upon a basic shape introduced in mm. 1–3. The basic shape contains not only motivic material for what follows in the sonata, but also its fundamental harmonic and rhythmic elements. The primary harmonic components are dissonant chords that prefigure important formations in Berg's later atonal harmonic vocabulary, although in the Sonata they primarily represent diatonic chords in the key of B minor.

475. Shipley, Linda P. "A Performer's Analysis of Berg's Piano Sonata, Opus 1." *New Journal for Music* 1/2 (1990): 33–46. In English.

476. Vogt, Harry. "Die Kunst des kleinsten Überganges: Interpretationsvergleich und Diskographie von Alban Bergs Klaviersonate Op. 1." *Neue Musikzeitung* 34/2 (1985): 34. In German.

Comparison of the interpretations of Berg's Piano Sonata in thirty commerical recordings of the work from the 1950s to the 1980s.

String Quartet, Op. 3

477. Holland, Dietmar. "Dialektik der musikalischen Freiheit: Alban Bergs freie 'Atonalität' in seinem Streichquartett Op. 3." MK 9 (1979): 29–37. In German.

Discusses the String Quartet, Op. 3, assessing Berg's reaction to the freedom implicit in the style of "free atonality" and his intention to maintain coherence.

478. Maegaard, Jan. "Anton Webern, Fem satser for strygekvartet, Opus 5 (1909). Alban Berg, Strygekvartet, Opus 3 (1910)." *Nutida musik* 26/3 (1982–83): 41–42. In Danish.

Overview of the two works.

479. Porter, Charles Edwin. "Interval Cycles and Symmetrical Formations as Generators of Melody, Harmony, and Form in Alban Berg's String Quartet Opus 3." Dissertation, City University of New York, 1989. UMI order no. 9000059. 246 p. In English.

Applies the notion of interval cycles (see Perle no. 876) to local and long-range spans within Berg's String Quartet, Op. 3. Finds the second movement of this work to be the earliest of Berg's compositions in which such symmetrical formations are importantly operative.

480. ———. "Interval Cycles in Alban Berg's String Quartet Opus 3." *Theory and Practice* 14–15 (1989–90): 139–77. In English.

Systematic analysis of the String Quartet using Perle's theory of interval cycles.

481. Rockmaker, Jody Darien. "Articulating Form in Alban Berg's String Quartet, Opus 3: An Analysis of the First Movement and the Sketches." Dissertation, Princeton University, 1989. UMI order no. 8920357. 166 p. In English.

The analyses focus on elements of continuity in the first movement of the String Quartet, Op. 3, which differ from comparable elements in earlier tonal music.

482. Zeller, Hans Rudolf. "Text und Interpretation: Zur Handlungsanalyse von Op. 3." MK 9 (1979): 38–48. In German.

Analysis of the opening of the first movement of the String Quartet, Op. 3, and how it influences thematic material for the entire work.

Four Pieces, Op. 5

483. Berry, Wallace. Chapter 4 ("Second Case: Berg, No. 3 of Four Pieces for Clarinet and Piano, Op. 5"). In Berry, *Musical Structure and Performance*, 83–143. New Haven and London: Yale University Press, 1989. In English.

Discussion of interpretive choices influenced by form and expressive character in the Four Pieces, Op. 5, no. 3.

484. Borris, Siegfried. "Vergleichende Stilanalyse: Alban Berg—Paul Hindemith." In *Versuche musikalischer Analysen*, 35–41. Darmstadt: Institut für Neue Musik und Musikerziehung, 1967. Another version ("Vergleichende Werkanalyse. Alban Berg: Op. 5 Nr. 1. Paul Hindemith: aus der Violinsonate 1939") in *Musik und Bildung* 5 (1973): 138–41. In German.

A descriptive analytic comparison of Berg's Clarinet Piece, Op. 5, no. 1, and Hindemith's Violin Sonata, second movement. Berg's work is found "irrational" and open in form, Hindemith's clear, linear, polyphonic, and tonal.

485. DeFotis, William. "Berg's Op. 5: Rehearsal Instructions." PNM 17 (1978): 131–37. In English. German language version

("Vier   Stücke   für   Klarinette   und   Klavier,   Op.   5:
Probenanweisungen") MK 9 (1979): 49–53.

> Reflections upon performance problems encountered in
> Berg's Op. 5 in light of the composer's applying formal
> procedures from large forms within the minuscule
> dimensions of these works.

486. Fisher, George, and Judy Lochhead. "Analysis, Hearing
and Performance." *Indiana Theory Review* 14 (1993): 1–36. In
English.

> An "analytic hearing" of Berg's Clarinet Pieces, Op. 5, nos.
> 1–2. The first is "cast as two interrelated stories in which
> musical actors enact two strands of a musical narrative."

487.   La Motte, Diether de.   "Voraussetzungslose Analyse.
Alban Berg: Vier Stücke für Klarinette und Klavier Op. 5, Nr. 1."
In La Motte, *Musikalische Analyse* (Textteil), 131–45.   Kassel:
Bärenreiter, 1968. In German.

> Concludes that a work such as Berg's Clarinet Piece, Op. 5,
> no. 1, is unanalyzable using normal formal categories and
> requires a new conception of form unencumbered by
> traditional assumptions. The analysis proceeds by ad hoc
> description and comparison, beginning with observations on
> tempo changes and continuing with attention to melodic,
> harmonic, and rhythmic elements.

488.   Lefkowitz, David Samuel.   "Alban Berg's Op. 5 Clarinet
and Piano Pieces."   Dissertation, University of Rochester, 1994.
UMI order no. 9426799. 76 p. In English.

> Analysis of pitch and rhythmic structures in the Four Pieces,
> Op. 5, finding that the opening gesture of the first piece is
> the unifying basis for the entire work. The author's approach
> to harmonic analysis involves set theory.

489. Lewis, Christopher. "Tonal Forms in Atonal Music: Berg's
Op. 5/3." MTS 3 (1981): 84–97. In English.

An analysis of pitch structures in the third of the Clarinet Pieces, Op. 5, using aspects of reductive tonal analysis and post-tonal set theory. The work is found "tonal" in the sense that there is persistent directed motion toward a tonic of D, although the harmonic language is characterized by the presence of sets that do not behave like tonal harmonies.

490. Perone, James. "Tonal Implications and the Role of the Symmetrical Hexachord in Alban Berg's Four Pieces for Clarinet and Piano, Opus 5, no. 2." *Interface* 16 (1987): 49–54. In English.

Argues for tonality in the work (based on B♭), which is revealed by Schenkeresque graphs and prominent uses of the pitch-class set (10 1 2 5 6).

491. Schaffer, Sarah. "Analytical Issues in the Segmentation of Atonal Music: An Investigation Based on Selected Pre-Serial Works of Schoenberg, Berg, and Webern." Dissertation, Indiana University, 1992. UMI order no. 9231508. 308 p. In English.

Discusses various approaches to segmentation in set-theory analysis, with application to Berg's Clarinet Piece, Op. 5, no. 3.

492. Schatt, Peter W. "Zahl, Symbolik und Kryptogrammatik in Alban Bergs Vier Stücken für Klarinette und Klavier." *Archiv für Musikwissenschaft* 43 (1986): 128–35. In German.

Finds prominent usages of the number 5 and the musical letters B, B♭, and A in various parts of the Clarinet Pieces, Op. 5.

Chamber Concerto

493. Adorno, Theodor W. "Alban Bergs Kammerkonzert." MK 9 (1979): 54–62. Reprinted in AGS 18 (1984): 630–40. In German.

Written in 1954 as a lecture for a general audience. Adorno approaches the Chamber Concerto as a work of great complexity, a "thicket," but one with features drawn from

Viennese classicism. These include a texture of theme plus accompaniment (the theme quickly passing from instrument to instrument) and an integrated continuity that is the opposite of contemporary pointillistic music.

494. Boulez, Pierre. [Untitled notes on the Chamber Concerto]. Sleeve notes to Boulez's recording of the Chamber Concerto, DGG 2531007. In French, English, and German. French text reprinted ("Berg: Le Kammerkonzert") in Boulez, *Points de repère*, 362–64, edited by Jean-Jacques Nattiez (Paris: Christian Bourgois, Éditions du Seuil, 1981). English translation ("Berg: The Chamber Concerto") in Boulez, *Orientations*, 372–73, translated by Martin Cooper, edited by Jean-Jacques Nattiez (Cambridge: Harvard University Press; London: Faber and Faber, 1986). Italian translation in Boulez, *Punti di riferimento* (Turin: Einaudi, 1984).

The Chamber Concerto combines constructivist tendencies (a love for palindrome, patterns based on the number three, preserialized elements) and pure expressivity.

495. Brauneiss, Leopold. "Überlegungen zur Rhythmik im Kammerkonzert Alban Bergs." ÖMZ 41 (1986): 553–59. In German.

Analysis of rhythm in the finale of the Chamber Concerto, finding a notable independence of rhythmic figures.

496. Congdon, David. "Composition in Berg's *Kammerkonzert*." PNM 24 (1985): 234–69. In English.

Detailed analysis of musical materials in the first two movements of the Chamber Concerto, finding similar compositional strategies and "a delicately crafted network of contrasts, communalities, partitions and symmetries within and between" these two sections.

497. ———. "*Kammerkonzert*: Evolution of the Adagio and the Trio Transcription." ABS 2 (1981): 145–60. In English, synopsis in German.

In 1935 Berg arranged the second movement of the Chamber Concerto for clarinet, violin, and piano. A sketch of this arrangement shows Berg's thinking about musical materials, which helps to clarify not only the evolution of the arrangement but also Berg's intentions in the substance of the movement itself.

498. Crawford, Robert Sheldon. "Dynamic Form and the Adagio of Alban Berg's Chamber Concerto." Dissertation, Washington University, 1982. UMI order no. 8314006. 121 p. In English.

The author distinguishes between "dynamic" and "architectonic" perceptions of a musical work, finding the two often separated in analyses of modern compositions. A synthetic analysis is proposed for Berg's Chamber Concerto.

499. Dalen, Barbara. "'Freundschaft, Liebe, und Welt': The Secret Programme of the Chamber Concerto." In *The Berg Companion* (no. 803): 141–80. In English.

Using evidence from musical and verbal sketchings in the Berg Collection at the Austrian National Library, the author concludes that the Adagio of the Chamber Concerto contains secret allusions to the illness and death of Mathilde Schoenberg as well as to her affair with Richard Gerstl, the latter presented by covert references to Maeterlinck's *Pelléas et Mélisande*. Also see the article by Floros (no. 502).

500. Deutsch, Max. "Le concerto de chambre d'Alban Berg." SMZ 89 (1949): 328–333. In French.

A general description and analysis of the Chamber Concerto, interpreting the content of Berg's "open letter" to Schoenberg (no. 39).

501. Floros, Constantin. "Das Kammerkonzert von Alban Berg: Hommage à Schönberg und Webern." MK 9 (1979): 63–90. In German.

A semantic analysis of the Chamber Concerto, concluding
that the work is a tribute to Webern as well as to Schoenberg
and that Schoenberg's Serenade, Op. 24, was a model.

502.   ————.   "Das   verschwiegene   Programm   des
Kammerkonzerts von Alban Berg: Eine semantische Analyse."
NZM 148/11 (1987): 11–22. In German.

An interpretation of the secretive content of the Chamber
Concerto, going beyond the autobiographical details
contained in the work that Berg himself made public.
Specifically, the author finds references in the first movement
to students in Schoenberg's circle other than himself and
Webern and, in the second movement, references to Mathilde
Schoenberg and Schoenberg's grief over her untimely death.
See the related findings of Dalen (no. 499).

503.   ————.   "Zum Beethoven-Bild Schönbergs, Bergs und
Weberns." In *Beethoven und die zweite Wiener Schule*, 8–24. Edited
by Otto Kolleritsch. Studien zur Wertungsforschung, volume 25.
Vienna,   Graz: Universal   Edition   for   the   Institut   für
Wertungsforschung, 1992. In German.

Berg's use of models from Beethoven is attested by a sketch
to the Chamber Concerto, which cites the rondos of
Beethoven's Piano Sonatas, Op. 13, and Op. 31, no. 1, as
models.

504. **Hansen, Mathias.** "'Aller guten Dinge. . .': Alban Berg im
Kreis der Wiener Schule." In *Alban Berg (1885–1935) und Kurt
Weill   (1900-1950):   Zwei   große   Komponisten   der   ersten
Jahrhunderthälfte*, 7–12. Edited by Günther Eisenhardt. Referate
der Dessauer Symposien, volume 10. Dessau: Musikschule
Dessau, 1986. In German.

General study of the Chamber Concerto, finding the work
balanced between the vocal idiom of Mahler and the
instrumental style of Schoenberg.

505. Hilmar, Rosemary. "Metrische Proportionen und serielle Rhythmik im Kammerkonzert von Alban Berg." SMZ 120 (1980): 355–60. In German, summary in French.

In the Chamber Concerto Berg "created a rigorous rhythmic proportionality based on the serial idea." All three movements are connected by proportional relations, the third being a summation of the previous two.

506. Lambert, Philip. "Berg's Path to Twelve-Note Composition: Aggregate Construction and Association in the Chamber Concerto." MA 12 (1993): 321–42. In English.

Studies the emergence of twelve-tone composition in Berg's works of the 1920s, reviews literature on the subject, and seeks out the formation and principles of association of aggregates in the Chamber Concerto.

507. Neuwirth, Gösta. "Themen- und Zeitstrukturen in Alban Bergs Kammerkonzert." ABS 2 (1981): 161–70. In German.

Numerological computations primarily concerning durations (in numbers of seconds and numbers of quarter-note values) in the Chamber Concerto, finding that these numbers exhibit simple arithmetic proportions.

508. Pinkas, Sally. "A Rhythmic and Metric Analysis of the Rondo Ritmico, the Third Movement of the Chamber Concerto by Alban Berg." Dissertation, Brandeis University, 1991. UMI order no. 9118713. 149 p. In English.

Study of the rhythm and meter of the movement, which is found to articulate musical form in the absence of an autonomous pitch system. The form of the movement is closer to sonata form than to rondo form.

509. Redlich, Hans F. "Alle guten Dinge." MEL 22 (1955): 39–40. In German.

Excerpts from Berg's correspondence with Schoenberg and Webern concerning the Chamber Concerto. Extracted from Redlich's book (no. 908).

510. Votta, Michael, Jr. "Pitch Structure and Extra-Musical References in Alban Berg's Kammerkonzert." *Journal of Band Research* 26/2 (1990-91): 1–32. In English.

> Analytic survey of the Chamber Concerto, especially as regards programmatic references and Berg's eclectic musical language.

511. Walgraeve, Gustaaf. "Het kamerconcert van Alban Berg." *Mens en melodie* 23 (1968): 234–37. In Dutch.

> General account of the Chamber Concerto emphasizing its twelve-tone aspects and thematic materials.

Lyric Suite

512. Adorno, Theodor W. "Berg: Drei Stücke aus der Lyrischen Suite für Streichorchester." AGS 18 (1984): 641–44 (incomplete version); AGS 20 (1986): 797–801 (complete). In German.

> Written in 1934 as a lecture for the British Broadcasting Corporation, Adorno presents an elementary description of the three orchestrated movements from the Lyric Suite. He asserts that the work is not a simple arrangement of a quartet but a reinstrumentation of a "lyric-dramatic" action.

513. Ashby, Arved. "Of *Modell-Typen* and *Reihenformen*: Berg, Schoenberg, F. H. Klein, and the Concept of Row Derivation." JAMS 48 (1995): 67–105. In English.

> Berg's use of multiple twelve-tone rows is attributed to the influence of Fritz Heinrich Klein, whose Variations for piano, Op. 14, provided a model that Berg developed in the Lyric Suite.

514. Bouquet, Fritz. "Alban Bergs Lyrische Suite: Eine Studie über Gestalt, Klang und Ausdruck." MEL 15 (1948): 227–31. In German.

> Analysis of formal elements of the Lyric Suite.

515. Bozzetti, Elmar. "'. . . Ein kleines Denkmal. . . einer großen Liebe': Alban Bergs Lyrische Suite." *Music und Bildung* 21 (1989): 29–36. In German.

Summary of the secretive programmatic content of the Lyric Suite and discussion of the significance of biographical allusions for the understanding of a musical work.

516. Buch, Estebán. *Histoire d'un secret: A propos de la Suite lyrique d'Alban Berg.* Arles: Actes Sud, 1994. ISBN 2742701990. ML410.B47B9 1994. In French.

Discussion and interpretation of the secretive, autobiographical content of Berg's Lyric Suite. There are no musical examples, and the author concludes with a discussion of strategies by which the listener interprets the semantic content of the work.

517. Budday, Wolfgang. *Alban Bergs Lyrische Suite: Satztechnische Analyse ihrer zwölftönigen Partien.* Dissertation, University of Tübingen, 1978. Tübinger Beiträge zur Musikwissenschaft, volume 8. Neuhausen-Stuttgart: Hänssler-Verlag, 1979. 106 p. ISBN 3775104895. ML410.B47 B8. Abstract in ÖMZ 41 (1986): 261. In German. Reviewed by Rudolf Klein, ÖMZ 36 (1981): 57–58; Jürg Stenzl, MF 34 (1981): 380; Rudolf Stephan, NZM 141 (1980): 478.

An analytic study of the Lyric Suite, emphasizing twelve-tone phenomena. The programmatic aspects of the work are reviewed.

518. Carner, Mosco. "The Berg Affair, Venice 1934." MT 110 (1969): 1129–31. In English.

At the Venice International Music Festival in 1934, a planned performance of the Lyric Suite was cancelled because the work had already been performed in Italy, thus contradicting the statutes of the festival. Berg's response to the cancellation is contained in a letter of 17 July 1934 to Francesco Malipiero. See also Morazzoni (no. 853).

519. Enns, Leonard. "Reflections on the First Movement of Berg's Lyric Suite." *Canadian University Music Review* 1 (1980): 147–55. In English.

Analysis of the Lyric Suite intending to show how structural principles from diatonic music are still present. Errors in musical examples in the article are pointed out by the author in the same journal, 2 (1981): 238.

520. Floros, Constantin. "Das esoterische Programm der Lyrischen Suite von Alban Berg: Eine semantische Analyse." HJM 1 (1974): 101–45. Reprinted (in abridged form) in MK 4 (1978): 5–48. In German. Italian translation ("Il programma esoterico della Lyrische Suite di Alban Berg: Un' analisi semantica") in *Com'era dolce il profumo del tiglio: La musica a Vienna nell'età di Freud*, 233–77, edited by Carlo de Incontrera (Monfalcone: Teatro Communale di Monfalcone, 1988).

A broad inquiry into the programmatic content of the Lyric Suite, touching on number symbolism, quotations from Richard Wagner and Alexander Zemlinsky, and autobiographical allusions (although not to the specifics of Berg's relation with Hanna Fuchs-Robettin).

521. García Torres, Fernando. "Zemlinsky, Berg y Fuchs-Robbetin: 'Relaciones' en la *Suite Lírica* de Berg." *Pauta* 4/15 (1985): 52–56. In Spanish.

Brief account of programmatic elements of the Lyric Suite.

522. Gerlach, Reinhard. "Zemlinsky und Berg: Lyrische Symphonie und Lyrische Suite." In *Alexander Zemlinsky: Tradition im Umkreis der Wiener Schule*, 145–54. Edited by Otto Kolleritsch. Studien zur Wertungsforschung, volume 7. Graz: Universal Edition for the Institut für Wertungsforschung, 1976. In German.

Analysis of Zemlinsky's Lyric Symphony with mention of its quotation in Berg's Lyric Suite. Written before the revelation of a vocal text associated with the Lyric Suite, the author concludes: "The human voice singing of spiritual love is consciously taken over [from Zemlinsky] into Berg's Lyric Suite."

523. Green, Douglass M. "The Allegro misterioso of Berg's *Lyric* Suite: Iso- and Retrorhythms." JAMS 30 (1977): 507–16. In English.

Analysis of rhythmic practices in the third movement of the Lyric Suite, supported by a sketch of the music in the Austrian National Library. Berg uses two brief rhythmic motifs, derived from pitches of the set, which are presented isorhythmically in the first half of the movement and in retrograde in the second half in forms suggested by serial transformation rather than by the more classical reversal of note values. Also see the commentary on this article in a letter from Michael Taylor, JAMS 32 (1979): 170-72, and Green's response, JAMS 33 (1980): 211–12.

524. ————. "Berg's De Profundis: The Finale of the Lyric Suite." BSN 5 (1977): 13–23. In English. German translation ("Das Largo desolato der Lyrischen Suite von Alban Berg") ÖMZ 33 (1978): 79–85.

Discusses a manuscript of the Lyric Suite in the Austrian National Library (labelled *Studienpartitur* by Helene Berg). Music of the finale is presented here in a formative stage. The manuscript also contains Berg's notes concerning twelve-tone usage and, entered beneath various staves, the text of Baudelaire's "De profundis clamavi" in a translation by Stefan George. This text suggests a hopeless passion to which the work refers, but its exact nature is unknown. (See Perle no. 532 for an explanation of this issue based on documents then unknown to Green.)

525. Gülke, Peter. "'Musik, die fürs erste . . . überhaupt wie keine anmutet': Zu Alban Bergs Lyrischer Suite." NZM 147/9 (1986): 14–21. In German.

General appraisal of the work and its programmatic content.

526. Harris, Donald, and Mark DeVoto. "Berg's Notes for the Lyric Suite." BSN 2 (1971): 5–7. In English.

Translation of an enclosure to a letter from Berg to Schoenberg (13 July 1926), headed "Komposition mit 12 Tönen." Berg discusses the properties of the all-interval row that he was using in the Lyric Suite. The letter is also translated in *The Berg-Schoenberg Correspondence* (no. 704): 349–51, and its contents are dealt with in Maegaard (no. 528).

527. Levin, Walter. "Textprobleme im dritten Satz der Lyrischen Suite." MK 9 (1979): 11–28. In German.

Analysis of row distortions in the repeat of the misterioso section of the Lyric Suite, movement 3, and their relation to longstanding principles of atonal composition.

528. Maegaard, Jan. "Ein Beispiel des atonalen Kontrapunkts im Frühstadium." *Zeitschrift für Musiktheorie* 3 (1972): 29–34. In German. English translation ("Berg's Seventeen Four-Part Canons: The Mystery Solved") BSN 3 (1975): 4–7.

Explains the meaning of Berg's reference to seventeen admissible four-part canons that can be derived from the row as used in the third movement of the Lyric Suite (see Harris and DeVoto, no. 526).

529. Mersemann, Hans, Hans Schultze-Ritter, and Heinrich Strobel. "Neue Musik aus dem Schönbergkreise." MEL 7 (1928): 479–80. In German.

A brief review of the newly published Lyric Suite.

530. Metzger, Heinz-Klaus, and Rainer Riehn. "Statt eines Nachworts zur Kontroverse." MK 9 (1979): 8–10. In German.

Summarizes the claims of Floros and Perle (see no. 534) concerning discovery of the secret program of the Lyric Suite and quotes from Theodor Adorno on Berg's relations with Hanna Fuchs-Robettin.

531. Parish, George David. "Motivic and Cellular Structure in Alban Berg's Lyric Suite." Dissertation, University of Michigan, 1970. UMI order no. 7115262. 328 p. In English.

Analysis of the Lyric Suite that deals with row manipulations and the deployment of pitch cells. A four-note cell in the third movement is found to be especially important. Reductive graphic analyses are included.

532. Perle, George. "The Secret Programme of the Lyric Suite." MT 118 (1977): 629–32, 709–13, 809–13. Reprinted in *Twentieth-Century Music*, 277–89, Garland Library of the History of Western Music, volume 10 (New York and London: Garland, 1985), and in *The Right Notes: Twenty-Three Selected Essays by George Perle on Twentieth-Century Music* (Stuyvesant, N.Y.: Pendragon Press, forthcoming ca. 1996). A shortened version is in BSN 5 (1977): 4–12. In English. German translation ("Das geheime Programm der Lyrischen Suite") in ÖMZ 33 (1978): 64–79, 113–19; and in MK 4 (1978): 49–74.

Brings to light the existence and contents of a miniature score of the Lyric Suite extensively annotated by the composer and given to Hanna Fuchs-Robettin. The annotations explain secretive programmatic references to Berg, Hanna, and her family.

533. ———. *Style and Idea in the Lyric Suite of Alban Berg.* Stuyvesant, N.Y.: Pendragon Press, 1995. xiv, 68 p. ISBN 0945193653. MT145.B47 P47 1995. In English.

An analytic study of the Lyric Suite, bringing back and updating several of the author's earlier writings on this work. The twelve-tone element is analyzed and Berg's annotated score given to Hanna Fuchs-Robettin is discussed. The texted version of the finale is also analyzed.

534. Perle, George, and Constantin Floros. "Kontroverse über das Programm der Lyrischen Suite." MK 9 (1979): 3–7. In German.

Both authors affirm the validity and independence of their discoveries concerning the program of the Lyric Suite, as enunicated in Perle no. 532 and Floros no. 520.

535. Petazzi, Paolo. "'. . . Du fond du gouffre obscur où mon coeur est tombé. . .'." In *Com'era dolce il profumo del tiglio: La musica a Vienna nell'età di Freud*, 279–97. Edited by Carlo de Incontrera. Monfalcone: Teatro Communale di Monfalcone, 1988. In Italian.

Discussion of the secretive programmatic aspects of the Lyric Suite.

536. Schneider, Frank. "Eine Suite für Berg: Zum 100. Geburtstag des Komponisten." *Musik und Gesellschaft* 35 (1985): 79–84. In German.

Interpretive analysis of the Lyric Suite, completely avoiding reference to its underlying autobiographical or formalistic elements.

537. Smith Brindle, Reginald. "The Symbolism in Berg's Lyric Suite." *The Score and I.M.A. Magazine* 21 (1957): 60–63. In English.

Notes the prominence of the number 23 in the Lyric Suite and hypothesizes that certain important rhythmic figures come from the rhythm of the words "von Zemlinsky" and "Alban Berg."

538. Stein, Erwin. [Untitled preface]. Alban Berg, *Lyrische Suite für Streichquartette.* Philharmonia Partituren, no. 173. Vienna and London: Universal Edition, 1927. In German, English, and French.

A brief formal sketch, emphasizing the free and nonsymphonic aspect which tends to the lyric and dramatic. A brief sketch of the twelve-tone idea is added.

539. Straus, Joseph N. "*Tristan* and Berg's Lyric Suite." *In Theory Only* 8/3 (1984): 33–41. In English.

Analysis of covert uses in the Lyric Suite of pitch structures from Richard Wagner's *Tristan und Isolde.*

540. Walgraeve, Gustaaf. "De Lyrische Suite van Alban Berg." *Mens en melodie* 24 (1969): 310–13. In Dutch.

General description of the work.

541. Zentner, Wilhelm. "Alban Berg: Lyrische Suite für Streichquartett." In *Reclams Kammermusikführer*, 585–86. Edited by Hans Renner. Stuttgart: Reclam, 1955. In German.

Brief description of the Lyric Suite.

542. Zervos, George. "Allegro misterioso tou Alban Berg." *Moussicologhia* 1/3 (1985): 72–87. In Greek, summary in English.

Using Berg's Lyric Suite, movement 3, as an example, the author discusses the innovative concept of theme in works of the Viennese School and its relation to theme in Renaissance polyphony.

7

Writings on
Berg's Orchestral Music

This chapter contains citations of writings that are primarily concerned with Berg's orchestral music (Orchestral Pieces, Op. 6; concert aria *Der Wein*; Violin Concerto). Studies of the Three Fragments from *Wozzeck* and Symphonic Pieces from *Lulu* are found in Chapters 4 and 5, respectively. The citations in this chapter are arranged alphabetically by author, or title if an author's name is lacking. Since information on the orchestral works is also contained in writings cited in other chapters of this book, the reader is urged to consult the Index under "Berg, Alban: works" for a complete list of sources.

Orchestral Pieces, Op. 6

543. Archibald, Bruce. "The Harmony of Berg's 'Reigen'." PNM 6 (1968): 73–91. In English.

> Harmonic analysis of Op. 6, no. 2, especially as regards treatment of the key of D minor and use of quartal and whole-tone harmonies.

544. Brandt, Maarten. "Een mahleriaanse mars die Mahler niet geschreven zou hebben." *Mens en melodie* 39 (1984): 424–29. In Dutch.

> Description of the Berg's March, Op. 6, no. 3, dealing primarily with themes.

545. Chadwick, Nicholas. "Franz Schreker's Orchestral Style and its Influence on Alban Berg." MR 35 (1974): 29–46. In English.

> Comparisons are drawn between the orchestration of Berg's Orchestral Songs, Op. 6, and Schreker's *Der ferne Klang* and *Vorspiel zu einem Drama*. Similarities include the treatment of the orchestra as a chamber ensemble, fragmentation of lines, and distinctive uses of harp and celesta.

546. DeVoto, Mark. "Alban Bergs Drei Orchesterstücke Op. 6: Struktur, Thematik und ihr Verhältnis zu *Wozzeck*." ABS 2 (1981): 97–106. In German.

> Investigation of the thematic element of the Orchestral Pieces and its relevance to overall structure. Tabulates with analytic commentary the main motifs of the entire work and surveys their recurrences. Although the often recondite thematic transformations used in Op. 6 recur in later works such as *Wozzeck*, the opera represents a degree of simplification in thematic processes in that unnecessary complications of the musical surface are avoided.

547. ———. "Alban Berg's 'Marche macabre'." PNM 22 (1983–84): 386–447. In English.

> Analysis of the March from the Orchestral Pieces, Op. 6, no. 3, focusing on thematic issues, "creeping" chromaticism, overall form, harmony, and tonality.

548. Jameux, Dominique. "Interminable analyse. Études atonales III: La première pièce de l'opus 6 de Berg—Präludium." *Musique en jeu* 20 (1975): 49–70; 21 (1975): 33–41. In French.

> Discussion of the Orchestral Piece, Op. 6, no. l, using a method said to be partly descriptive, partly analytic. The piece is seen as being organized around a climax occurring between mm. 36 and 37.

549. Micznik, Vera. "Gesture as Sign: A Semiotic Interpretation of Berg's Op. 6, no. 1." *In Theory Only* 9/4 (1986): 19–35. In English.

Proposes a model for analyzing meaning in atonal works such as Berg's Orchestral Piece, Op. 6, no. 1, based on Roland Barthes's theory of connotative rather than denotative signs.

550. Redlich, Hans F. "Der Symphoniker Alban Berg: Die Entstehungsgeschichte der Drei Orchesterstücke Op. 6 und ein Symphonie-Plan." ÖMZ 9 (1954): 148–54. In German.

The Orchestral Pieces, Op. 6, are related more to the symphonic style of Mahler than to the Orchestral Pieces of Schoenberg or Webern. (Material from this article is incorporated in Redlich's book, no. 908.) Quotes from letters by Berg to Webern and Schoenberg from the time of Berg's Op. 6.

551. Rost, Cornelia. "Im Konzertsaal gehört: Alban Berg, Drei Orchesterstücke Op. 6." NZM 143/12 (1982): 37–40. In German.

Brief general appraisal of Op. 6.

552. Taylor, Michael. "Musical Progression in the Präludium of the Three Orchestral Pieces Op. 6." In *The Berg Companion* (no. 803): 123–39. In English.

A discussion of elements of continuity in the Prelude of the Orchestral Pieces, Op. 6, based on listening and study. Brief passages at the beginning are isolated as "events," which begin with little information, but then grow and build upon one another, leading to a sense of "progression" that ultimately spans and unifies the entire movement.

Der Wein

553. Adorno, Theodor W. "Konzertarie *Der Wein.*" In Reich 1937 (no. 919): 101–106. Reprinted in AGS 13 (1971): 509–14. In German.

Adorno was apparently unsatisfied with this analysis of *Der Wein*, written for Reich's 1937 study. It was the only analysis prepared for Reich that was not reused in Adorno's own book on Berg (no. 667).

554. ———. "Zum Rundfunkkonzert vom 8. April 1931." AGS 20 (1986): 793–96. In German.

Concerns Berg's *Der Wein*, asserting its cyclic form, motivic construction, and distance from the spirit of neoclassicism.

555. **Headlam, David.** "Row Derivation and Contour Association in Berg's *Der Wein*." PNM 28 (1990): 256–92. In English.

Methods for deriving row forms from a basic row applied in *Lulu* are located in *Der Wein*. The author also studies the contour given to rows in *Der Wein*, finding that the associations that they produce mark off formal areas and underscore the relationships existing within the musical materials.

556. **Jarman, Douglas.** "Some Row Techniques in Alban Berg's *Der Wein*." *Soundings* 2 (1971–72): 68–56. In English.

Analysis of harmonic and thematic structures in *Der Wein*, showing their derivation from row forms. Ends with a comparison of row techniques in *Der Wein* with those in *Lulu*.

557. **Knaus, Herwig.** "Alban Bergs Skizzen und Vorarbeiten zur Konzertarie *Der Wein*." In *Festschrift Othmar Wessely zum 60. Geburtstag*, 355–79. Edited by Manfred Angerer, et al. Tutzing: Hans Schneider, 1982. Reprinted (shortened) in *Musikerziehung* 38 (1984–85): 195–204. In German.

Detailed analysis of the musical and textual manuscripts for *Der Wein*.

558. ———. "Kompositionstechnik und Semantik in Alban Bergs Konzertarie *Der Wein* nebst einem Anhang zum Violinkonzert." ABS 2 (1981): 136–44. In German.

The author applies his theory of "row tonality" to the row forms of *Der Wein*, concluding that certain tonal areas express ideas from the text. The tonal interpretation of rows is supported by Berg's own musical examples drawn up for the use of Willi Reich in writing program notes for the first performance of the work in 1930. These examples are reproduced in facsimile.

559. Mooser, R.-Aloys. "*Der Wein* d'Alban Berg." SMZ 72 (1932): 502–503. In French.

Report on the 1932 festival of the International Society for Contemporary Music in Vienna, where Berg's *Der Wein* was heard. The work is described and praised.

560. Paclt, Jaromir. "Berg wünschte sich einen Tenor für die Weinarie." MEL 33 (1966): 114–15. In German.

Transcription and facsimile of a letter from Berg (18 October 1935) to K. B. Jirák expressing Berg's wish to have *Der Wein* sung by a tenor ("in text the aria is clearly a man's song").

561. Redlich, Hans F. "Bergs Konzertarie *Der Wein*: Zur Erstveröffentlichung der Partitur im Jahre 1966." ÖMZ 21 (1966): 284–91. In German.

Credits Universal Edition with a belated attempt to make Berg's music available, although he finds several spurious changes in the 1966 edition of *Der Wein*. Analytic remarks are added concerning the twelve-tone element of the aria.

562. Reich, Willi. "Alban Berg und Anton von Webern in ihren neuen Werken." *Der Auftakt* 10 (1930): 132–35. In German. English translation ("Berg's New Work: *Der Wein*"), *Modern Music* 7/3 (1930): 41–43. Dutch translation ("*Der Wein*, een nieuw werk van Alban Berg") in *De muziek* 4 (1929–30): 215–17.

Brief description of *Der Wein*.

563. Schroeder, David P. "Berg, Strindberg, and D Minor." *College Music Symposium* 30/2 (1990): 74–89. In English.

An analysis of *Der Wein* that looks for references to D minor in conjunction with C major, suggesting conflict and transcendence. The same conjunction is found in several works by Beethoven in D minor, whose conflicts may have provoked Strindberg to imbue his writings with a similar ethos.

Violin Concerto

564. Adorno, Theodor W. "Alban Berg: Violinkonzert." In Adorno, *Der getreue Korrepetitor: Lehrschriften zur musikalischen Praxis*, 187–216. Frankfurt: Suhrkamp, 1963. Reprinted in AGS 15 (1976): 338–68. In German. Italian translation in Adorno, *Il fido maestro sostituto: Studi sulla communicazione della musica*, translated by G. Manzoni (Turin: Einaudi, 1969): 206–40.

A detailed "interpretive" analysis of the Violin Concerto, which Adorno finds easily misinterpreted given the work's "tension between poles of chaos and transparent organization." An ideal performance is impossible, but must still be properly informed, first of all by a microscopic analysis of the work's motivic structure.

565. ———. "Berg-Gedenkkonzert im Londoner Rundfunk." AGS 20 (1986): 802–803. In German.

Notice concerning a London BBC broadcast in 1936 of Berg's works, including the Violin Concerto, conducted by Webern. The Concerto is described as Berg's Mahlerian farewell. "It has the simplicity of haste, spoken by one who knows that he has no time to lose to say what must be said."

566. Barcaba, Peter. "Zur Tonalität in Alban Bergs Violinkonzert." *Musikerziehung* 32 (1978–79): 158–64. In German.

Discussion of the harmonic and pseudotonal elements of the Violin Concerto, finding in the work a merger of styles.

567. Bauer, Hans-Joachim. "Alban Berg: 'Dem Andenken eines Engels'." *Das Orchester* 33 (1985): 916–20. In German.

General analysis of the Violin Concerto touching on the historical background, programmatic content, and differing critical assessments.

568. Berger, Gregor. "Alban Bergs Violinkonzert." In *Musik und Musikerziehung in der Reifezeit: Vorträge der dritten Bundesschulmusikwoche*, München 1959, 222–31. Edited by Egon Kraus. Mainz: B. Schott's Söhne, n.d. (ca. 1959). In German.

Analysis of the Violin Concerto intending to show that the work "is pertinent to the final year of German high school." The analysis focuses on the twelve-tone element of the concerto, "which is bound up with functional relations and thus forms a bridge to the nineteenth century."

569. Blasl, Franz. "Das Violinkonzert von Alban Berg." *Musikerziehung* 19 (1965–66): 111–16. In German.

Text of a radio broadcast in which the programmatic content of the Violin Concerto is analyzed.

570. Carner, Mosco. "Alban Berg (1885–1935)." In *The Concerto*, 362–79. Edited by Ralph Hill. Baltimore: Penguin Books, 1952. In English.

Analysis of the Violin Concerto for general readers. Berg's twelve-tone method in the work represents "a move from the abstraction and 'Ivory Tower' attitude of a Schönberg and a Webern to a more humane plane."

571. Conridge, Graham. "A Wrong Note in Berg's Violin Concerto?" MT 130 (1989): 205–207. In English.

Notes a probable misprint in the orchestral score at m. 143 in the finale of the Violin Concerto (in the bass clarinet part).

572. Delaigue, Olivier. "Le Requiem d'Alban Berg: Quelques éléments pour l'analyse du Concerto à la mémoire d'un ange." *Analyse musicale* 18 (1990): 58–60. In French.

Analysis of the Violin Concerto emphasizing serial procedures, number symbolism, and programmatic implications.

573. Fiedler, Achim. "Is This Enough? Divine Chance or Carefully Structured Programme?" MT 134 (1993): 444–45. In English.

Notes that in 1914 Berg heard a performance of Bach's cantata *O Ewigkeit du Donnerwort*, BWV 60 (containing the chorale melody "Es ist genug"), which may have influenced his use of the melody in the Violin Concerto.

574. Floros, Constantin. "Alban Bergs Requiem: Das verschwiegene Programm des Violinkonzerts." NZM 146/4 (1985): 4–8. In German.

An interpretation of the Violin Concerto as a tribute to Manon Gropius, finding Berg's use of a Lutheran chorale to be "a personal religious confession." For an entirely different interpretation of the secret programmatic content, see Jarman (no. 581).

575. ―――. "Die Skizzen zum Violinkonzert von Alban Berg." ABS 2 (1981): 118–35. In German.

Analytic examination of the sketches for the Violin Concerto in the Austrian National Library (including sketches entered into Berg's date book for 1935). The sketches are of four types: characteristic passages for violin from other violin concertos, "chords, cadenzas, and scales" derived from the tone row, discontinuous themes and motives, and verbal indications of the general formal conception with programmatic allusions. The sketches contain no information that conflicts with the accepted chronology of the work. The sketches have valuable information concerning Berg's working methods, techniques, and extramusical intentions. As to programmatic allusions, the sketches support Reich's interpretation (no. 918).

576. Flothuis, Marius. "Musik über 'Musik über Musik': Bemerkungen zur Berceuse élégiaque von Ferruccio Busoni und dem Violinkonzert von Alban Berg." In *Florilegium musicologicum: Hellmut Federhofer zum 75. Geburtstag,* 95–102. Edited by Christoph-Hellmut Mahling. Tutzing: Hans Schneider, 1988. In German.

> Draws a comparison between Busoni's *Berceuse élégiaque* and Berg's Violin Concerto: both works have a memorial character and draw meaning from existing pieces of music.

577. Foreman, Lewis. "Webern, the BBC and the Berg Violin Concerto." *Tempo* 178 (1991): 2–10. In English.

> Information concerning Webern's conducting Berg's Violin Concerto with the BBC Orchestra in 1936. Highly critical of Webern's abilities. (He was reportedly known to the English players as "Kapellmeister Zig-Zag.")

578. Forneberg, Erich. "Der Bach-Choral in Alban Bergs Violinkonzert." MEL 23 (1956): 247–49. Reprinted in Forneberg, *Der Geist der neuen Musik: Das neue Klang im Spiegel der traditionellen Harmonielehre,* 110–13, Literarhistorisch-musikwissenschaftliche Abhandlungen, volume 15 (Würzburg: K. Triltsch, 1957). In German.

> Discussion of the hymn tune quoted in Berg's Violin Concerto and its relation to the row.

579. Fuhrmann, Robert. "Alban Berg (1885–1935): Violinkonzert (1935)." In *Perspektiven neuer Musik: Material und didaktische Information,* volume 1: 73–109. Edited by Dieter Zimmerschied. Mainz: B. Schott's Söhne, 1974. In German.

> General analysis of the Violin Concerto touching on form, row usages, number and pitch symbolism, source materials, and pedagogical questions.

580. Hall, Anne Carothers. "Texture in Violin Concertos of Stravinsky, Berg, Schoenberg, and Bartók." Dissertation,

University of Michigan, 1971. UMI order no. 7114884. 356 p. In English.

Develops terminology and method for analyzing musical texture. Berg's Violin Concerto is one of four works studied.

581. Hurd, Michael. "Berg: Violin Concerto." *Music in Education* 38 (1974): 270–73. In English.

General discussion of the form, program, and twelve-tone aspects of the Violin Concerto, which the author finds "saturated in the kind of emotion that would gladden the heart of the most cynical ad-man."

582. Jarman, Douglas. "Alban Berg, Wilhelm Fliess and the Secret Programme of the Violin Concerto." BSN 12 (1982): 5–11. Reprinted in *The Berg Companion* (no. 803): 181–94. In English. German translation ("Alban Berg, Wilhelm Fliess und das geheime Programm des Violinkonzerts") in ÖMZ 40 (1985): 12–21.

Traces Berg's ideas concerning numerology to the writings of Wilhelm Fliess and gives examples of numerological phenomena in the Violin Concerto, suggesting simultaneous references both to Hanna Fuchs and to Berg's early affair with Marie Scheuchl. Jarman also suggests that Berg may have viewed the Violin Concerto as his own Requiem. The content of this article is discussed in Jordan Mejias, "Denkmal für sich selbst," *Frankfurter allgemeine Zeitung* (23 July 1983): 21.

583. Jiránek, Jaroslav. "Das Violinkonzert von Alban Berg: Modell einer Analyse." BMW 21 (1979): 143–88. In German. (The article originated in a Czech version in *Hudebni věda* 14 [1977]: 3–50.)

A lengthy, systematic analysis of the Violin Concerto seeking to reveal both the "historical" and the "individual" styles. The analysis touches on matters of tonality, tone rows, rhythm, motif, form, and semantic content. "Berg's Violin

Concerto is a great humanistic work from the bourgeois era, whose time is now over."

584. Kastner, Rudolf. "Alban Berg och hans violinkonsert." *Musikrevy* 14 (1959): 230–34. In Swedish.

Historical background of the Violin Concerto and its programmatic content.

585. Knab, Armin. "Alban Berg und Georg Trakl: Gedanken über zeitgenössische Kunst." *Musica* 5 (1951): 345–48. Reprinted in Knab, *Denken und Tun: Gesammelte Aufsätze über Musik*, 100–104 (Berlin: Verlag Merseburger, 1959). In German.

The author expands upon a remark heard on the radio, that Berg's Violin Concerto must be heard in the same way that one hears a poem by Trakl. Analogies between the two artists are not to be found in form and material, but instead in content, both relating to Expressionism, melancholy, and isolation.

586. Knaus, Herwig. "Die Kärntner Volksweise aus Alban Bergs Violinkonzert." *Musikerziehung* 23 (1969–70): 117–18. In German. English translation by Mosco Carner ("Berg's Carinthian Folk Tune") MT 117 (1976): 487.

Identifies the Carinthian folk song used in Berg's Violin Concerto as "A Vögele af'n Zweschpm-bam" in an 1892 collection, *Wulfenia-Blüten*, edited by Karl Leibleitner. Also see the related findings in Ernst Krenek's review of Redlich (no. 908).

587. ———. "Die Reihenskizzen zu Alban Bergs Violinkonzert." ÖMZ 37 (1982): 105–108. In German.

Examination of the contents of two of Berg's row charts for the Violin Concerto.

588. ———. "Studien zu Alban Bergs Violinkonzert." In *De ratione in musica: Festschrift Erich Schenk zum 5. Mai 1972*, 255–74. Edited by Theophil Antonicek, Rudolf Flotzinger, Othmar

Wessely. Kassel: Bärenreiter, 1975. Reprinted in *Die Wiener Schule*, 256–78, edited by Rudolf Stephan (Darmstadt: Wissenschaftliche Buchgesellschaft, 1989). In German.

Analysis of the Violin Concerto, especially concerning row usage and Berg's application of motivic symbols from the nineteenth century (such as the "Les adieux" thematic type).

589. Krasner, Louis. "The Origins of the Alban Berg Violin Concerto." ABS 2 (1981): 107–17. In English, synopsis in German.

Reminiscences of the commissioning, composition, and early performances of the Violin Concerto by its first solo interpreter.

590. ———. "The Violin Concerto in Vienna." BSN 12 (1982): 3–4. In English.

Recollection of playing Berg's Violin Concerto with the Vienna Philharmonic Orchestra under Otto Klemperer in October, 1936. As a form of protest against the work, the orchestra marched off the stage immediately upon its conclusion.

591. ———. "Violinist Krasner Relates Story behind Berg Concerto." *Musical Courier* 149 (1 May 1954): 43. In English.

Brief news item.

592. Krasner, Louis, and Don C. Seibert. "Some Memories of Anton Webern, the Berg Concerto, and Vienna in the 1930s." *Fanfare* 11 (1987): 335–47. In English. French translation of excerpts ("Souvenirs: Anton Webern, le Concerto de violon de Berg et la Vienne des années 30"), *Dissonance: La nouvelle revue musicale suisse* 27 (1991): 4–9.

Recollections about early performances of Berg's Violin Concerto under Webern's direction; also contains references to Webern's support for the Nazis. See also Laugwitz (no. 593).

593.   Laugwitz, Burkhard.   "Das Konzert war eine Demonstration: Louis Krasner und die Uraufführung von Bergs Violinkonzert." NZM 152/10 (1991): 4–10. In German.

Interview focusing on Krasner's training, his contact with Oskar Adler, the history of Berg's Violin Concerto, his contact with Webern, and Webern's Nazi sympathies.

594. Lorkovic, Radovan (abridged by Douglas Jarman). "Berg's Violin Concerto: Discrepancies in the Published Score." MT 130 (1989): 268–71. In English.

Virtually a translation of no. 595, although the list of "discrepancies" in the score of the Violin Concerto is considerably shortened.

595.   ———.   "Später Versuch einer Textkorrektur im Violinkonzert von Alban Berg."   ÖMZ 44 (1989):611–19.   In German.

Based on a study of manuscript materials and analytic readings of Berg's Violin Concerto, the author constructs a list of corrections in the score of the first edition. Similar material found in the Lorkovic's book, no. 596, and in the author's article, no. 594, although in this version the list of corrections to be made in the Violin Concerto is considerably longer.

596.   ———.   *Das Violinkonzert von Alban Berg: Analysen, Textkorrekturen, Interpretation.*   Musikreflektionen, volume 3. Edited by the Musik-Akademie der Stadt Basel.   Winterthur: Amadeus, 1991. 220 p. ISBN 3905049481. ML410.B47 L6 1991. In German. Reviewed by Stephen Hinton, *Notes* 49 (1992–93): 1459–62; Anthony Pople, MT 134 (1993): 337; Rudolf Stephan, NZM 153/5 (1992): 53; Manfred Wagner, ÖMZ 48 (1993): 379–80.

Study of form, dodecaphonic elements and textual discrepancies in published sources of the Violin Concerto. Much of the analysis and interpretation is made from the perspective of the performer.

597. Newman, Ernest. "Alban Berg's Violin Concerto: Tonality and Atonality." *Sunday Times,* 10 May 1936. In English.

Newman is critical of atonal and twelve-tone composition in general and of Berg's Violin Concerto in particular, given its "unsuccessful" attempt to merge tonality and atonality. Berg is depicted as a composer divided against himself: the quotation of a Bach chorale harmonization amid the atonalism of the Concerto "is to fall between two stools." See the response to this article by Willi Reich, "An Ernest Newman," no. 604.

598. Panofsky, Walter. "Alban Berg: Violinkonzert." In Panofsky, *Die hundert schönsten Konzerte,* 127–29. Berlin and Munich: Gebrüder Weiss, n.d. (ca. 1958). In German.

Brief and general account of the Violin Concerto.

599. Pople, Anthony. *Berg: Violin Concerto.* Cambridge Music Handbooks. Cambridge: Cambridge University Press, 1991. ix, 121 p. ISBN 0521390664 (hardback), 0521399769 (paperback). ML410.B47 P6 1991. In English. Reviewed by Bruce Archibald, ML 73 (1992): 474–75; Nick Chadwick, MT 132 (1991): 516–17; Michael Graubart, *Tempo* 180 (1992): 36–41; Stephen Hinton, *Notes* 49 (1992–93): 1459–62; Robert Morgan, MA 12 (1993): 400–406.

A broad appraisal of the Violin Concerto touching on Berg's earlier compositions from the time of the Orchestral Pieces, Op. 6, contemporary work on *Lulu,* the historical background of the Concerto, programmatic elements and theories, form and musical materials, serial aspects, and critical reception. The analysis finds that the music has an "affinity with extended tonal resources," although aspects of set and serial theory are used as well.

600. Puetter, Hugo. "Wiederbegegnung mit Alban Berg: Deutsche Erstaufführung seines Violinkonzertes in Frankfurt am Main." MEL 14 (1947): 85. In German.

Discussion of the Violin Concerto following an early German performance.

601. Redlich, Hans F. "Alban Bergs Violinkonzert." MEL 24 (1957): 316–21; 352–57. In German.

Detailed analysis extracted from Redlich's book (no. 908).

602. Reich, Willi. "Alban Bergs neues Werk: 'Dem Andenken eines Engels'." *Neues Wiener Journal*, 31 August 1935, p. 11. In German.

Brief notice and description.

603. ———. "Alban Bergs neuestes Werk." SMZ 75 (1935): 735–37. In German.

General description of the Violin Concerto.

604. ———. "An Ernest Newman." *23: Eine Wiener Musikzeitschrift* 28–30 (1936): 20–28. In German, quotations in English.

A response to Ernest Newman's critique (no. 597) of Berg's Violin Concerto in which Reich dismisses Newman's idea that atonal composition is opposed to the context of tonal composition.

605. ———. "Requiem für Manon." MBA 17 (1935): 250–52. In German.

Describes a programmatic element in the Violin Concerto as it relates to Manon Gropius. Also notes on the derivation of the tone row.

606. Rostal, Max, and Hans Keller. "Berg's Violin Concerto: A Revision." MT 95 (1954): 87–88. In English.

The violinist Rostal suggests rewriting the violin cadenza in the Allegro of Part 2 of the Violin Concerto to clarify its implicit voice leading. Keller adds support for the idea.

607. Schneider, Frank. "Alban Bergs Violinkonzert: Metaphern zu einer transzendierenden Musik." BMW 18 (1976): 219–33.

Reprinted in *Musikalischer Analyse in der Diskussion*, 20–28 (Berlin, 1982). In German.

Analysis of the chorale quotation in the Violin Concerto and its mode of integration into the body of the work, suggesting both syntactic and semantic issues that ultimately lend a societal meaning to the work.

608. Shreffler, Theodore Wilson, III. "An Analysis of the Violin Concerto (1938) by Alban Berg." Dissertation, University of California, Los Angeles, 1979. UMI order no. 8001423. 161 p. In English.

Analysis of form, thematic and row usages, and orchestration in the Violin Concerto.

609. Smith, Moses. "Alban Berg—Finale: A Requiem." *Modern Music* 13/3 (March/April 1936): 29–34. In English.

Surveys Berg's Violin Concerto and other late works with sarcastic reflections upon American critics who reject all nontonal music as nonsense.

610. Stahmer, Klaus Hinrich. "Analytische Orchestration: Bach-Transkriptionen von Schönberg, Webern und Berg." In *57. Bachfest der Neuen Bachgesellschaft: Bach und die Barockkunst*, 151–54. Edited by Christian Kabitz. Würzburg: Johann Sebastian Bachgesellschaft; Leipzig: Neue Bachgesellschaftfest Internationale Vereinigung, 1982. In German.

Distinguishes between the Bach arrangements by Schoenberg and Webern, which are analytic in character, and Berg's use of Bach's chorale harmonization in Berg's Violin Concerto, which is pure quotation.

611. Stefan, Paul. "Alban Bergs 'Requiem für Manon'." MBA 18 (1936): 233–34. In German.

Praises the work after its premiere with the Vienna Philharmonic. "The orchestra played as beautifully and perfectly as ever." See Louis Krasner's description of this concert in no. 590. The article has no byline, although Stefan was the editor of MBA at this time (Ploebsch, no. 227, attributes it to Willi Reich).

612.   Stephan, Rudolf.   *Alban Berg: Violinkonzert (1935).* Meisterwerke der Musik, volume 49.   Munich: Wilhelm Fink Verlag, 1988. 56 p. ISBN 3770524837. MT130.B46 S7 1988. In German.

Concise sketch of the Violin Concerto touching on its historical background, the accuracy of the score, twelve-tone practices, the issue of tonality, interpretation, documents, and a movement-by-movement analysis.

613.   Taylor, Clifford.   "The Contemporaneity of Music in History." MR 24 (1963): 205–17. In English.

Compares the communicative power of Berg's Violin Concerto with works of Mozart, concluding that all are products of their time, a contemporaneity distilled into a symbolic "idea" present in each.

614. Thomson, Virgil. "Gloomy Masterpiece." *New York Herald Tribune*, 16 December 1949. Reprinted in Thomson, *A Virgil Thomson Reader*, 330–31. New York: E. P. Dutton, 1981.   In English.

Review of a performance by the New York Philharmonic of Berg's Violin Concerto.   Thomson found the work "expressionism at its most intense and visceral" although he admits that the piece is far removed from his own artistic sensibilities.

615.   Walgraeve, Gustaaf. "Het vioolconcert van Alban Berg." *Mens en melodie* 22 (1967): 108–11. In Dutch.

General account of the work and its programmatic content.

616. Winkler, Klaus. "Bach-Choralzitate in Kompositionen des 20. Jahrhunderts." In *Alte Musik als ästhetische Gegenwart: Bericht über den internationalen musikwissenschaftlichen Kongreß, Stuttgart*

1985, volume 1: 535–43. Edited by Dietrich Berke and Dorothee Hanemann. Kassel: Bärenreiter, 1987. In German.

Finds in Berg's chorale quotation in the Violin Concerto a model for later composers (including Bernd Alois Zimmermann and Helmut Barbe) in the portrayal of suffering and death.

617. Yates, Peter. "Music: The Alban Berg Violin Concerto." *Arts and Architecture* 63 (January 1946): 9, 14, 18. In English.

Description of the Violin Concerto for general readers.

618. "Zur Entstehung des Violin-Konzertes von Alban Berg." MBA 18 (1936): 196–97. In German.

Excerpts from five letters and cards from 1935 (28 March, 16 July, 27 July, 13 August, 13 September) from Berg to Louis Krasner concerning the Violin Concerto. The letter of 16 July reports that composition of the work had been completed the previous day and its orchestration could now begin.

8

Writings on
Berg's Songs

This chapter contains citations of writings that are primarily concerned with Berg's songs (Seven Early Songs; Four Songs, Op. 2; Orchestral Songs, Op. 4; other songs). The citations are arranged alphabetically by author, or title if an author's name is lacking. Since information on the songs is also contained in writings cited in other chapters of this book, the reader is urged to consult the Index under "Berg, Alban: works" for a complete list of sources.

Seven Early Songs

619. Adorno, Theodor W. "Alban Berg frühe Lieder." MBA 11 (1929): 90–92. Reprinted in AGS 18 (1984): 465–68. In German.

Reviews the stylistic significance of the Seven Early Songs, shortly after they were published, concluding that they are evidence of Berg's humanity, purity, and genuineness.

620. ———. "Berg: Sieben frühe Lieder für eine Singstimme und Klavier." *Die Musik* 21 (1929): 761–62. Reprinted in AGS 18 (1984): 469–71. In German.

Closely related to Adorno's remarks in no. 619, concluding that the songs share content with music of the late romantic period but begin the changes in musical form that would bring the downfall of romanticism.

621. ———. "Zur Instrumentation von Bergs frühen Liedern." SMZ 72 (1932): 158–62, 196–200. Reprinted (in revised form and retitled "Die Instrumentation von Bergs frühen Liedern") in Adorno, *Klangfiguren*, 138–56 (Berlin and Frankfurt: Suhrkamp, 1959); AGS 16 (1978): 97–109. In German.

> The 1928 instrumentation of the Seven Early Songs does not mix two different styles; instead, it reveals the substance of the music. The homogeneous sound of the romantic orchestra is avoided in favor of a constantly changing, refined use of color.

622. Eberle, Gottfried. "Im Konzertsaal gehört: Alban Berg, Sieben frühe Lieder." NZM 146/2 (1985): 23–26. In German.

> General background and stylistic appraisal of the Seven Early Songs.

Four Songs, Op. 2

623. Ayrey, Craig. "Berg's 'Scheideweg': Analytical Issues in Op. 2/ii." MA 1 (1982): 189–202. In English.

> Berg's "Schlafend trägt man mich" (Op. 2, no. 2) is portrayed as Berg's "crossroads" connecting tonal and atonal composition. The song can be analyzed in either context, based on a tonal reading of the opening French sixth chord or its equally viable alternative reading as a nontonal, centric formation that is subsequently prolonged throughout the entire work.

624. Gerlach, Reinhard. "Der Traum ein Leben—Der Leben ein Traum: Die innere Biographie der frühen Berg in Stadien seines musikalischen Bewußtseins." In Gerlach, *Musik und Jugendstil der Wiener Schule, 1900–1908*, 223–74. Laaber: Laaber–Verlag, 1985. In German.

> Detailed analysis of musical form, style, and expression in the Four Songs, Op. 2.

625. Kett, Stephen W. "A Conservative Revolution: The Music of the Four Songs Op. 2." In *The Berg Companion* (no. 803): 67–87. In English.

An analytic and documentary study of each of the Four Songs and their totality as a cycle. Emphasis on three chords (labelled A, B, and C), which provide continuity throughout the cycle. Chord B ("an incomplete minor seventh, with both a major and minor third") is said to unify the cycle.

626. Metz, Paul W. "Set Theory, Clock Diagrams, and Berg's Op. 2, no. 2." *In Theory Only* 12/1–2 (1991): 1–17. In English.

Analysis of Berg's "Schlafend trägt man mich," Op. 2, no. 2, as to tonal plan, motif, and especially harmony. The author uses a clocklike schema to illustrate pitch-class sets and their transformations.

627. Simms, Bryan R. "Alban Berg's Four Songs, Op. 2: A Tribute to Schoenberg." In *Musical Humanism and its Legacy: Essays in Honor of Claude V. Palisca*, 487–502. Edited by Nancy K. Baker and Barbara R. Hanning. Stuyvesant, N.Y.: Pendragon Press, 1992. In English.

Analysis of the songs of Op. 2 in order to find cryptographic allusions to Schoenberg's name and oeuvre.

628. Stuckenschmidt, H[ans] H[einz]. "Daneben der Andere lebt." *Frankfurter allgemeine Zeitung*, 30 April 1965. Reprinted in MEL 33 (1966): 41–44, and in Stuckenschmidt, *Die Musik eines halben Jahrhunderts, 1925–1975*, 230–34 (Munich and Zurich: R. Piper, 1976). In German.

Surveys the stylistic similarities in music by Berg and Debussy, especially a shared harmonic progression in Berg's Op. 2, no. 3, and Debussy's *Six épigraphes antiques*, no. 4. This similarity is dealt with in more detail in Stuckenschmidt (no. 629).

629. ——. "Debussy or Berg? The Mystery of a Chord Progression." MQ 51 (1965): 453–59. In English.

A succession of five chords in the piano part of Berg's song "Nun ich der Riesen," Op. 2, no. 3, recurs almost exactly in Debussy's "Pour la danseuse aux crotales" from the *Six épigraphes antiques*, perhaps an unconscious borrowing by the French composer.

630. **Wennerstrom, Mary H.** "Pitch Relationships in Berg's Songs, Op. 2." *Indiana Theory Review* 1 (1972): 12–22. In English.

A detailed analysis of pitch structures in the songs of Op. 2, using reductive procedures to reveal aspects of functional tonality but also noting the presence of a freer, nontonal use of pitches whose coherence comes from the handling of interval sets.

Orchestral Songs, Op. 4

631. **Chadwick, Nicholas.** "Thematic Integration in Berg's Altenberg Songs." MR 29 (1968): 300–304. In English.

Brief survey of systematic usages of themes and motifs in Berg's Orchestral Songs, Op. 4.

632. **Danuser, Hermann.** "Zu den Altenberg-Liedern von Alban Berg." *Musik und Bildung* 17 (1985): 837–45. In German.

Analysis of the Orchestral Songs, Op. 4, especially regarding Altenberg's texts. The music of the work both prefigures aspects of twelve-tone composition and reflects upon tonal composition.

633. **DeVoto, Mark.** "Alban Berg's Picture-Postcard Songs." Dissertation, Princeton University, 1967. UMI order no. 6713487. 222 p. In English.

Historical background and analysis of the Orchestral Songs, Op. 4, with information on editions and sources.

634. ———. "Alban Berg's Picture Postcard Songs." *Essays in Modern Music* 1 (1984): 11–19. In English.

Information on the history and structure of the Orchestral Songs, Op. 4, their first performances, and Berg's own thoughts about them.

635. ———. "Some Notes on the Unknown Altenberg Lieder." PNM 5 (1966): 37–74. In English.

Historical background and analysis (primarily of thematic content and practice) in the Orchestral Songs, Op. 4.

636. Fanselau, Rainer. "Zur Beziehung von Text und Musik in Alban Bergs Altenberg-Liedern: Eine didaktische Erfahrung." *Musik und Bildung* 17 (1985): 845–52. In German.

Survey of relationships between Altenberg's poetry and Berg's Orchestral Songs, Op. 4, emphasizing song no. 3. The analysis is highly systematic, progressing through six stages, observing goals in each and noting teaching methods concerning the work.

637. Leibowitz, René. "Alban Berg's Five Orchestral Songs After Postcard Texts by Peter Altenberg, Op. 4." MQ 34 (1948): 487–511. Reprinted in MQ, 75/4 (1991): 125–31. In English.

History of the songs, the stormy 1913 performance, and an analysis concentrating primarily on song no. 5. The piano-vocal score of this song is reproduced.

638. Mattenklott, Gert. "'Keine Ansiedlungen': Peter Altenbergs Texte der fünf Orchesterlieder Alban Bergs Op. 4." *Hofmannsthal-Blätter* 27 (1983): 74–91. In German.

Discussion of Altenberg's poems for Berg's Op. 4, including reproductions of the picture postcards with which the poems were first associated. The formal and expressive intentions in these texts are seen as paralleling Berg's musical treatment.

639. Mayer-Rosa, Eugen. "Alban Bergs Altenberg-Lieder im Unterricht." *Musik und Bildung* 4 (1972): 123–28. In German.

General analysis of the Orchestral Songs, Op. 4, aimed at developing teaching strategies.

640. Orbán, Ottó. "Alban Berg: Opus 4, The Altenberg Songs." Translated by George Szírtes. *Times Literary Supplement*, 4599 (24 May 1991): 11. In English.

A poem concerning Berg.

641. Redlich, Hans F. "Alban Berg's 'Altenberg' Songs Op. 4: Editorial Problems and No End." MR 31 (1970): 43–53. In English.

Concludes that "Seele" (no. 1) and "Sahst du" (no. 2) from the Orchestral Songs were performed at the tumultuous Viennese concert in 1913, not songs 2 and 4 or 2 and 3, as previously thought. Redlich compares the piano-vocal edition of 1953 and the miniature score of 1966 against Berg's autograph materials, finding many discrepancies.

642. Ringger, Rolf Urs. "Zur formbildenden Kraft des vertonten Wortes: Analytische Untersuchungen an Liedern von Hugo Wolf und Alban Berg." SMZ 99 (1959): 225–29. In German.

Analyses and comparison of Wolf's "Das verlassene Mägdlein" and Berg's "Sahst du," Op. 4, no. 2.

643. Schroeder, David P. "Alban Berg and Peter Altenberg: Intimate Art and the Aesthetics of Life." JAMS 46 (1993): 261–94. In English.

Examines Berg's close affinity for the works and literary methods of Altenberg, with an analysis of the Orchestral Songs, Op. 4, showing how the composer's perception of the texts influenced musical form.

644. Stenzl, Jürg. "Franz Schreker und Alban Berg: Bemerkungen zu den Altenberg–Liedern, Op. 4." In *Franz Schreker: Am Beginn der neuen Musik*, 44–58. Edited by Otto Kolleritsch. Studien für Wertungsforschung, volume 11. Graz: Universal Edition for the Institut für Wertungsforschung, 1978. In German.

In addition to Berg's use of Schoenbergian thematic work in the Orchestral Songs, Op. 4, the composer also invoked an orchestrational style closer to that of Franz Schreker, one involving "static chordal textures."

645. Stephan, Rudolf. "Die Altenberglieder von Alban Berg." In *Almanach der Kleinen Vandenhoeck-Reihe 1957/58*, 38–42. Göttingen: Vandenhoeck and Ruprecht, 1957. In German.

646. Stroh, Wolfgang Martin. "Alban Bergs Orchesterlieder." NZM 130 (1969): 89–94. In German.

Analysis of the Orchestral Songs, Op. 4, with the intention of finding elements that prefigure Berg's later adaptation of the twelve-tone method.

647. Wellesz, Egon. "An Alban Berg Manuscript at Oxford." *Tempo* 15 (1946): 3–4. In English.

In July 1945 Wellesz received from Berg's widow an autograph manuscript of the full score of the Orchestral Songs, Op. 4, songs 4 and 5, which was deposited at Oxford University. The manuscript also contains a phrase in Schoenberg's hand.

Other Songs

648. Ayrey, Craig. "Tonality and the Series: Berg." In *Models of Musical Analysis: Early Twentieth-Century Music*, 81–113. Edited by Jonathan Dunsby. Oxford: Basil Blackwell, 1993. In English.

Discussion of the possibility of combining elements of tonal and serial music, focusing analytically upon Berg's "Schließe mir die Augen beide" (1925). Here a tonal background is found, transfigured in the foreground, and row forms are seen as imitating tonal scale steps. Berg does not systematically reinforce these connections.

649. Broekema, Andrew J. "A Stylistic Analysis and Comparison of the Solo Vocal Works of Arnold Schoenberg,

Alban Berg, and Anton Webern." Dissertation, University of Texas, 1962. UMI order no. 6204822. 351 p. In English.

A general appraisal and comparison, finding the word central to the musical language in the songs of the three composers.

650. **Chadwick, Nicholas.** "Berg's Unpublished Songs in the Österreichische Nationalbibliothek." ML 52 (1971): 123–40. In English. Italian translation ("I Lieder inediti di Berg nella Österreichische Nationalbibliothek") in Monte and Segreto (no. 851): 387–410.

A discussion of style in seventy-three early songs. These fall into four stylistic-chronological periods and, in general, rely upon relatively conservative models (such as found in the songs of Brahms). The song "Das stille Königreich" is cited as the outstanding one of the group. The content of the article is drawn from the author's unpublished dissertation, "A Survey of the Early Songs of Alban Berg," Oxford University, 1972.

651. **DeVoto, Mark.** "Berg the Composer of Songs." In *The Berg Companion* (no. 803): 35–66. In English.

An analytic and general assessment of Berg's songs, primarily the Seven Early Songs; Four Songs, Op. 2; and Orchestral Songs, Op. 4.

652. **Dopheide, Bernhard.** "Zu Alban Bergs Zweitvertonung von Theodor Storms Gedicht 'Schließe mir die Augen beide'." *Musiktheorie* 7 (1992): 33–46. In German.

Analysis of the 1925 setting of Storm's "Schließe mir" based on sketches from the Austrian National Library, emphasizing row usage, connections with Berg's first setting of the same poem, and autobiographical hints.

653. ———. "Zum frühen Liedschaffen Alban Bergs." MF 43 (1990): 222–44. In German.

Historical background and stylistic analysis of Berg's early songs as represented in the *Jugendlieder* (no. 1) and Seven Early Songs. "Schließe mir die Augen beide" and "Traumgekrönt" receive special attention.

654.   Koivisto, Tiina.   "Joukkoteorian kehityksen ja sävellysstrategioidien välisestä suhteesta." *Musiikki* 20/3–4 (1990): 77–107. In Finnish.

Analytic remarks on "Schließe mir die Augen beide" (1925).

655.   Morazzoni, Anna Maria. "I Lieder di Berg: Orizzonte culturale e mondo poetico." In Monte and Segreto (no. 851): 411–38. In Italian.

Study of the poets and literary style favored by Berg in his songs.

656.   Pittman, Elmer Everett. "Harmony in the Songs of Alban Berg." Dissertation, Florida State University, 1966. UMI order no. 6700306. 74 p. In English.

A general discussion of the harmonic language of the songs, beginning with the 1925 version of "Schließe mir die Augen beide" and subsequently concentrating on the early tonal songs.

657. Redlich, Hans F. [Appendix]. In Berg, *Zwei Lieder (Theodor Storm)*. Vienna: Universal Edition, 1955. Reprinted in 1960. In German and English.

This edition is described as an extensive revision (by the composer) of the first edition in *Die Musik* (see no. 3). Evidence for the date of 1925 for the second setting of "Schließe mir die Augen beide" is brought forward from Berg's correspondence with Webern (although Redlich offers no evidence for a date of 1900 for the earlier setting, which is, in fact, erroneous). The tone row and its application in the second setting are described. Also see the critique of Redlich's remarks by Reich, no. 658.

658.   Reich,   Willi.   "Eine   sonderbare   Alban-Berg-Veröffentlichung." SMZ 95 (1955): 507–508. In German.

Criticizes Redlich's notes to the 1955 edition of the two settings of *Zwei Lieder: Schließe mir die Augen beide* (no. 657), reasserting that the earlier of the two songs dates from 1907, not 1900.

659. Schollum, Robert. "Arnold Schönberg, Alban Berg." In Schollum, *Das Österreichische Lied des 20. Jahrhunderts*, 55–68. Publikationen   des   Instituts   für   Österreichische Musikdokumentation, volume 3. Tutzing: Hans Schneider, 1977. In German.

A survey of song compositions by Schoenberg and Berg. Berg is dispatched in two pages.

660. Smith, Joan Allen. "Some Sources for Berg's 'Schliesse mir die Augen beide' II." BSN 6 (1978): 9–13. In English.

Comparison of a sketch and two autograph manuscript versions of the 1925 Storm song with the 1930 edition of this song in *Die Musik* and the 1955 Universal Edition printing.

661. Venus, Dankmar. "Vergleichende Untersuchungen zur melischen Struktur der Singstimmen in den Liedern von Arnold Schönberg, Alban Berg, Anton Webern und Paul Hindemith." Dissertation, University of Göttingen, 1965. 251 p. Identifying no. U 66.6217. ML2807 V45. In German.

Statistical comparison of intervals from the voice parts of twenty songs.

662. ⸺. "Zum Problem der Schlußbildung im Liedwerk von Schönberg, Berg und Webern." *Musik und Bildung* 4 (1972): 117–23. In German.

Distinguishes three types of cadences in songs by Schoenberg, Webern, and Berg (Op. 2, no. 2, and "Schließe mir die Augen beide," 1925 version).

663. Witzenmann, Wolfgang. "'Text von Theodor Storm': Zu den Klavierliedern Alban Bergs." MF 41 (1988): 127–41. In German.

> Surveys the early songs "Die Nachtigall," "Im Zimmer," and "Schilflied," finding models for each in the late romantic song literature. Although "Warm die Lüfte" (Op. 2, no. 4) is putatively atonal, the music suggests a simultaneous opposition of the tonal areas F and B. Similarly, Berg's first twelve-tone song, the second setting of Storm's "Schließe mir die Augen beide," contains a simultaneous opposition between the tonalities of F and C#.

9

Other Writings on
Berg's Life and Works

This chapter contains citations of writings on Berg that are not primarily concerned with a single composition. The citations are arranged alphabetically by author, or title if an author's name is lacking.

General Studies

664. Ackere, Jules E. van. "Alban Berg en zijn dramatisch werk." *Streven* 10 (March 1957). Reprinted in *Katoliek cultureel tijdschrift streven* 10 (1958): 515–20. In Dutch.

665. ————. "Alban Berg." *Vlaanderen: Tidjschrift voor kunst en kultuur* 164 (1978): 160–74. In Dutch.

A broad discussion of Berg's life and works for the general reader.

666. Adensamer, Eva. "Bergs geistige Umgebung: Briefe aus seinem Nachlaß." *ABS* 2 (1981): 181–88. In German.

Excerpts from letters addressed to Berg found in the Berg Collection at the Austrian National Library. The letters touch on several topics, foremost among them Berg's relations with Adorno.

667. Adorno, Theodor W. *Alban Berg: Der Meister des kleinsten Übergangs.* Österreichische Komponisten des XX. Jahrhunderts, volume 15. Vienna: Verlag Elisabeth Lafite, Österreichischer Bundesverlag, 1968. 144 p. ML410.B47 A63. Reprinted in AGS 13 (1971), and Frankfurt: Suhrkamp, 1977. In German. Reviewed by Mosco Carner, MT 110 (1969): 268–70; Carl Dahlhaus, NZM 130 (1969): 252; Martin Geck, *Musik und Kirche* 39 (1969): 231; Rudolf Heinemann, *Musica* 23 (1969): 607–608; Hans Hollander, *Das Orchester* 17 (1969): 175–76; Rudolf Stephan, MF 24 (1971): 110–11.

English translation: *Alban Berg: Master of the Smallest Link.* Translated by Juliane Brand and Christopher Hailey. Cambridge: Cambridge University Press, 1991. xviii, 156 p. ISBN 0521330165 (hardback), 0521338840 (paperback). ML410.B47 A6313 1991. Reviewed by Nick Chadwick, MT 132 (1991): 516–17; Michael Graubart, *Tempo* 182 (1992): 34–37; David Headlam, MTS 15 (1993): 273–85; Stephen Miles, *Notes* 49 (1992–93): 1419–23; Alan Street, ML 75 (1994): 113–15.

French translation: *Alban Berg: Le maître de la transition infime.* Translated by Rainer Rochlitz. Bibliothèque des Idées. Paris: Gallimard, 1989. ISBN 2070715272. 215 p.

Italian translation: *Alban Berg: Il maestro del minimo passaggio.* Translated by Paolo Petazzi. Milan: Feltrinelli, 1983.

Spanish translation: *Alban Berg: El maestro de la transición ínfima.* Translated by Helena Cortés and Arturo Leyte. Madrid: Alianza, 1990. 142 p. Reviewed by Blas Matamoro, *Cuadernos hispanoamericanos*, 498 (1991): 151.

Adorno's book on Berg is largely a compilation of earlier publications. The analyses of Opp. 1–3, 5–6, the Lyric Suite, and Seven Early Songs were written in 1937 for Reich's study, no. 919. Other passages were reused from articles and lectures from the 1930s through 1960s, and a few remaining sections were newly written in 1968. The analyses (dealing with all of Berg's major works except for the Violin Concerto) mix technical observations on motivic matters with impressions and interpretations distinctive of Adorno. These have added authority since they reflect Adorno's studies and conversations with Berg during the last decade of the composer's life. Many passages from this book have been reprinted separately.

668. ————. "Alban Berg." *Kontinente* 8/7 (1955): 1–5. Reprinted in Österreichische Gesellschaft für Musik, *Beiträge*, 11–18 (Kassel: Bärenreiter, 1967). In German. Dutch translation in Schönberger (no. 969): 58–67.

Berg's method of developing themes and motifs tended toward a relentless dissolution, a method that stands as a "metaphor of vanishing." Berg's relation to Wagner is outlined, and aspects of *Wozzeck* and *Lulu* are discussed. The material for this essay returns in the first chapter of Adorno's book on Berg, no. 667.

669. ————. "Alban Berg." *Merkur* 10 (1956): 643–51. Reprinted in Adorno, *Klangfiguren*, 121–37 (Berlin and Frankfurt: Suhrkamp, 1959); AGS 16 (1978): 85–96; Adorno, *Nervenpunkte der neuen Musik (Ausgewählt aus "Klangfiguren")*, 45–53 (Reinbek bei Hamburg: Rowohlts Deutsche Enzyklopädie, 1969). In German. Dutch translation in Schönberger (no. 969): 58–69.

Originally a lecture marking the twentieth anniversary of Berg's death, this article assesses Berg for the general reader, returning to ideas encountered in several of the author's other essays. Berg's traditionalism and innovative spirit are said to be in balance, and his relations to the art and music of the late romantic period and twentieth century are described.

670. ————. "Alban Berg und die Gegenwart." *Forum: Österreichische Monatsblätter für kulturelle Freiheit* 8 (1961): 153–55, 187–90. Reprinted ("Bergs kompositionstechnische Funde") in Adorno, *Quasi una fantasia*, 245–73 (Frankfurt: Suhrkamp, 1963); in AGS 16 (1978): 413–32. In German. English translation ("Berg's Discoveries in Compositional Technique") in *Quasi una Fantasia: Essays on Modern Music*, 179–200, translated by Rodney Livingstone (London, New York: Verso, 1994).

Asserts Berg's relevance for composers of the 1960s who were inclined to bypass him in favor of Webern. Berg's music is all rigorously constructed and organically interconnected, eschewing everything arbitrary. The early works tend to be chaotic, the later ones cautious. The author's main analytic remarks concern the finale of the String Quartet, Op. 3, and the March from the Orchestral Pieces, Op. 6.

671. ———. "Analyse und Berg." ÖMZ 23 (1968): 601–606. In German.

Extract from Adorno's book on Berg (no. 667). Adorno's approach to analysis was based on following the transformations of themes and motifs. He viewed Berg's music itself as an embodiment of an analytic process that tended toward dissolution into minimal motivic particles.

672. ———. "Berg and Webern: Schönberg's Heirs." *Modern Music* 8/2 (January-February 1931): 29–38. Reprinted in AGS 18 (1984): 446–55. In English. German translation ("Berg und Webern") in ÖMZ 39 (1984): 290–95; reprinted in AGS 20 (1986): 782–92.

Berg and Webern are depicted as polar opposites within Schoenberg's stylistic domain. Berg's works are surveyed, emphasizing their relation to nineteenth-century styles and their organic elements. (Adorno's original German text is lost.)

673. ——— [Hektor Rottweiler]. "Erinnerung an den Lebenden." *23: Eine Wiener Musikzeitschrift* 24–25 (1936): 19–29. In German.

Reflections upon the composer shortly after his death, his relation to the nineteenth century, and an assessment of his work. This article was expanded for use in Adorno's book on Berg (no. 667).

674. ———. "Für Alban Berg." *Die neue Rundschau* 62/1 (1951): 134–36. Reprinted in AGS 18 (1984): 483–86. In German.

Written shortly after the fifteenth anniversary of Berg's death, Adorno recalls with great intensity Berg the man and a body of music which should be a model for continued study and development.

675. ———. "Im Gedächtnis an Alban Berg." AGS 18 (1984): 487–512. In German.

This reminiscence, written in 1955, is a revision of Adorno's "Erinnerung an den Lebenden" (no. 673) and was itself revised for inclusion in Adorno's book on Berg (no. 667). The author expressly forbade the publication of this version—which in some areas is more explicit than the two others—as long as he or others mentioned in it were still alive. Among other sensitive topics is Adorno's description of his role in the Hanna Fuchs-Robettin affair. An excerpt from this article appeared in Csampai and Holland (no. 333): 8–10.

676. ———. "Werk." In Reich 1937 (no. 919): 21–43, 47–64, 91–106. In German.

Analyses of Berg's Opp. 1–3, 5–6, Lyric Suite, Seven Early Songs, and *Der Wein*. Adorno's analyses are general and descriptive in nature, dealing technically primarily with motivic-thematic processes. The discussion of *Der Wein* is reprinted in AGS 13, and the other analyses for Reich's 1937 book were reused in Adorno's own *Alban Berg* (no. 667).

677. **"Alban Berg."** *Neues Musikblatt* 15/14 (1936): 2. In German.

Brief obituary notice. Berg is a "representative of extreme twelve-tone constructivism."

678. **"Alban Berg."** *Le monde musical* 47 (1936): 21–22. In French.

679. *Alban Berg zum Gedenken.* Special issue of *23: Eine Wiener Musikzeitschrift,* 24–25 (1936). 32 p. In German.

Contains brief tributes to the recently deceased composer by Willi Reich, Heinrich Jalowetz, Theodor Adorno, Erwin Stein, Soma Morgenstern, Hugo Winter, and Ernst Krenek (most of these are reprinted in Reich 1959 [no. 917]: 79–85). Two longer articles by "Hektor Rottweiler" (Theodor Adorno) are cited in this bibliography as nos. 307 and 673.

680. Alcaraz, José Antonio. "Su vehemencia, su lucidez. Alban Berg: 1885–1935." *Pauta* 4/15 (1985): 12–14. In Spanish.

Brief account of the composer's life and works.

681. Altenberg, Peter. "Bekanntschaft." In Altenberg, *Neues Altes*, 87–88. Berlin: Fischer, 1911. Reprinted in Reich 1959 (no. 917): 17–18. In German.

Poem in prose alluding to Berg and to Helene Nahowski, much admired by Altenberg. Also see Schroeder 1993 (no. 643).

682. Archibald, Bruce. "Berg's Development as an Instrumental Composer." In *The Berg Companion* (no. 803): 91–122. In English.

Analysis of Opp. 1, 3, 5, and 6, describing selected compositional materials in general terms.

683. Bach, David Josef. "New Music by Berg, Webern, Krenek." *Modern Music* 12 (1934–35): 31–38. In English.

"The twelve-tone scale has taken possession of modern music," declares the author, by which he refers to the "twelve-tone system." A brief description of Berg's *Lulu* follows, among other works by Webern and Krenek.

684. Baier, Christian. "Fritz Heinrich Klein: Der 'Mutterakkord' im Werk Alban Bergs." ÖMZ 44 (1989): 585–600. In German.

Information about Berg's student Fritz Heinrich Klein, Klein's *Die Maschine*, Op. 1 (composed in 1921 using a form of twelve-tone composition), his theorizing on the resources of the chromatic scale, and the use of his "mother chord" by Berg in "Schließe mir die Augen beide" (1925) and the Lyric

Suite. Letters from Berg to Klein are excerpted, and a letter of 18 August 1931 is shown in facsimile.

685. Banda, Daniel. *L'atteinte vaine: "Wozzeck" & "Lulu."* Arles: Actes Sud, 1992. 115 p. ISBN 2868698182. ML 410.B47 B3 1992. In French.

An interpretive study of Berg's two operas for the nonspecialist reader. There is little in the way of technical musical analysis and no musical examples.

686. Barilier, Étienne. *Alban Berg: Essai d'interprétation.* Lausanne: l'Age d'Homme, 1978. 255 p. ML410.B47 B4. In French. Reviewed by Philippe Albéra, SMZ 119 (1979): 292–93.
Second edition. Lausanne: l'Age d'Homme, 1992. 335 p. ML 410.B47 B4 1992.

Barilier (known primarily as a novelist and literary critic) writes for the nonspecialist, covering Berg's life, cultural milieu, and major works in general terms. His objective is "to reflect as little poorly as possible the light that shines from an exemplary body of work and to attempt to clarify with it the conditions and the sense of contemporary artistic creativity." The second edition dispenses with musical examples and technical descriptions.

687. Bauer-Mengelberg, Stefan, and Melvin Ferentz. "On Eleven-Interval Twelve-Tone Rows." PNM 3 (1965): 93–103. In English.

Discusses the mathematics of deriving all possible all-interval rows, of which there are 1,928.

688. Beaujean, Alfred. "Selbstdarstellung von Komponisten: Der Komponist als Selbstporträtist." *Hifi-Stereophonie* 20 (1981): 690–92. In German.

A brief though synoptic article concerning music that has been a medium for statements by composers about themselves. Berlioz, Tchaikovsky, Strauss, Pfitzner, Berg, Hindemith, Shostakovich, Boulez, Henze, and Stockhausen are touched on. Berg's self-portrait in the character of Alwa from *Lulu* is described.

689. Bek, Josef. "'Alban Berg nennt sich mein neuer Freund'." ÖMZ 48 (1993): 469–76. In German.

Concerns Erwin Schulhoff and his contact with Schoenberg and Berg. A letter from Berg to Schulhoff dated 24 February 1921 is cited concerning Berg's ideas on jazz and musical prose.

690. Bellingardi, Luigi. [In memoriam Helene Berg]. *Nuova rivista musicale italiana* 10 (1976): 537–38. In Italian.

Notice concerning the passing of Helene Berg.

691. Berg, Erich Alban, editor. *Alban Berg: Leben und Werk in Daten und Bildern.* Frankfurt: Insel, 1976. 257 p. ISBN 3458018948. ML88.B473 A4. In German. Reviewed by Hans Hollander, *Das Orchester* 24 (1976): 750; Walter Szmolyan, ÖMZ 33 (1978): 99; Konrad Vogelsang, MF 32 (1979): 240.
    Second edition, revised. Insel Taschenbuch. Frankfurt: Insel, 1985. 264 p. In German.

Short biography with pictures from all periods of Berg's life.

692. ———. "Bergiana." SMZ 120 (1980): 147–55. In German, summary in French.

Identifies Albine Scheuchl Manninger (1902–54) as Berg's natural daughter and discusses Helene Berg's refusal to have *Lulu* completed, which the author (Berg's nephew) attributes to artistic considerations.

693. ———. *Der unverbesserliche Romantiker: Alban Berg, 1885–1935.* Vienna: Österreichischer Bundesverlag, 1985. 200 p. ISBN 3215054590. ML410.B47 B5 1985. In German. Reviewed by Ernst Scherzer, *Opernwelt* 26/9 (1985): 63; Klaus Schweizer, NZM 147/10 (1966): 73.

Collection of vignettes seeking to capture the man Berg. Contains the text of a biography of the composer by Hermann Watznauer from 1927, selections from Berg's letters (1907–35), and Erich Berg's own recollections. The author is Berg's nephew.

694. **Berg, Helene.** "Ein Nachtrag zu Bergs Briefe an seine Frau." ÖMZ 21 (1966): 727. In German.

Helene Berg's response to an article by Redlich (no. 909) that was critical of her edition of Berg's *Briefe an seine Frau* and of her last-minute withdrawal of the original edition overseen by Franz Willnauer. See Willnauer (no. 1052).

695. **Berl, Christine, and Paul Lansky.** "An Alban Berg Bibliography, 1966–1968." BSN 1 (1968): 7–9. In English.

A general bibliography, including book reviews.

696. **Bischof, Rainer.** "Versuch über die philosophischen Grundlagen von Alban Berg." ABS 2 (1981): 209–15. In German. Italian version ("Ipotesi sui fondamenti filosofici di Alban Berg") in Monte and Segreto (no. 851): 511–22.

An assessment of philosophical ideas in existence in Berg's milieu by which he was attracted and apparently influenced. Friedrich Nietzsche and Karl Kraus are discussed in their relation to music of the turn of the century. From a survey of Berg's correspondence, the author surmises that Berg was most interested in philosophical ideas stemming from Kraus, Otto Weininger, Henrik Ibsen, and August Strindberg, although Berg admitted to being no theoretician in philosophical thought. The content of a letter from Berg to Hermann Watznauer from October 1906 is examined as to the composer's ideas on the relation of nature and art.

697. **Bond, Bruce.** "Alban Berg." *New Republic* 203/16 (1990): 46. Reprinted in *Quarterly Review of Literature* 30 (1990): 21. In English.

A poem concerning Berg.

698. Boucourechtliev, André. "Alban Berg et les problèmes de l'opéra moderne." *La table ronde* 67 (1953): 168–71. In French.

Compares *Wozzeck* and *Lulu*, finding them very different as concerns form. *Lulu* more resembles a single homogeneous musical form than does *Wozzeck*, which amounts to a succession of small forms.

699. Boulez, Pierre. "Alban Berg heute gesehen." MEL 27 (1960): 33–36. In German.

Praises Berg's refinement of technique and organization, but notes the greater relevance of Webern for contemporary composers.

700. ———. S.v. "Berg, Alban." In *Encyclopédie de la musique.* Paris: Fasquelle, 1958. Reprinted in Boulez, *Relevés d'apprenti,* 307–25 (Paris: Éditions du Seuil, 1966). In French. English translation in Boulez, *Notes of an Apprenticeship,* 313–33, translated by Herbert Weinstock (New York: Alfred A. Knopf, 1968); in Boulez, *Stocktakings from an Apprenticeship,* 243–58, translated by Stephen Walsh (Oxford: Clarendon Press, 1991). German translation in Boulez, *Anhaltspunkte: Essays,* 335–56, translated by Josef Häusler (Kassel: Bärenreiter; Munich: Deutscher Taschenbuch Verlag, 1979). Spanish translation in *Pauta* 4/15 (1985): 15–32. Italian translation in Boulez, *Note di apprendistato* (Turin: Einaudi, 1968).

Survey of the composer and his works, without the critical polemics that earlier characterized Boulez's writings on Berg.

701. ———. Chapter 3 ("Défense de Berg"). In Boulez, *Par volonté et par hasard: Entretiens avec Célestin Deliège,* 25–30, Paris: Éditions du Seuil, 1975. In French. English translation ("In Defence of Berg") in Boulez, *Conversations with Célestin Deliège,* 23–26, translator not identified (London: Eulenburg Books, 1976). Italian translation in Boulez, *Per volontà et per caso* (Turin: Einaudi, 1977, reprinted 1984).

Boulez recants some of the criticism of Berg from an earlier period (see no. 702) and is now more inclined to value Berg's complexity, density, and esotericism (especially in the Chamber Concerto). But Boulez is still "aware that to discover a new vocabulary it was no use looking to Berg."

702. ———. "Incidences actuelles de Berg," *Polyphonie* 2 (1948): 104–108. Reprinted in Boulez, *Relevés d'apprenti*, 235–40 (Paris: Éditions du Seuil, 1966). In French. English translation ("Present-Day Encounters with Berg") in Boulez, *Notes of an Apprenticeship*, 235–41, translated by Herbert Weinstock (New York: Alfred A. Knopf, 1968); ("The Current Impact of Berg") in Boulez, *Stocktakings from an Apprenticeship*, 183–87, translated by Stephen Walsh (Oxford: Clarendon Press, 1991). German translation ("Misverständnisse um Berg") in Boulez, *Anhaltspunkte: Essays*, 318–24, translated by Josef Häusler (Kassel: Bärenreiter; Munich: Deutscher Taschenbuch Verlag, 1979). Italian translation ("Incidenze attuali di Berg") in Boulez, *Note di apprendistato*, 207–11 (Turin: Einaudi, 1968).

Attacks Berg for his romanticism, closeness to the spirit of Puccini, and incongruity of quotations of tonal music in an atonal context.

703. Brand, Juliane, and Christopher Hailey. "Catalogue of the Correspondence between Alban Berg and Arnold Schoenberg." JASI 11 (1988): 70–97. In English.

Catalog of the entire known correspondence passing between Schoenberg and Berg (794 items, 1906–36). Each item is described by its date, format, addresses of both correspondents, and present location. Also gives the texts (in English) of four letters not included in *The Berg-Schoenberg Correspondence* (no. 704).

704. Brand, Juliane, Christopher Hailey, and Donald Harris, editors and translators. *The Berg-Schoenberg Correspondence: Selected Letters.* New York, W. W. Norton; Basingstoke: Macmillan, 1987. xxviii, 497 pp. ISBN 0393029295. ML410.B47A4 1987. In English. Reviewed by Paul Banks, MT 130 (1989): 84–85; Robert Craft, *New York Review of Books* 34/17 (1987–88): 30–33; Christopher Hatch, *Opera Quarterly*, 6/1

(1988–89): 553–55; Mark S. Laporta, *Opera News* 53/2 (1988): 45; Judith Meibach, *Notes*, 45 (1988–89): 274–76; Claudio Spies, *College Music Symposium* 28 (1988): 134–42; Peter Stadlen, *Opera* 39 (1988): 553–55; Arnold Whittall, ML 69 (1988): 547–49.

English translation of the texts (sometimes abbreviated) of 341 pieces of correspondence between Schoenberg and Berg spanning the years 1911 to 1936, annotated by the editors.

705.   [———].   "The   Berg-Schoenberg   Correspondence: *Gurrelieder* and *Lulu*." MT 129 (1988): 8–13. In English.

Extracts from no. 704.

706. **Breuer, János.** "Budapesti interjú Alban Berggel." *Muzsika* 19/10 (1976): 1–3. In Hungarian.

Information about Berg's visit to Budapest in February 1928 to hear a performance of the Lyric Suite organized by Alexander Jemnitz. An interview with Berg that appeared in the *Pesti napló* (24 February 1928) (no. 45) is reprinted.

707.   ———.   "Jemnitz Sándor levelezése Alban Berggel." *Muzsika* 30/1 (1987): 8–11. In Hungarian.

Texts of eleven letters (in Hungarian only) from Jemnitz to Berg, 1926–35, with summaries of Berg's responses. Most of the letters concern Jemnitz's requests for Berg's assistance in advancing Jemnitz's music. Also see Lampert (no. 827).

708. **Briner, Andreas.** "Eine Zeitschrift der Neuen Wiener Schule: Zum Reprint von *23: Eine Wiener Musikzeitschrift*." SMZ 112 (1972): 205–10. In German.

Discusses the journal *23: Eine Wiener Musikzeitschrift*, which was edited by Willi Reich in Vienna from 1932 to 1937.

709. **Brook, Barry S.** "Berg Research in America." ABS 2 (1981): 46–55. In English, synopsis in German.

The author represents the International Alban Berg Society, recounting its founding and discussing its *Newsletter*. He summarizes recent Berg conferences held in the United States, Berg sources in America, and presents an annotated bibliography (prepared by Arthur Maisel) of Berg publications and dissertations, 1960–80.

710. Buchanan, Herbert H. "An Investigation of Mutual Influences Among Schoenberg, Webern and Berg (With an Emphasis on Schoenberg and Webern, ca. 1904–1908)." Dissertation, Rutgers University, 1974. UMI order no. 7427592329. 335 p. In English.

Emphasizes the influence passing among Schoenberg, Berg, and Webern during the years in which the atonal language emerged. Stresses the influence of Webern upon Schoenberg.

711. Burkholder, J. Peter. "Berg and the Possibility of Popularity." In *Alban Berg: Historical and Analytical Perspectives* (no. 746): 25–53. In English.

Berg's popularity rests on his adoption of the "familiar rhetoric of tonal music" while at the same time avoiding cliché and organizing the music according to new structural principles to insure inner coherence. These two dimensions are coordinated to the satisfaction of both the naive and sophisticated listener. Analytic examples are drawn mainly from the Violin Concerto.

712. Busch, Regina. "Wie Berg die richtige Reihe fand." MK Sonderband: *Anton Webern II*, 365–87. Edited by Heinz-Klaus Metzger and Rainer Riehn. Munich: Edition text + kritik, 1984. In German.

Reproduces and discusses Berg's analytic sketches concerning row techniques in Webern's String Trio, Op. 20, made in 1927 and sent to Webern as a Christmas gift in December of that year.

713. Cahn, Peter. "Klassizismen bei Alban Berg?" In *Colloquium Klassizität, Klassizismus, Klassik in der Musik 1920–1950*, 95–129. Edited by Wolfgang Osthoff and Reinhard Wiesend. Würzburger

Musikhistorische Beiträge, volume 10. Tutzing: Hans Schneider, 1988. In German.

> Discussion of neoclassical elements in Berg's music, emphasizing the appearance of symmetrical forms.

714. Carner, Mosco. *Alban Berg: The Man and the Work.* London: Duckworth, 1975; New York: Holmes & Meier, 1977. xv, 255 p. ISBN 0715607693. ML410.B47 C4. In English. Reviewed by Douglass M. Green, *Notes* 35 (1978–79): 71–72; Paul Griffiths, MT 117 (1976): 405; Max Harrison, *Composer* 58 (1976): 47; Robert Henderson, *Opera* 28 (1977): 481–82; Hans Hollander, MEL/NZM 2 (1976): 240; Douglas Jarman, ML 57 (1976): 320–22; Derrick Puffett, *Tempo* 117 (1976): 39–42; Klaus Schweizer, SMZ 16 (1976): 403–404; Arnold Whittall, MR 37 (1976): 238–39.

Second edition, revised. London: Duckworth; New York: Holmes & Meier, 1983. 314 p. ISBN 0841908419 (hardback), 0841912564 (paperback). ML410.B47 C4 1983. Reviewed by Andrew Clements, MT 125 (1984): 28; Mark DeVoto, *Opera Quarterly* 3/3 (1985): 170–72; George Martin, *Opera Quarterly* 1/4 (1983): 164–67.

French translation: *Alban Berg: L'homme, l'oeuvre.* Translated by Dennis Collins. Paris: J. C. Lattès, 1979. 368 p.

> A major biographical and analytic study of the composer and his works. The analyses seek to reveal "imaginative content" more than technical features. The second edition is extensively revised, especially as regards the completion of Act 3 of *Lulu* and details of Berg's relations with Hanna Fuchs-Robettin.

715. ———. "Alban Berg and Anton Webern." In *The New Oxford History of Music*. Volume 10: *The Modern Age, 1890–1960*, 362–86. Edited by Martin Cooper. London, New York, Toronto: Oxford University Press, 1974. In English.

> A general appraisal focusing on *Wozzeck*, *Lulu*, the Chamber Concerto, and the Violin Concerto.

716. ———. "Alban Berg in His Letters to His Wife." ML 50 (1969): 365–75. In English.

Survey of the published collection of letters (no. 67), a "human document." Helene was a "woman of superior intelligence, noble, self-sacrificing."

717. ———. "Pfitzner versus Berg." MT 118 (1977): 379–80. Reprinted in *Musical Newsletter* 7/2 (1977): 3–5; Carner, *Major and Minor*, 253–57 (London: Duckworth; New York: Holmes & Meier Publishers, 1980). In English.

Brief review of Berg's response to Pfitzner (see no. 34), concluding that Pfitzner had the stronger argument in his assertion that rational analysis cannot reveal the roots of beauty in music.

718. Cervello, Marcelo. "Alban Berg: El expresionismo en clave lírica." *Monsalvat* no. 48 (1978): 136–38. In Spanish.

719. Chadwick, Nicholas. "Alban Berg and the BBC." *British Library Journal* 11 (1985): 46–59. In English.

Traces Berg's contact with musicians of the BBC, primarily Edward Clark and Adrian Boult, from 1930 to 1935. Berg first came to England to participate in a jury for the International Society of Contemporary Music, and he was hopeful that a performance of *Wozzeck* at Covent Garden would materialize in 1935. His correspondence with Clark and Boult is reproduced.

720. Clements, Andrew. "Berg: The Hidden Agenda." *Opera* 41 (1990): 1043–46. In English.

Review of recent literature and discussion of tendencies since 1970 to reevaluate Berg.

721. Conrath, Ernest. "Einführung in die Musik von Alban Berg." *Musikerziehung* 16 (1962–63): 182–87. In German.

Brief sketch of Berg's life and his major compositions (with bibliography).

722. Cooper, Martin. "Alban Berg (1888 [sic]-1935)." In *The Music Masters: The Twentieth Century*, volume 4, 35–41. Edited by A. L. Bacharach. London: Cassell & Company, 1954. In English.

General sketch, written for the nonspecialist, of Berg's life and music.

723. ———. "Schubert and Berg." *The London Mercury* 32/187 (1938): 59. In English.

Reviews recent concerts, including a performance of the Symphonic Pieces from *Lulu*. The work "appeals to a perfectly unexploited region of the human emotions."

724. Corte, Andrea della. "La morte di Alban Berg." *Musica d'oggi* 18/1 (1936): 7–9. In Italian.

Notice concerning Berg's recent death and late works.

725. Curl, James Stevens. "Decadence in Four Twentieth-Century Operas." MR 31 (1970): 158–62. In English.

Survey of the esthetic of decadence and Naturalism as documented by the texts of *Lulu, Wozzeck, Salome,* and *Elektra*.

726. Dace, Wallace. Chapter 4 ("Spoken Drama into Music Drama: Alban Berg"). In Dace, *Opera as Dramatic Poetry*, 139–73. New York: Vantage Press, 1993. In English.

Discussion of literary questions concerning the libretti of *Wozzeck* and *Lulu*.

727. Dahlhaus, Carl. "Oper und neue Musik." In Dahlhaus, *Vom Musikdrama zur Literaturoper: Aufsätze zur neueren Operngeschichte*, 145–52. Munich and Salzburg: Musikverlag Emil Katzbichler, 1983. In German.

The author proposes a model for constructing a history of twentieth-century opera by addressing questions of genre, techniques of avant-garde composition, libretti, and

Regietheater. *Wozzeck* and *Lulu* are analyzed from these viewpoints.

728. Delaere, Mark. Chapter 5 ("Analytische Beispiele"). In Delaere, *Funktionelle Atonalität: Analytische Stratagien für die frei-atonale Musik der Wiener Schule*, 53–158. Veröffentlichungen zur Musikforschung, volume 14. Wilhelmshaven: Florian Noetzel Verlag, 1993. In German.

The author's approach to analyzing atonal music is eclectic, seeking the existence of ostinati, complementarity of pitch formations, contrapuntal or variational forms, and recurrent pitch-class constellations (using elements of set theory). Berg's "Hier ist Friede," Op. 4, no. 5, and the Clarinet Piece, Op. 5, no. 2, are analyzed.

729. DeVoto, Mark. "Alban Berg and Creeping Chromaticism." In *Alban Berg: Historical and Analytical Perspectives* (no. 746): 57–78. In English.

"Creeping" is defined as stepwise movement in one or more parts with the possibility that additional parts remain stationary. It is said to subvert harmonic progression. Examples of the phenomenon are brought forward from all periods of Berg's music and in music by other composers.

730. ———. "Berg and Pacifism." BSN 2 (1971): 8–11. In English.

Translation of a letter (27 November 1919) from Berg to Erwin Schulhoff (see Vojtěch, no. 1031, for the original German text). The letter, rambling and intemperate, speaks of Berg's bitterness regarding events leading to World War I and of his own antimilitaristic sentiments.

731. Donat, Misha. "Mathematical Mysticism." *Listener* 83 (2 April 1970): 458–59. In English.

Finds "a strong element of mathematical mysticism" in Berg's music, looking primarily at the Chamber Concerto and *Wozzeck*.

732. Dümling, Albrecht. "Alban Berg und Robert Schumann: Die versteckte Verwandschaft." *Musik und Bildung* 17 (1985): 861–66. In German.

Berg's admiration for Schumann had to be muted in Schoenberg's circle, where Schumann was not held in the highest esteem. Berg's positive attitude toward Schumann's music is expressed in the essay on Pfitzner (no. 34).

733. Eigeldinger, Jean-Jacques. "Une lettre inédite d'Alban Berg à Ernest Ansermet." *RM Suisse romande* 33 (1980): 2–7. In French, letter in German.

Letter from Berg to Ansermet (27 February 1923) analyzing the derivation of musical materials from tone rows in the Lyric Suite.

734. Eitan, Zohar. "Style and Gesture: A Study of Melodic Peaks." Dissertation, University of Pennsylvania, 1991. UMI order no. 9125635. 502 p. In English.

Empirical analysis of melodic contour as an expressive and structural factor in music by Haydn, Chopin, and Berg's Lyric Suite and *Lulu*.

735. Esslin, Martin. "Berg's Vienna." In *The Berg Companion* (no. 803): 1–12. In English.

A brief survey of the social and artistic milieu in Vienna in which Berg lived.

736. Falkner, Johannes B. "Alban Berg: Tjugofem år efter hans död." *Musikrevy* 16 (1961): 258–60. In Swedish.

Brief report on *Wozzeck* and *Lulu*.

737. Federhofer, Hellmut. "Meine Erinnerungen an Alban Berg." *Festschrift Othmar Wessely zum 60. Geburtstag*, 113–19. Edited by Manfred Angerer, et al. Tutzing: Hans Schneider, 1982. In German.

Recollections of the author's studies in composition with Berg, beginning in 1932.

738. Fellinger, Imogen. "Aufführungen von Werken Alban Bergs im Urteil zeitgenössischer Musikkritik." ABS 2 (1981): 251–64. In German.

A survey of the critical reception of Berg's music in leading German-language newspapers and periodicals. The discussion is introduced by a survey of leading musical periodicals in existence during Berg's lifetime. Excerpts from journalistic writing emphasize the better-known critics (e.g., H. H. Stuckenschmidt, Paul Stefan, Julius Weismann, Klaus Pringsheim, Richard Specht).

739. Fiechtner, Helmut A. "Atonalität und Zwöltonmusik: Ihre Begründung durch Arnold Schönberg und ihre Verzauberung durch Alban Berg." *Wissenschaft und Weltbild: Zeitschrift für Grundfragen der Forschung und Weltanschauung* 7 (1954): 375–82. Reprinted with revisions ("Schönberg und Berg: Die Grundlagen der Zwölftonmusik") in *Hochland* 5 (1962–63): 534–41. In German.

Deals mainly with Schoenberg's aim in the formulation and practice of the twelve-tone idea, holding that the adoption of the method represented more of a leap into the future than a gradual evolution. A brief discussion of Berg touches on all compositions, whose differences from Schoenberg are stressed.

740. ———. "In memoriam: Helene Berg." ÖMZ 31 (1976): 623. In German.

Brief notice concerning Helene Berg's death.

741. Floros, Constantin. *Alban Berg: Musik als Autobiographie.* Wiesbaden, Leipzig, and Paris: Breitkopf & Härtel, 1992. 376 p. ISBN 3765102903. ML 410.B47 F5 1992. In German. Reviewed by Hartmut Krones, ÖMZ 49 (1994): 75–76; Claus-Steffen Mahnkopf, NZM 155 (1994): 76–77; Anthony Pople, MT 135 (1994): 243.

A broad study of Berg's life, music, and aesthetics as they
pertain to the composer's incorporation of autobiographical
reference in his music. The analytic portions focus on the
String Quartet, Op. 3; March, Op. 6, no. 3; *Wozzeck*; Chamber
Concerto; "Schließe mir die Augen beide" (1907 and 1925);
Lyric Suite; *Lulu*; and Violin Concerto.

742. ————. "Alban Berg und Hanna Fuchs: Die Geschichte
einer unglücklichen Liebe und ihre Auswirkungen auf Bergs
Schaffen." ÖMZ 49 (1994): 768–93. In German.

Reviews the content of Berg's correspondence with Hanna
Fuchs-Robettin, finding his relation with her central to his
personal and artistic life during his last ten years. The letter
to Hanna of 23 October 1926 is cited as containing the earliest
version of the program of the Lyric Suite, and Berg's
references to Hanna in *Der Wein* are also noted. The letters
are now in the Austrian National Library.

743. **Flothuis, Marius.** "Alban Berg." *Kroniek van kunst en
kultuur* 20 (1960): 75–79. In Dutch.

General appraisal of Berg's music on the occasion of a
performance of the Violin Concerto at the Holland Festival.

744. **Fuchs, Anton.** "Alban Berg: Auf seinen Spuren in
Kärnten." *Die Brücke*, 1975. Reprinted in Fuchs, *Auf ihren Spuren
in Kärnten: Alban Berg, Gustav Mahler, Johannes Brahms, Hugo
Wolf, Anton Webern*, 5–19. Klagenfurt: Kärntner Druck- und
Verlagsgesellschaft, 1982. In German.

General biography emphasizing Berg's activities in Carinthia.
Many illustrations and facsimiles.

745. **Fuss, Hans-Ulrich.** *Musikalisch-dramatische Prozesse in den
Opern Alban Bergs.* Dissertation, University of Hamburg, 1990.
Hamburger Beiträge zur Musikwissenschaft, volume 40.
Hamburg and Eisenach: Verlag der Musikalienhandlung Karl
Dieter Wagner, 1991. 308 p. ISBN 3889790569. ML410.B47 F87
1991. In German.

Discussion of processes in music—accumulation, homogenization, sonorous and dynamic development, tempo formation, developing variation, shaping of vocal lines—using *Wozzeck* and *Lulu* as examples. Since both music and drama are temporal in nature, they must result from such processes.

746. Gable, David, and Robert P. Morgan, editors. *Alban Berg: Historical and Analytical Perspectives.* Oxford: Clarendon Press; New York: Oxford University Press, 1991. viii, 296 pp. ISBN 0193113384. ML410.B47 A777 1990. In English. Reviewed by Nick Chadwick, MT 132 (1991): 516–17; Michael Graubart, *Tempo* 180 (1992): 36–41; David Headlam, MTS 15 (1993): 273–85; Peter A. Hoyt, *Notes* 49 (1992–93): 578–81; Anthony Pople, ML 74 (1993): 463–66; Rudolf Stephan NZM 153/6 (1992): 50.

Contains ten articles on different subjects, most of which are based on papers read at a conference on Berg at the University of Chicago in 1985. Four of the ten articles concern *Lulu*.

747. García-Alcalde, Guillermo. "Música, expresión y sentimiento de la forma en el centenario de Alban Berg." *Los cuadernos del norte* 6/31 (1985): 18–25. In Spanish.

A general aesthetic statement about Berg's merging of form and expressivity within a modernist musical idiom.

748. Gatti, Guido M. "In memoria di Alban Berg." *Scenario: Rivista mensile delle arti della scena,* 14 (1936): 65–67. In Italian.

Tribute to Berg shortly after his death. Emphasizes *Wozzeck*.

749. ———. "Note e commenti: Alban Berg." *Rassegna musicale* 9 (1936): 27–28. In Italian.

Brief appreciation of Berg shortly after his death.

750. ———. [Untitled passage]. In Gatti, *L'opera di Gian Francesco Malipiero,* 382–84. [Bologna]: Edizioni di Treviso, 1952. In Italian.

Texts of letters from Berg to Malipiero dated 17 July 1934 and 19 September 1934 concerning the cancellation of music by Berg from the Venice Festival. See also Carner (no. 518) and Morazzoni (no. 853).

751. Gibson, Roland, and Raymond Harvey. "Delius in his Historical Setting: Delius and Berg." *Delius Society Journal* 62 (1979): 12–15. In English.

752. Girardi, Michele. "Composizioni vocali e strumentali di Alban Berg." In Monte and Segreto (no. 851): 261–385. In Italian.

Musical analysis of Berg's principal compositions other than *Wozzeck* and *Lulu*.

753. Glaser, Werner Wolf. "Möten med Alban Berg." *Musikrevy* 40 (1985): 156–60. In Swedish.

Recollections of a meeting with Berg.

754. Glück, Franz. "Briefe von Anton von Webern und Alban Berg an Adolf Loos." ÖMZ 30 (1975): 110–13. In German.

Letter from Berg to Adolf Loos of 12 December 1920 and note addressed to Berg ca. 1924.

755. Godwin, Paul Milton. "A Study of Concepts of Melody, with Particular Reference to Some Music of the Twentieth Century and Examples from the Compositions of Schoenberg, Webern, and Berg." Dissertation, Ohio State University, 1972. In English. UMI order no. 7302003. 238 p.

The author's objective is "to provide the basis for further investigation of melody in both traditional and contemporary music."

756. Goléa, Antoine. Chapter 3 ("Le dodécaphonisme"). In Goléa, *Esthétique de la musique contemporaine*, 48–71. Paris: Presses Universitaires, 1954. In French. German translation ("Die Zwölftonmusik: Ein erster Versuch der Synthese. Die Musik

Alban Bergs"), in Goléa, *Musik unserer Zeit*, 63–68 (Munich: Beck, 1955).

The twelve-tone usages of Schoenberg, Webern, and Berg (pp. 66–71) are outlined. Berg is described as the least doctrinaire and most eclectic of the three.

757. Graf, Max. "Alban Berg zu seinem 50. Geburtstag," "Alban Berg: Nachruf," "Gespräch im Musikerhimmel anläßlich der ersten Aufführung des *Wozzeck* bei den Salzburger Festspielen," "Eine neue Wiener Musikergeneration." In Graf, *Die Wiener Oper*, 359–71. Vienna: Humboldt Verlag, 1955. In German.

Reprint of four of Graf's journal notices concerning Berg. The last two were prompted by the performance of *Wozzeck* at the Salzburg Festspiel in 1951.

758. Grasberger, Franz. "Der Bestand Alban Berg." In *Der künstlerische Nachlaß Alban Berg* (no. 1061): 5–7. In German.

Text of a speech given in December 1977 on the occasion of the transfer of materials from Berg's legacy to the Austrian National Library.

759. Gratzer, Wolfgang. "'Es hat mich ja unermeßliche Mühe gekostet': Alban Berg als Dichter zweier Akrostichen." *Glasba in poezija: 130 letnica rojstva Huga Wolfa*, 148–55. Edited by Prinoz Kuret and Julijan Strajnar. Ljubljana: Festival Ljubljana 1990. In German, summary in Slovene.

Analyzes numerological aspects of Berg's acrostic poems (nos. 52 and 55) honoring the sixtieth birthdays of Karl Kraus and Arnold Schoenberg.

760. ———. *Zur "wunderlichen Mystik" Alban Bergs.* Dissertation, University of Salzburg, 1989. Stichwort Musikwissenschaft. Vienna: Bohlau Verlag, 1993. 290 p. ISBN 3205980883. ML410.B47 G73 1993. Abstract in ÖMZ 45 (1990): 199. In German.

Extended discussion of Berg's apparent interest in the occult and irrational, including number symbolism. Superstition is investigated in works esteemed by Berg, including writings by August Strindberg, Emanuel Swedenborg, Oskar Adler, Honoré de Balzac, Otto Weininger, and Maurice Maeterlinck; evidence of Berg's interests is gathered from works in his personal library and passages from the correspondence with Webern and Schoenberg.

761.   Green, Douglass M.   "Cantus Firmus Techniques in the Concertos and Operas of Alban Berg." ABS 2 (1981): 56–68. In English, synopsis in German.

Analysis of passages in works by Berg that use a "cantus firmus," meaning a preexistent melodic line that is presented as a "foil against which other parts are to sound." Cantus firmus was an important element in the contrapuntal training that Berg received at the hands of Schoenberg. The analysis focuses on *Wozzeck*, Act 2, scene 4; the Adagio from the Chamber Concerto; *Lulu*, Act 1, scene 3 and Act 3, scene 1; and the Adagio of the Violin Concerto. The appearance of cantus firmus was not intended by Berg as a neoclassical gesture, rather as a continuation of a German-Austrian tradition that he inherited from his immediate forerunners.

762.   Gruber, Gernot.   "Die Musik der Wiener Schule im Münchner Musikleben vor 1933." ABS 2 (1981): 245–50. In German.

Assessment of the journalistic reception of music by the Viennese School (mainly Schoenberg) in Munich to 1933. Reviews are extracted primarily from the *Münchener neueste Nachrichten* (no musical journal was published then in Munich). Before World War I Schoenberg's music was received with tolerance, which was dispelled following the war by an increasingly vitriolic and politically motivated tone. Repertory in the 1920s in Munich was conservative, and modern music was dominated by the works of Hans Pfitzner. Berg was little heard—*Wozzeck* was premiered in Munich only in 1957.

763. Hába, Alois. "Alban Berg." *Klíč* 2/6 (1932): 82–84. In Czech. German translation by Jiří Kozelka in MEL/NZM 3 (1977): 115–16.

A general appreciation of Berg's futuristic stance, which provided models for the works of Hába.

764. Hailey, Christopher. "Between Instinct and Reflection: Berg, Opera and the Viennese Dichotomy." In *The Berg Companion* (no. 803): 221–34. In English.

Finds Viennese culture filled with "awkward discrepancies" that were expressed strikingly in operatic works and tastes of the early twentieth century. These dichotomies take differing forms of expression—classical versus modern, high art versus *Kleinkunst*, the mundane versus the ecstatic—whose tension is evident in such operas as Franz Schreker's and Schoenberg's. Berg defuses this tension in operatic works whose drama and music are equally coherent and comprehensible.

765. Halasz, Gabor. "Des Ausdrucks Übermaß: Zur 100. Wiederkehr von Alban Bergs Geburtstag am 9. 2. 85." *Musikhandel* 36 (1985): 72–73. In German.

General appreciation.

766. Halbreich, Harry. "Berg en mémoire." *Diapason-Harmonie* 307 (1985): 20–27. In French.

Annotated, interpretive discography of Berg's major works.

767. ———. "Discographie critique: Alban Berg parmi nous." *Harmonie* 146 (April 1979): 80–99. In French.

Annotated discography.

768. Hamilton, David. "Berg on Records: A Centenary Survey." *Opus: The Classical Music Magazine* 2/2 (1986): 22–26. In English.

Annotated discography.

769. Hamilton, Iain. "Alban Berg and Anton Webern." In *European Music in the Twentieth Century*, 94–117. Edited by Howard Hartog. London: Routledge and Kegan Paul; New York: Praeger, 1957. In English.

General survey of Berg's music.

770. Harris, Donald. "Berg and Frida Semler." BSN 8 (1979): 8–12. In English.

Lengthy quotations from and discussion of five letters sent from Berg to Frida Semler (Seabury) in 1907 and 1908. The letters, now at the Library of Congress, deal primarily with Berg's attitudes toward modern music and culture.

771. ———. "Berg and Miss Frida: Further Recollections of His Friendship with an American College Girl." ABS 2 (1981): 198–208. In English, synopsis and quotations from correspondence in German.

Deals with Frida Semler (Seabury), who visited the Berghof in 1903 and 1904, striking up a friendship with Berg. This article (like nos. 770 and 976) quotes from and discusses the content of documents from the Seabury materials at the Library of Congress: five letters from Berg to her (1907–1908), a memoir (ca. 1936) by Mrs. Seabury concerning her contact with the composer, three songs by Berg (autograph manuscripts, one to Seabury's own poem "Traum"), and miscellaneous items.

772. ———. "The Berg-Schoenberg Correspondence: A Preliminary Report." BSN 9 (1980): 11–14. In English.

An overview of and excerpts from the Berg-Schoenberg correspondence, preliminary to the publication of *The Berg-Schoenberg Correspondence* (no. 704).

773. ———. "Ravel Visits the Verein: Alban Berg's Report." JASI 3 (1979): 75–82. In English.

Translates and discusses the content of a letter from Berg to Schoenberg (dated 28 October 1920) concerning a recent concert sponsored by the Verein für musikalische Privataufführungen in Vienna in which music by Ravel was performed.

774. ———. "Some Thoughts on the Teacher-Student Relationship between Arnold Schoenberg and Alban Berg." PNM 15 (1977): 133–44. In English.

Outline of Berg's efforts on Schoenberg's behalf as revealed in the Berg-Schoenberg correspondence.

775. Hassler, Marianne. "Weibliches Komponieren." *Musikpsychologie: Jahrbuch der deutschen Gesellschaft für Musikpsychologie* 8 (1991): 32–45. In German, summary in English.

By comparing music of Berg and Dora Pejačevic, categories for a general comparison of music by men versus music by women are advanced.

776. Häusler, Josef. "Alban Berg." In *Musik im 20. Jahrhundert von Schönberg zu Penderecki*, 99–115. Bremen: Schünemann Verlag, 1969. In German.

General survey of Berg's life and works.

777. Haußwald, Günter. "Im Memoriam: Alban Berg zur 75. Wiederkehr seines Geburtstages." *Musica* 14 (1960): 111–12. In German.

Brief appreciation.

778. Heinsheimer, Hans W. "Alban Berg: As I Knew Him." *Opera News* 41/21 (1977): 10–13. In English.

Personal recollections and quotations from letters from Berg to the author.

779. Hill, Richard. "Music." *Library of Congress: Quarterly Journal of Current Acquisitions* 10/1 (1952): 33–44. In English.

Concerns the acquisition by the Library of Congress of segments of the Schoenberg-Berg correspondence. The article touches on Berg only in passing.

780. Hilmar, Rosemary. *Alban Berg: Leben und Wirken in Wien bis zu seinen ersten Erfolgen als Komponist.* Dissertation, University of Vienna, 1974. Wiener Musikwissenschaftliche Beiträge, volume 10. Vienna, Cologne, and Graz: Verlag Hermann Böhlaus Nachf., 1978. 196 p. ISBN 3205082389. ML410.B47 H5. In German. Reviewed by Luigi Bellingardi, *Nuova rivista musicale italiana* 16 (1982): 243–44; Paul Pisk, PNM 18 (1979–80): 422–25; Volker Scherliess, MF 34 (1981): 116–17; Walter Szmolyan, ÖMZ 34 (1979): 166–67.

Biography of Berg during his youth, apprenticeship, studies with Schoenberg, experiences in World War I, work for Schoenberg's Verein für musikalische Privataufführungen, and early recognition as a composer through a performance of his String Quartet in Salzburg in 1923.

781. ———. "Alban Berg's Studies with Schoenberg." JASI 8 (1984): 7–29. In English.

Survey of Berg's compositional studies with Schoenberg, based on Berg's written musical exercises (now found in the Berg Collection at the Austrian National Library). His course of study moved from harmony to counterpoint, to strict counterpoint, finally, to free composition (the last emphasizing variation forms). Early string quartets and piano sonatas are discussed.

782. ———. "Dr. Adorno war nur ein Schüler von Alban Berg." In *Adorno in seinen musikalischen Schriften: Beiträge zum Symposion "Philosophische Äußerungen über Musik. Adorno in seinen musikalischen Schriften," vom 20.-21. September 1985 in der Westfälischen Wilhelms-Universität Münster, im Auftrag der Gesellschaft für Musikpädagogik GMP,* 107–37. Edited by Brunhilde Sonntag. Musik im Diskurs, volume 2. Regensburg: Gustav Bosse Verlag, 1987. In German.

A wide-ranging article based on the correspondence between Berg and Adorno now in the Austrian National Library. The author concludes that Adorno was not among Berg's closest students but that his analytic essays, especially those concerning the music of Schoenberg, were influential upon Berg. Adorno's strained relations with Helene Berg are also investigated.

783. ———. "Das Edelweiß und der Schmetterling: Alban Bergs Briefe an seine Frau im neuen Licht. Versuch eines Psychogramms." *Musikerziehung* 41 (1987–88): 108–22. In German.

Discusses the contents of hitherto unpublished letters (1907–1909) passing between Berg and Helene Nahowski.

784. ———. "Das Sprachrohr: Eine Erläuterung zu einem falsch identifizierten Aufsatz von Anton Webern." SMZ 122 (1982): 326–32. In German.

Concerns a typescript titled "Der neue Stil Arnold Schönbergs" in the Berg Collection of the Austrian National Library, with handwritten entries by Webern and Erwin Stein. The item is a version of Berg's essay "Warum ist Schönbergs Musik so schwer verständlich" (no. 38), in which Berg apparently sought the editorial assistance of Webern and Stein.

785. ———, editor. *Katalog der Musikhandschriften, Schriften und Studien Alban Bergs im Fonds Alban Berg und der weiteren handschriftlichen Quellen im Besitz der Österreichischen Nationalbibliothek.* ABS 1. Vienna: Universal Edition, 1980. 212 p. ISBN 3702401474. ML134.B46 H5 1981. In German. Reviewed by Douglas Jarman, ML 63 (1982): 285–88; Wulf Konold, NZM 143/1 (1982): 74; Claudio Spies, *Notes* 38 (1981): 401–406; Manfred Stahnke, NZM 143/3 (1982): 76; Jürg Stenzl, SMZ 121 (1981), 268–69.

Catalog of Berg's writings and music in the Austrian National Library.

786. ———, **editor.** *Katalog der Schriftstücke von der Hand Alban Bergs, der fremdschriftlichen und gedruckten Dokumente zur Lebensgeschichte und zu seinem Werk.* ABS 1/2. Vienna: Universal Edition, 1985. 161 p. ISBN 3702401741. ML134.B465 H53 1985. In German. Reviewed by Constantin Floros, NZM 147/11 (1986); Douglas Jarman, ML 67 (1986): 438.

> Catalog of writings (mainly drafts of correspondence) from Berg's legacy, now in the Austrian National Library. An appendix gives the texts of numerous letters.

787. Hirsbrunner, Theo. "Richard Wagners Musikdramen und ihr Fortwirken bei Debussy, Strauss, Schönberg und Berg." In *Gattungen der Musik und ihre Klassiker*, 271–85. Edited by Hermann Danuser. Publikationen der Hochschule für Musik und Theater Hannover, volume 1. Laaber: Laaber-Verlag, 1988. In German.

> Traces the Wagnerian element in operas of Debussy, Strauss, Schoenberg, and Berg, focusing on text, dramaturgy, orchestration, and treatment of voices.

788. Holland, Dietmar. "Auswahldiskographie." MK 9 (1979): 96–100. In German.

> Critical report on recordings of the String Quartet; Four Pieces, Op. 5; Chamber Concerto; and Lyric Suite. Also see the "Nachbemerkung der Herausgeber [Heinz-Klaus Metzger and Rainer Riehn] zu Dietmar Hollands Diskographie," same volume, pp. 101–102.

789. Holländer, Hans. "Alban Berg." MQ 22 (1936): 375–82. In English.

> General appraisal of Berg's music. Includes a facsimile of a card (21 June 1934) from Berg to Carl Engel concerning the sale of the manuscript of *Wozzeck* to the Library of Congress.

790. Honolka, Kurt. "Alban Bergs freie Atonalität"; "Berg, der Zwölfton Romantiker." In Honolka, *Das vielstimmige Jahrhundert:*

Musik in unserer Zeit, 103–105 and 129–32. Stuttgart: Cotta-Verlag, 1960. In German.

The two articles briefly survey Berg's atonal and twelve-tone works. The latter discussion focuses on the use of quotations in the Violin Concerto and ciphers in the Chamber Concerto.

791. Hübner, Herbert. S.v. "Berg, Alban." *Die Musik in Geschichte und Gegenwart* (1951). In German.

Notable for its scant treatment of Berg. "Berg belongs to the narrow circle of Austrian composers who were trained at the hands of Arnold Schoenberg at the beginning of our century. His music grew entirely from the spirit of this exemplary personality and matured soon into its own style." The bibliography lists eight items.

792. Humphrey, Mary Lou. "An Alban Berg Bibliography, 1969–1977." BSN 6 (1978): 14–15; 7 (1978): 12–15. In English.

A general bibliography including reviews.

793. *International Alban Berg Society Newsletter.* Published irregularly, 1968– . In English.

794. Jameux, Dominique. "Alban Berg." *Musique de notre temps* 1 (1973): 33–40. In French.

General study of Berg touching on his life, music of his "atonal period (1907–21)" and his "dodecaphonic period (1923–35)." *Wozzeck* and *Lulu* are briefly analyzed and compared.

795. ———. "Alban Berg, le provocateur." *Revue d'esthétique* 21/special issue ("Musiques nouvelles") (1968): 317–28. In French.

Asserts the relevance of Berg for contemporary composers of the 1960s, holding that "Berg is not explained by Wagner, Brahms, or Arnold Schoenberg, but by Varèse, Stockhausen, Boulez." An analysis of the Sonata, Op. 1, finds ambiguities that prefigure serial composition.

796. ———. *Berg.* Solfèges, volume 38. Paris: Éditions du Seuil, 1980. 192 p. ISBN 2020055155. ML410.B47 J32. In French. Reviewed by Peter J. Pirie, MR 43 (1982): 72–73.

> Study of Berg's life and works. Each of the major compositions is analyzed as to form, pitch structure, and expressive content. An abbreviated bibliography, work list, discography, and French translation of the texts of the Four Songs, Op. 2, and Orchestral Songs, Op. 4, are appended.

797. ———. "Entendre Berg et le voir: Notes sur les relations entre structure, écriture et audition dans l'oeuvre d'Alban Berg." *Critique* 37 (1981): 485–95. In French. Spanish translation ("Escuchar y ver a Berg") *Heterofonia* 16 (1983): 40–49.

> Deals with the relation of hearing Berg's music, following the score, and understanding. Understanding is "the faculty for transforming auditory information into structural meaning."

798. ———. "Une ville fatale." *Arc* 40 (1970): 57–64. In French.

> Comparisons between Berg and Beethoven and their relation to the city Vienna.

799. **Jarman, Douglas.** "Alban Berg: The Origins of a Method." MA 6 (1987): 273–88. In English.

> An analytic study of symmetrical pitch formations in *Lulu*, the second of the Orchestral Songs, Op. 4, and the song "Schlafend trägt man," Op. 2, no. 2.

800. ———. "'Man hat auch nur Fleisch und Blut': Towards a Berg Biography." In *Alban Berg: Historical and Analytical Perspectives* (no. 746): 11–23. In English.

> Takes stock of the needs in future Berg research, especially for a biography that will question longstanding assumptions, be more accurate in facts than Willi Reich's, and include reliable chronologies of the composition of works such as *Lulu*.

801. ————. *The Music of Alban Berg*. London: Faber & Faber; Berkeley and Los Angeles, University of California Press, 1979. xii, 266 p. ISBN 0520034856. ML 410.B47 J33. In English. Reviewed by Nicholas Chadwick, *Tempo*, 130 (1979): 29–31; Carmelo Comberiati, *In Theory Only* 4/7 (1979): 34–37; Mark DeVoto, JAMS 33 (1980): 407–12, and *Opera Quarterly* 3/3 (1985): 67–68; Jan Maegaard, *Dansk musiktidsskrift* 56 (1981–82): 189; Peter J. Pirie, MR 41 (1980): 71–73; Derrick Puffett, MT 120 (1979): 1000–1001; Gottfried Scholz, ÖMZ, 34 (1979): 645–46; Joan Allen Smith, *Notes*, 36 (1980); 881–83; Rudolf Stephan, NZM 141 (1980): 479; John Warrack, *Times Literary Supplement*, 4002 (1979): 71–72; Glenn Watkins, *Michigan Quarterly Review* 20 (1981): 134–43; Arnold Whittall, ML 60 (1979): 328–31.

Paperback edition of 1985 differs in details from the edition of 1979. ISBN 0520049543. ML410.B47 J33 1985. In English.

An analytic study focusing on the atonal and twelve-tone works and their structural properties, rhythmic techniques, and formal patterns.

802. ————. "Two Unpublished Letters from Berg." MT 113 (1972): 350–52. In English.

Translation of letters from Berg to Ruzena Herlinger and her husband, dated 23 July 1929 and 14 August 1935, concerning *Der Wein*.

803. ————, editor. *The Berg Companion*. Basingstoke: Macmillan Press; Boston: Northeastern University Press, 1989. xii, 301 pp. ISBN 1555530680. ML410.B47 B53 1990. In English. Reviewed by Nick Chadwick, MT 131 (1990): 659; Douglass M. Green, JASI 14 (1991): 107–17; Dave Headlam, *Notes* 47 (1990–91): 1139–42; Susan Kagan, *Fanfare* 14/6 (1990–91): 415–16; Anthony Pople, ML 72 (1991): 313–15.

Contains thirteen articles intended "to give the reader some idea of the range and excitement of the work being done in the field of Berg studies at the moment."

804. **Johnson, Carl.** "Helene and Alban: The Story of a Great Love." *Opera Journal* 13/4 (1980): 16–20. In English.

Brief description of Berg's "ideal marriage."

805. **Jost, Werner.** "Pierre-Jean Jouve und Alban Berg: Vom 'Blick in jene Freude'." *Universitas: Zeitschrift für Wissenschaft, Kunst und Literatur* 41 (1986): 1179–83. In German.

Discusses the attachment of the writer Jouve (1887–1976) to the music of Berg as an example of the affinity of literature and music.

806. **Kaczyński, Bogusław.** *Ucieczki do Karyntii: Rzecz o Albanie Bergu i jego operach* [Flight to Carinthia: Study of the Operas of Alban Berg]. Warsaw: Wydawnictwa Radia i Telewizji, 1987. 168 p. ISBN 832120483X. In Polish.

Survey of *Wozzeck* and *Lulu* for the general reader including summaries of the libretti and musical overview. The bibliography lists twenty-eight items.

807. **Kars, Gustave.** "De Mahler à l'école sérielle: Rupture ou continuité?" RM 298–99 (1977): 107–36. In French.

Mainly a discussion of Schoenberg's relations with Mahler, briefly about Berg's.

808. **Kassowitz, Gottfried.** "Lehrzeit bei Alban Berg." ÖMZ 23 (1968): 323–30. In German.

Recollections about Berg by a former student. The author studied with both Berg and Schoenberg, finding Berg the more sympathetic teacher. Kassowitz also recounts memories concerning the composition of *Wozzeck*, the scandalous concert of 31 March 1913 when songs from Berg's Orchestral Songs, Op. 4, were first heard, and other matters. Two letters from Berg to Kassowitz are reproduced (dated 21 July 1920 and 5 March 1929).

809. **Kaufmann, Harald.** "Rede in Alban Bergs Landschaft: Anläßlich der Übergabe einer Erinnerungstafel." In

Fingerübungen: Musikgesellschaft und Wertungsforschung, 66–71. Vienna: Verlag Elisabeth Lafite, 1970. In German.

Text of a lecture praising Berg's love of the Carinthian land.

810. Keller, Hans. "Three Half-Truths." *Music and Musicians* 17/10 (1969): 24–25. In English.

Dismisses the concept of a "Second Viennese School," all three terms of which constitute half-truths when used to refer collectively to Schoenberg, Berg, and Webern. Keller attributes the idea of a Second Viennese School to Hans F. Redlich.

811. Kerner, Dieter. "Alban Bergs Ende." *Hessische Ärzteblätter* 21 (1960): 610–12. Reprinted in MEL 29 (1962): 112–13. In German. Spanish translation ("El fin de Alban Berg") in *Folia humanistica* 2/issue 24 (1964): 1041–1048.

Information (the sources for which are unspecified) concerning Berg's final illness and its medical treatment.

812. Kett, Stephen W. "An Alban Bibliography, 1978–80." BSN 11 (1982): 9–17. In English.

813. ———. "An Alban Bibliography, 1982." BSN 12 (1982): 17–21. In English.

Both bibliographies are subdivided by composition and include reviews.

814. Klebe, Giselher. "Zuneigung mit Widersprüchen." *Oper 1985* (yearbook of the journal *Opernwelt*): 46. In German.

Klebe admits that Berg's music was earlier influential upon his own works, but his more recent encounters with the music of Webern have made both Berg and Schoenberg seem hyperemotional, "like a meal that is too fatty and indigestible."

815. Klein, Elisabeth. "Alban Berg: Den moderne klassiker." *Norsk musikerblad* 77/6 (1990): 6. In Norwegian.

816. Klein, Fritz Heinrich. "Die Grenze der Halbtonwelt." *Die Musik* 17 (1925): 281–86. In German.

A report on Klein's statistical studies regarding harmonic properties of chromatic collections of pitches, including his identification of a "mother chord" that contains all of the pitch and interval classes. This theory was influential upon Berg's choice of a basic row in "Schließe mir die Augen beide" (1925) and Lyric Suite.

817. Klein, Rudolf, editor. *Alban Berg Symposion Wien 1980: Tagungsbericht.* ABS 2. Vienna: Alban Berg-Stiftung in der Universal Edition, 1981. 272 p. ISBN 370240158X. ML410.B47 A78 1980. In German or English. Reviewed by Theo Hirsbrunner, MF 38 (1985): 131; Peter Revers, ÖMZ 37 (1982): 655–56; Klaus Schweizer, SMZ 122 (1982): 295–97.

Contains the texts of twenty-seven brief articles originating as papers read at the International Alban Berg Symposium in Vienna in June 1980. The conference was sponsored by the Alban Berg-Stiftung and the Wiener Festwochen and brought together Berg scholars from Europe and America. The papers dealt in general with the themes "Documentation—Analysis—Reception," and they touched upon Berg's mature works (primarily *Lulu, Wozzeck,* Violin Concerto, Chamber Concerto, and Orchestral Pieces) as well as aspects of his life and cultural milieu. The articles appear in either English or German, with the English-language articles followed by a German abstract. Each of the articles is cited elsewhere in this bibliography.

818. *Klíč* 2/6 (1932). Special issue devoted to Berg. In Czech.

Articles include a contribution by Alois Hába (no. 763).

819. Kolleritsch, Otto. "Aspekte der Berg-Rezeption in Österreich." ABS 2 (1981): 265–68. In German.

Berg's music was in general not accepted by the Austrian public because, in a time of political and social insecurity, people were unwilling to give up music as a refuge of order.

The music of Joseph Marx was an example of what they sought with its overt evocation of the affects of nature and landscape.

820. Krämer, Ulrich. "Quotation and Self-Borrowing in the Music of Alban Berg." *Journal of Musicological Research* 12 (1992): 53–82. In English.

Discussion of techniques of quotation in Berg's music, primarily the folk-song quotation in the Violin Concerto and quotations from Berg's own early piano sonata fragments (1908–1909) in *Wozzeck* and the String Quartet, Op. 3. An appendix summarizes such quotations and the literature about them.

821. Kraus, Egon. "Bibliographie: Alban Berg." *Musik und Bildung* 5 (1973): 142–45. In German.

Brief bibliography and discography, emphasizing German sources.

822. Krause, Ernst. "*Wozzeck*—heute," "Berg *Lulu* Berlin." In Krause, *Schreiben über Musik: Essays, Berichte, Kritiken*, 48–51, 324–26. Berlin: Henschelverlag Kunst und Gesellschaft, 1981. In German.

Reprints of reviews of stagings of *Wozzeck* (1965) and *Lulu* (1975) at the East Berlin Staatsoper. The works are said to unite the opposites of euphoria and construction.

823. Krones, Hartmut. "'Wiener' Symbolik? Zu musiksemantischen Traditionen in den beiden Wiener Schulen." In *Beethoven und die zweite Wiener Schule*, 51–79. Edited by Otto Kolleritsch. Studien zur Wertungsforschung, volume 25. Vienna and Graz: Universal Edition for the Institut für Wertungsforschung, 1992. In German.

Surveys traditional musical devices among early Viennese composers and their continued use by Schoenberg, Berg, and Webern. An example is the use of musical letters to form extramusical allusions.

824. Kullberg, Erling. "Alban Berg." *Dansk musiktidsskrift* 58 (1983–84): 182–87. In Danish.

Reviews recent trends in Berg research toward revealing secretive autobiographical allusions.

825. ———. "Alban Berg: Kærligheden og dyneløfterne." *Dansk musiktidsskrift* 58 (1983–84): 182–87. In Danish.

Survey of musical cryptograms in Berg's Lyric Suite and Violin Concerto, summarizing the theories of Constantin Floros and George Perle.

826. Lakatos, István. "Ein unbekannter Brief von Alban Berg." *Studia musicologica* 12 (1970): 319–21. Reprinted MEL 38 (1971): 412–13. In German.

Facsimile and transcription of a letter from Berg (6 March 1931) to the Lakatos Quartet concerning music to the Lyric Suite; also recollections by the author of meeting Berg.

827. Lampert, Vera. "Schoenbergs, Bergs und Adornos Briefe an Sándor (Alexander) Jemnitz." *Studia musicologica* 15 (1973): 355–73. In German.

Gives the texts of letters from Berg, Schoenberg, and Adorno to Sándor Jemnitz (1890–1963), who had been a student of Schoenberg in Berlin from 1921 to 1924. Eight letters are from Berg (dated 1923–35), dealing briefly with various performances. See also Breuer (no. 707).

828. Leibowitz, René. Chapters 7–8 ("Alban Berg"). In Leibowitz, *Schönberg et son école: L'étape contemporaine du langage musical*, 137–88. Paris: J. B. Janin, 1947. In French. English translation (*Schoenberg and His School: The Contemporary Stage of the Language of Music*), 135–86, translated by Dika Newlin (New York: Philosophical Library, 1949); reprint New York: Da Capo, 1975.

An analytic survey of all of Berg's major compositions, emphasizing pitch organization, counterpoint, form, and relations with the style of Schoenberg. Leibowitz credits

Adorno with inspiring his analytic viewpoint, although his conclusions often differ notably from Adorno's.

829. ———. "Alban Berg et l'essence de l'opéra. Réflexions sur la musique dramatiques *sub una specie.*" *L'arche* 3/13 (1946): 130–34. In French.

Considers *Wozzeck* and *Lulu* in the context of the history of opera, concluding that they constitute a peak in the development of modern dramatic music.

830. ———. "Innovation and Tradition in Contemporary Music: III. Alban Berg: Or the Seduction to Truth." *Horizon: Review of Literature and Art* 16 (1947): 140–52. In English.

Compares and contrasts the works and musical instincts of Berg with the music and teaching of Schoenberg.

831. ———. "Les opéras d'Alban Berg ou le synthèse de l'art lyrique." In Leibowitz, *L'histoire de l'opéra*, 369–88 (Paris: Buchet/Chastel, 1957). In French. German translation ("Alban Bergs *Wozzeck*: Eine Einführung") in Csampai and Holland (no. 103): 210–20. Spanish translation ("Las óperas de Alban Berg o la síntesis del arte lírico") in *Pauta* 4/15 (1985): 70–89.

Survey of *Wozzeck* and *Lulu*, holding that these two works achieve greatness by "synthesizing the principal means of expression and the great traditions of the past."

832. Lewinski, Wolf-Eberhard von. "Der Zwölftöne-Klassiker: Zum 25. Todestag von Alban Berg." *Musica* 14 (1960): 806–807. In German.

Brief appreciation.

833. Lindlar, Heinrich. "'Mir fehlt die grosse Freude. . .': Zum 20. Todestag Alban Bergs (24.12)." *Musica* 9 (1955): 594–96. In German.

Brief appreciation.

834. Linke, Karl. "Anton von Webern und Alban Berg." *Das musikfestliche Wien*, 1912. Reprinted in Reich 1959 (no. 917): 21–23. In German.

One of the earliest published articles on Berg. Contrasts Berg and Webern: "If with Webern the moment of quiet is represented in its emotionality, then with Berg emotionality—with all of its intensifications, climaxes, subsidiary phenomena—becomes the object of representation."

835. Machabey, Armand. "Alban Berg." *Le ménestrel* (22 August 1930): 28–30. In French.

836. Mahler Werfel, Alma. Chapter 9 ("A House in Venice") and passim. In Mahler Werfel, *And the Bridge Is Love*, 167–88 and passim. In collaboration with E. B. Ashton. New York: Harcourt, Brace, 1958. In English. German version (*Mein Leben*), Frankfurt: Fischer, 1960.

References to Helene and Alban Berg are found throughout Mahler Werfel's memoirs. The Bergs are described as her "closest friends," and she relates anecdotes about the premiere of *Wozzeck*, its stormy performance in Prague in 1926, and Berg's relations with Schoenberg. The German version has a section on Berg, pp. 171–75.

837. Mancini, Tamara. *Alban Berg*. I grandi musicisti del XX secolo. Milan: Targa Italiana Editore, 1990. ISBN 8871110226. ML410.B47 M36 1990. In Italian.

A concise general study of Berg covering his life and selected works (*Wozzeck, Lulu, Lyric* Suite, and Chamber Concerto). Four of Berg's essays are translated, taken from Berg's *Écrits* (no. 64).

838. Mantelli, Alberto. "Elenco delle opere di Berg." *Rassegna musicale* 9 (1936): 163–64. In Italian.

Highly abbreviated list of Berg's works.

839. ———. "Note su Alban Berg." *La rassegna musicale* 9 (1936): 117–32. Reprinted in *Musica/realtà* 42 (1993): 186–201, and in Monte and Segreto (no. 851): 559–77. In Italian.

A general survey and description of all of Berg's works, emphasizing *Wozzeck*.

840. Maul, Andreas. "'Es war eine Freundschaft vom ersten Augenblick an': Eleonore Vondenhoff im Gespräch mit Andreas Maul über ihre Erinnerungen an Alban und Helene Berg." ÖMZ 44 (1989): 601–10. In German.

Eleonore Vondenhoff's recollections of Berg begin in November 1930, when the composer visited Gera. Her husband, Bruno, was to conduct *Wozzeck*. The two families were frequently in contact thereafter. Her reminiscences include Berg's remarks on Mahler, Webern, Schoenberg, and Wagner.

841. Mayer, Harry. "De brieven van Alban Berg aan zijn vrouw." *Mens en melodie* 22 (1967): 50–53. In Dutch.

Commentary upon and excerpts from Berg's *Briefe an seine Frau* (no. 67).

842. Mayer, Otto. "Apunts sobre Alban Berg." *Revista musical catalana* 33 (1936): 154–57. In Catalan.

General remarks on Berg's works, especially on the musical language of *Wozzeck* and *Lulu*.

843. *Melos* 22/2 (1955). Special Berg issue.

Contains articles by Willi Reich, Hans Redlich, Helmut Schmidt-Garre, and Josef Rufer.

844. Mertens, Pierre. *Lettres clandestines, un récit.* Paris: Éditions du Seuil, 1990. In French.

A novella based on the fictitious thoughts of Berg on his death bed. His mind turns alternately to his sister, Schoenberg, his wife, and Hanna Fuchs.

845. **Metzger, Heinz-Klaus, and Rainer Riehn, editors.** MK 4 (1978): *Alban Berg Kammermusik I.* Munich: Edition text + kritik. 76 p. ISBN 3921402662. MT145.B47 A4 volume 1. In German. Reviewed by Dieter Rexroth, ÖMZ 35 (1980): 494–95.

846. ———, **editors.** MK 9 (1979): *Alban Berg: Kammermusik II.* Munich: Edition text + kritik. 104 p. ISBN 3883770159. MT145.B47 A4 volume 2. In German. Reviewed by Klaus Hinrich Stahmer, *Das Orchester*, 28 (1980): 437.

The two issues of *Musik-Konzepte* concerning Berg's chamber music include new, reprinted, and translated articles. Bibliographies and discographies are included.

847. **Meyer, Gustav William.** "Berg—Bloch—Honegger." *Kunst und Kritik* (Chemnitz, 1929): 149. In German.

848. **Mikorey, Stefan.** *Klangfarbe und Komposition: Besetzung und musikalische Faktur in Werken für großes Orchester und Kammerorchester von Berlioz, Strauss, Mahler, Debussy, Schönberg und Berg.* Dissertation, University of Munich, 1980. Minerva Fachserie Kunst. Munich: Minerva, 1982. 306 p. In German. Reviewed by Peter Nitsche, *Musica* 38 (1984): 374.

Discussion of tone color in selected nineteenth- and twentieth-century orchestral works.

849. **Möller, Eberhard.** "Ein unveröffentlicher Briefwechsel zwischen Alban Berg und Georg Göhler." *Beiträge zur Musikwissenschaft* 31 (1989): 279–82. In German.

Transcription of a letter of recommendation from Berg to Göhler dated 5 July 1924 concerning Berg's student Josef Schmid.

850. **Monson, Karen.** *Alban Berg.* Boston: Houghton Mifflin, 1979; London: Macdonald and Jane's, 1980. xvi, 396 p. ISBN 0395277620. ML410.B47 M6. In English. Reviewed by Mosco Carner, *Opera* 31 (1980): 247–48; Christopher Hailey, *Opera Quarterly* 3/3 (1985): 168–70; Douglas Jarman, ML 61 (1980): 446–49; Umberto Padroni, *Nuova rivista musicale italiana* 17 (1983):

615; Derrick Puffett, MT 121 (1980): 564; Joan Allen Smith, *Notes* 36 (1989–80): 881–83; Patrick J. Smith, *High Fidelity/Musical America* 30/1 (1980): MA 18; Michael Taylor, *Times Literary Supplement* 4039 (1980): 941; Glenn Watkins, *Michigan Quarterly Review* 20 (1981): 134–43.

German translation: *Alban Berg: Musikalischer Rebell im kaiserlichen Wien*. Translated by Ursula Stiebler. Frankfurt: Ullstein, 1989. 336 p. Reviewed by Theo Hirsbrunner, *Das Orchester* 39/1 (1991): 59–61.

Italian translation: *Berg*. Translated by D. de' Paoli. Milan: Rusconi, 1982. 412 p.

A biographical survey written primarily for the general reader.

851. Monte, Claudio Del, and Vincenzo Raffaele Segreto, editors. *Alban Berg*. Parma: Grafiche STEP Editrice, 1989. 604 p. In Italian. Reviewed by Umberto Padroni, *Nuova rivista musicale italiana* 26 (1992): 102–103.

Collection of articles—some reprinted, some new—concerning various aspects of Berg's life, milieu, and work. The publication of the volume was prompted by a staging of *Wozzeck* in Parma's Teatro Regio in April 1989.

852. Montrul, Mario. "'Schlafend traegt man mich in mein Heimatland. . .': Culto a la memoria de Alban Berg." *Buenos Aires musical* 27/issue no. 437 (1972): 2. In Spanish.

Report on an interview by the author with Helene Berg in January 1972. Their conversation touched on Berg's courtship, everyday life, and the incomplete state of *Lulu*.

853. Morazzoni, Anna Maria. "Berg and Italy in the Thirties." BSN 13 (1985): 10–31. In English.

A detailed study, based on correspondence, of Berg's personal and professional relations in the 1930s with Italy's major musical figures, primarily Gian Francesco Malipiero, Alfredo Casella, and Adriano Lualdi. The abortive plan to perform the Lyric Suite at the 1934 Venice International

Music Festival is investigated, and the text of Berg's correspondence during these years with Casella, Malipiero, Lualdi, and Luigi Dallapiccola is reproduced. See also Carner, no. 518.

854. ———. "Berg e l'Italia." In Monte and Segreto (no. 851): 525–42. In Italian.

Closely related in content to the author's no. 853, also including information about Berg in Italian musical life following World War II.

855. **Morgan, Robert P.** "The Eternal Return: Retrograde and Circular Form in Berg." In *Alban Berg: Historical and Analytical Perspectives* (no. 746): 111–49. In English.

An analytic investigation of retrograde and circular forms in Berg's music, with special attention to *Wozzeck*, Act 1, scene 1; passages from *Lulu*; the song "Schlafen" (Op. 2, no. 1); and Seven Early Songs. Nietzsche's idea of eternal recurrence is cited as a possible influence upon the composer in his use of circular form.

856. **Mössmer, Günter.** "Autobiographische und private Verweisungsrelationen in Werken Alban Bergs." In *Musica privata: Die Rolle der Musik im privaten Leben. Festschrift zum 65. Geburtstag von Walter Salmen*, 271–82. Edited by Monika Fink, Rainer Gstrein, and Günter Mössmer. Innsbruck: Edition Helbling, 1991. In German.

Reviews the secretive autobiographical symbols in Berg's late works, finding them different from such allusions in medieval and Renaissance music due to their highly private nature.

857. **Müller, Thomas.** "Alban Berg, Sonata für Klavier op. 1: Verbindlichkeit der Tradition und Sprengkraft des Neuen," "Alban Berg, Vier Stücke für Klarinette und Klavier, op. 5: Atonales Widerspruch und Veränderung," "Alban Berg, Lyrische Suite für Streichquartett: Zwölftontechnik zwischen objektiver

Setzung und subjektivem Programm," "Alban Berg, Drei Orchesterstücke, op. 6, 3—Marsch: Konstruktion und Ausdruck in der kritischen Immanenz zur Warengesellschaft." In Müller, *Die Musiksoziologie Theodor W. Adornos: Ein Modell ihrer Interpretation am Beispiel Alban Bergs*, 88–161. Campus Forschung, volume 642. Frankfurt and New York: Campus Verlag, 1990. In German.

> An attempt to explain Adorno's theories of music and society with analytic reference and application to selected works by Berg. The discussion deals primarily with Berg's use of time. In general, musical time conflicts with the social organization of time, a conflict that the author tries to resolve. That Berg's works stem from an existing political culture, capitalistic society, and the composer's own mind and intellect also suggests contradictions that Adorno does not fully address.

858. Müller-Naef, Monika. "Biographische Notizen zu Alban Berg." In Hanselmann, *Alban Berg Wozzeck* (no. 134): 31–36. In German.

> Brief biographical summary.

859. Murray, Robert. "A Closer Look at the Berg Quartets." *American String Teacher* 33/2 (1983): 16–20. In English.

> Overview of the String Quartet and Lyric Suite.

860. Nelson, Robert U. "Form and Fancy in the Variations of Berg." MR 31 (1970): 54–69. In English.

> Analysis of variational procedures in Berg's Twelve Variations for Piano on an Original Theme; sections of the Orchestral Songs, Op. 4; *Wozzeck*; Chamber Concerto; *Lulu*; and Violin Concerto. Also see a letter from Douglas Jarman, MR 32 (1971): 92, which comments on a discrepancy between Berg's formal chart and text in the "open letter" on the Chamber Concerto (no. 39).

861. Nicolodi, Fiamma. "Luigi Dallapiccola e la scuola di Vienna: Considerazioni e note in margine a una scelta." *Nuova rivista musicale italiana* 17 (1983): 493–528. In Italian.

Includes a chronicle (1933–41) of Berg's contact with Schoenberg and Webern and their music.

862. Nygren, Dennis. "The Chamber Music of Berg." *Clarinet* 13/2 (1985): 26–31. In English.

Analytic notes and historical background to the chamber music.

863. ———. "The Clarinet Chamber Music of Alban Berg." *Clarinet* 13/1 (1985): 22–25. In English.

Analytic notes and historical background to the Clarinet Pieces, Op. 5, and Adagio from the Chamber Concerto arranged for violin, clarinet, and piano.

864. Oesch, Hans. "Alban Berg, Arnold Schönberg und Anton Webern: Ihr Werk für die 'Neue Musik'." *Universitas: Zeitschrift für Wissenschaft, Kunst und Literatur* 28 (1973): 713–22. In German.

Finds a modernism in the works of the three composers that has endured while other modernistic trends in twentieth-century music now seem commonplace.

865. Olives, Juan José. "Alban Berg: In memoriam." *Revista musical catalana* 4 (1985): 25–31. In Catalan.

General survey of Berg's life and works and tribute on the hundredth anniversary of his birth.

866. Op de Coul, Paul. "Unveröffentliche Briefe von Alban Berg und Anton Webern an Daniel Ruyneman." *Tijdschrift van de Vereniging voor Nederlandse Muziekgeschiedenis* 22 (1972): 201–20. In German.

The efforts of Ruyneman to organize concerts of new music in Amsterdam are outlined, and the texts of letters from Berg and Webern to Ruyneman in 1929 (1 July, 30 July, 18 August, 23 September, 24 September, 26 November, 30 December, 29 December) and 1930 (12 March, 26 April) are reproduced. These concern two concerts of music by Schoenberg and his circle in March 1930.

867. *Österreichische Musikzeitung* 40/1 (1985). Special Berg issue. In German.

Contains articles by Rudolf Stephan, Douglas Jarman, and Jürg Stenzl commemorating the hundredth anniversary of the composer's birth.

868. Ostwald, David Frank. "The Integrated Opera: A Study of the Influence of Richard Wagner's Theories of Theatrical Production on Schoenberg, Berg and Stravinsky as Opera Composers." Dissertation, Carnegie-Mellon University, 1973. UMI order no. 7426650. 228 p. In English.

Chapter 7 deals with *Lulu* and *Wozzeck* as regards their relation to Wagner's theories and operatic practices.

869. Paap, Wouter. "Alban Berg." *Mens en melodie* 15 (1960): 14–18. In Dutch.

Brief appreciation on the twenty-fifth anniversary of Berg's death.

870. Pantijewlew, Grigori. "Opernprinzipien von Arnold Schönberg und Alban Berg in Opern aus der BRD." BMW 32 (1990): 34–37. In German.

Discusses the relevance of *Wozzeck*, *Lulu*, and Schoenberg's *Moses und Aron* for the operatic works of Bernd Alois Zimmermann, Aribert Reimann, and Wolfgang Rihm.

871. Pätzold, Sabine. "Alban Bergs Opern *Wozzeck* und *Lulu* in ihrer gesellschaftspolitischen Bedeutung." In *"Nach Frankreich zogen zwei Grenadier": Zeitgeschehen im Spiegel von Musik*, 64–105. Edited by Brunhilde Sonntag. Musik, Kunst & Konsum, volume 2. Münster and Hamburg: Lit Verlag, 1991. In German.

Based on Berg's correspondence with his wife, Gottfried
Kassowitz, Arnold Schoenberg, and others, the author
concludes that Berg constructed the texts of his two operas
so as to heighten their socio-political themes. A brief musical
analysis is also undertaken.

872. *Pauta: Cuadernos de teoria y critica musical*, 4/15 (1985).
Special Berg issue. In Spanish.

Commemorates the hundredth anniversary of the composer's
birth. Most of the articles (by Berg, René Leibowitz, Pierre
Boulez, Andrew Porter, and others) are reprinted from earlier
sources.

873. Paz, Juan Carlos. "Alban Berg y el expresionismo."
Cultura universitaria 82 (1963): 60–68. In Spanish.

Finds similarities in Berg's music and the spirit of German
Expressionism as it existed among painters including Vasili
Kandinsky and Oskar Kokoschka. "In Berg's typical
compositions, as in Schoenberg's, there is an exaltation and,
ultimately, a dissolution of the dramatic and musical
characteristics into pure expressive functions."

874. Pérez Maseda, Eduardo. *Alban Berg: Músicos de nuestro
siglo.* Colección 'Músicos de neustro siglo,' volume 3. Madrid:
Circulo de Bellas Artes, 1985. 103 p. ISBN 8486418038.
ML410.B47 P46 1985. In Spanish.

Life and works of Berg.

875. Perle, George. S. v. "Berg, Alban." *New Grove Dictionary
of Music and Musicians,* 1980. In English. Reprinted (revised) in
The New Grove Second Viennese School: Schoenberg, Webern, Berg,
135–97, The Composer Biography Series (London and New York:
W. W. Norton, 1983). German translation in *The New Grove.
Schönberg, Webern, Berg: Die zweite Wiener Schule* (Stuttgart and
Weimar: Metzler, 1992). Italian translation in *La seconda scuola di
Vienna (Schönberg, Webern, Berg)* (Florence: Giunti Barbera, 1986).

General study of Berg's life and music for both specialists and general readers.

876. ————. "Berg's Master Array of the Interval Cycles." MQ 63 (1977): 1–30. Reprinted in *Die Wiener Schule*, 279–310, edited by Rudolf Stephan (Darmstadt: Wissenschaftliche Buchgesellschaft, 1989). Reprinted in *The Right Notes: Twenty-Three Selected Essays by George Perle on Twentieth-Century Music* (Stuyvesant, N.Y.: Pendragon Press, forthcoming ca. 1996). In English.

> In a letter from Berg to Schoenberg dated 27 July 1920, Berg displays a "theoretical trifle": a 12–line score in which the notes in each line progress by a single interval, from minor second through octave. The succession of thirteen vertical collections that are produced in this matrix is symmetrical: the first chord (a unison) returns as the thirteenth; the second chord (a full chromatic collection) returns as the twelfth, and so forth. Perle calls each such line an "interval cycle" and observes the passing occurrence of music evidently derived from superimposing several such cycles in Berg's Four Songs, Op. 2; *Wozzeck*; and String Quartet, Op. 3. The article continues to explore the compositional potential of such cycles, introducing ideas that are developed in Perle's later theoretical writings.

877. ————. Chapter 20 ("Alban Berg's Master Array of the Interval Cycles"). In Perle, *Twelve-Tone Tonality*, 76–79. Berkeley: University of California Press, 1977. In English.

> Related in content to Perle's 1977 article no. 876. The author holds that pitch configurations derived from interval cycles "play a significant and persistent role in Berg's work, from the second song of Opus 2 through *Lulu*." Examples are drawn from the String Quartet, Op. 3.

878. ————. *The Listening Composer*. Berkeley, Los Angeles, Oxford: University of California Press, 1990. i, 202 p. ISBN 0520069919. ML410.P2925 A3 1990. In English.

Six Ernest Bloch Lectures at the University of California, Berkeley, given in 1989. Analytic discussions of Berg's music are found throughout, especially in Lecture 4 (on *Lulu* among other works) and Lecture 5 (on the Lyric Suite).

879. ———. "Martyr to His Profession." *Opera News* 49/9 (1985): 10–13. Reprinted in *The Right Notes: Twenty-Three Selected Essays by George Perle on Twentieth-Century Music* (Stuyvesant, N.Y.: Pendragon Press, forthcoming ca. 1996). In English.

Brief account of the revival of interest in Berg following World War II. Notes on *Wozzeck* and *Lulu*.

880. ———. "'Mein geliebtes Almschi'." BSN 7 (1978): 5–10. Reprinted in *The Right Notes: Twenty-Three Selected Essays by George Perle on Twentieth-Century Music* (Stuyvesant, N.Y.: Pendragon Press, forthcoming ca. 1996). In English. German translation ("'Mein geliebtes Almschi. . . ': Briefe von Alban und Helene Berg an Alma Mahler Werfel"), ÖMZ 35 (1980): 2–15.

Letters from Alban and Helene Berg to Alma Mahler Werfel, 1927–37, drawn from correspondence in the Alma Mahler Werfel Collection at the University of Pennsylvania. Some letters suggest Helene's knowledge of Berg's contact with another woman. The English language version of this article gives only paraphrases from the letters.

881. ———. *Serial Composition and Atonality: An Introduction to the Music of Schoenberg, Berg, and Webern.* Berkeley and Los Angeles: University of California Press, 1962. Sixth edition 1991. In English. First edition reviewed by Benjamin Boretz, PNM 1 (spring 1963): 125–36; Carl Dahlhaus, MF 18 (1965): 218–19; Thea Musgrave, MT 104 (1963): 113; Oliver Nieghbour, ML 43 (1962): 357–59; Dika Newlin, *Notes* (1961–62): 434–35; Mel Powell, *Journal of Music Theory* 6 (1962): 309–11; George Rochberg, JAMS 16 (1963): 413–18. Second edition reviewed by Mark DeVoto, *Notes* 26 (1969–70): 26–27; Humphrey Searle, *Composer* 31 (1969): 34, 36; Roger Smalley, *Tempo* 90 (1969): 2–7; Wolfgang Martin Stroh, NZM 130 (1969): 302–303; Hugh Wood, MT 110 (1969): 838. Fourth edition reviewed by Mark DeVoto, *Notes* 35 (1978–79):

294–95; Jonathan Dunsby, ML 60 (1979): 63–66; Peter Paul Nash, *Tempo* 127 (1978): 35–37; Arnold Whittall, MR 40 (1979): 57–63. Fifth edition reviewed by Wolfgang Seifert, NZM 143/10 (1982): 78–79.

> General study of the subject mentioned in the title, with emphasis upon twelve-tone music. Berg's works are discussed throughout the book, especially *Lulu*, the Lyric Suite, String Quartet, Four Pieces for Clarinet and Piano, Violin Concerto, *Der Wein*, and *Wozzeck*.

882. Pernye, András. *Alban Berg.* Kis zenei könyvtár, volume 35. Budapest: Gondolat Kiadó, 1967. 324 p. In Hungarian. ML410.B474 P37.

> A general life and works emphasizing *Wozzeck* and *Lulu* and Berg's relation to numerology.

883. ———. "Alban Berg und die Zahlen." *Studia musicologica* 9 (1967): 141–61. In German. Hungarian version, "Alban Berg és a számok," *Magyar zene* 8 (1967): 248–61.

> Surveys the prominence of the numbers 7, 21, and 23 in music by Berg. Extracted from Pernye's book, no. 882.

884. Petazzi, Paolo. *Alban Berg: La vita, l'opera, i testi musicali.* Milan: Feltrinelli, 1977. 358 p. ML410.B47 P5. In Italian.

> Petazzi's study deals with Berg's studies with Schoenberg, his meeting with Helene Nahowski, his wartime experiences, and his approach to twelve-tone composition. The musical analyses emphasize the Orchestral Pieces, Op. 6; *Wozzeck*; Chamber Concerto; Lyric Suite; *Der Wein*; *Lulu*; and the Violin Concerto. The complete libretti of the two operas are given in German and Italian (translated by M. T. Mandalari) as are selected song texts.

885. ———. "Il teatro musicale di Alban Berg." In Monte and Segreto (no. 851): 439–509. In Italian.

> An extensive though general account of the history, style, and form of *Wozzeck* and *Lulu*.

886. Petersen, Peter. "Volkstümliche Genres in der Musik Alban Bergs." In *Ich will aber gerade vom Leben singen. . . : Über populäre Musik vom ausgehenden 19. Jahrhundert bis zum Ende der Weimarer Republik*, 432–54. Edited by Sabine Schutte. Reinbek bei Hamburg: Rowohlt Taschenbuch Verlag, 1987. In German.

Survey of Berg's use of popular or folkloric musical idioms in music from the Orchestral Pieces, Op. 6, to the Violin Concerto. The popular genres include dance music, songs, and marches; these normally appear in Berg's compositions in a stylized manner and suggest programmatic content.

887. ———. "Zu einigen Spezifika der Dodekaphonie im Schaffen Alban Bergs." In *Bericht über den 2. Kongreß der Internationalen Schönberg-Gesellschaft: Die Wiener Schule in der Musikgeschichte des 20. Jahrhunderts*, 168–79. Edited by Rudolf Stephan and Sigrid Wiesmann. Vienna: Verlag Elisabeth Lafite, 1986. In German.

Studies Berg's interpretation and application of the dodecaphonic principle, primarily in *Lulu*. The rows of the work are analyzed in terms of their thematic, diastematic, and intervallic properties.

888. Pfluger, Rolf. "Diskographie der Wiener Schule." ÖMZ 24 (1969): 353–58. In German.

Brief coverage of recordings of complete works by Berg on long-playing discs.

889. Pijper, Willem. "Alban Berg." *Caecilia en de muziek* 93/10 (1935–36): 106–11. Reprinted in Schönberger (no. 969): 52–55. In Dutch. English translation ("Alban Berg") MT 77 (1936): 414–15.

Obituary asserting Berg's greatness and preeminence among modern atonal composers. With Berg's death, the author sees no immediate possibility that the idiom of atonality will significantly endure.

890. Pisk, Paul A. "[Alban Berg]: A Personal Note," "Berg." In David Ewen, *The Book of Modern Composers*, 338–49. New York: Alfred A. Knopf, 1943. In English.

Brief personal recollection of Berg and a survey of his music.

891. ———. "Alban Berg's leven en werken." *De muziek* 5 (1930–31): 4–7. In Dutch. English version ("The Life and Career of Alban Berg") in *Paul A. Pisk: Essays in His Honor*, 228–30, edited by John Glowacki, translated by D. C. Travis (University of Texas: College of Fine Arts, 1966).

Brief survey and general appreciation.

892. ———. "New Music in Austria during the 1920's." *Orbis musicae* 1 (1971): 83–87. In English.

Describes the various societies supporting modern music in Vienna in the 1920s, especially Schoenberg's Verein für musikalische Privataufführungen and the International Society for Contemporary Music.

893. ———. "Personal Recollections of Alban Berg." BSN 10 (1981): 12. In English.

Brief memoirs from a friendship that lasted from 1918 to 1935. Pisk mentions an unpublished article by Berg attacking music critics, which was intended for MBA but never used. This article is probably "Wiener Musikkritik" (no. 63).

894. ———. "The Viennese Triumvirate Remembered." *American Music Teacher* 23/1 (1973–74): 30–31. In English.

A brief personal recollection of Schoenberg, Berg, and Webern.

895. Plotkin, Frederick. "Berg's Sense of Terror." *Music Journal* 27 (1969): 33, 64–65. In English.

Finds a vivid expression of terror in Berg's music.

896. Polnauer, Josef. "Paralipomena zu Berg und Webern." ÖMZ 24 (1969): 292–96. In German.

Argues for the existence of a quotation in *Wozzeck* (Act 3, scene 1) from the Gloria of Bruckner's Mass in D minor and a second folk-song quotation in the second movement of the Violin Concerto (from the tune of "Es ritten drei Reiter zum Tore hinaus").

897. Poole, Geoffrey. "Alban Berg and the Fateful Number." *Tempo* 179 (1991): 2–7. In English.

Hypothesizes that Berg's identification with the number 23 had its origins in his horoscope.

898. Pople, Anthony. "Secret Programmes: Themes and Techniques in Recent Berg Scholarship." MA 12 (1993): 381–99. In English.

Critical assessment of recent analytic approaches to and specific writings on works by Berg.

899. Principe, Quirino. "Gustav Mahler e Alban Berg: L'eredità visibile e l'eredità segreta." In Monte and Segreto (no. 851): 241–58. In Italian.

Study of the personal and artistic relations between Berg and Gustav Mahler.

900. Prunières, Henry. "Nécrologie: Alban Berg." RM 17/issue 162 (1936): 79–80. Reprinted in RM 416–417 (1989): 123. In French.

An obituary notable for its assessment of Berg's enduring greatness as a composer and his essential independence from Schoenberg and Webern. "The death of Alban Berg deprives Austria of its greatest musician."

901. Puffett, Derrick. "Berg and German Opera." In *The Berg Companion* (no. 803): 197–219. In English.

A survey of the tradition of modern German opera—Wagner, Strauss, Schoenberg, Franz Schreker, Alexander Zemlinsky, and others—from which *Wozzeck* grows and which influenced the expressive dimension of its music. *Lulu* is compared to specific German operas of the 1920s and 1930s, including Strauss's *Intermezzo* and Kurt Weill's *Mahagonny*.

902. ———. "'Music That Echoes within One' for a Lifetime: Berg's Reception of Schoenberg's *Pelleas und Melisande*." ML 76 (1995): 209–64. In English.

Discussion of Berg's esteem for Schoenberg's *Pelleas* and a critique of the analytic viewpoint about the work put forth in Berg's analysis (no. 35). The author finds that Berg exaggerated the importance of absolute, symphonic elements in the work. An English translation of Berg's analysis is appended.

903. **Pulido, Esperanza.** "Con la viuda de Alban Berg en Viena." *Heterofonia* 11/62 (1978): 50–52. In Spanish.

Report on a visit in 1954 to Helene Berg.

904. **"14 lettres inédites d'Alban Berg."** *Panorama de la musique et des instruments* 14 (1976): 52–58. In French.

905. **Rauchhaupt, Ursula von, editor.** *Schönberg, Berg, Webern: Die Streichquartette. Eine Dokumentation.* Program book accompanying the recording by the LaSalle Quartet, "Neue Wiener Schule: Schönberg, Berg, Webern." Hamburg: Deutsche Grammophon Gesellschaft (recording no. 2720029), 1971. Separate editions in German, English, and French.

German edition reprinted separately (*Schönberg, Berg, Webern: Die Streichquartette der Wiener Schule: Eine Dokumentation*), Munich: Ellermann, 1972. 185 p. ISBN 3770776283. ML1160.R3. Reviewed by Volker Scherliess, MF 28 (1975): 360–61; Jürg Stenzl, MEL 41 (1974): 24–25; Walter Szmolyan, ÖMZ 27 (1972): 367–68.

Revised edition (in German with English translation by Eugene Hartzell) with Deutsche Grammophon Gesellschaft recording 419994–2, 1987.

Documents concerning the complete string quartets of Schoenberg, Berg, and Webern. Concerning Berg's String Quartet, Op. 3, and Lyric Suite, there are letters from Berg to Schoenberg (1912–27, those of 1912 concerning Berg's arrangement of movements from Schoenberg's String Quartet no. 2), to Anton Webern (1910–28), to Helene Berg (1910–34), to Universal Edition (1924–35), to Carl Engel (1934, concerning a project for a new quartet), and to Gustav Havemann (1929). Also facsimile and text of Berg's "Neun Blätter zur Lyrischen Suite" (no. 66), facsimiles of musical sketches, and (1971 edition only) Berg's essay "Warum ist Schönbergs Musik so schwer verständlich?"

906. Redlich, Hans F. "Alban Berg and Posterity: An Interim Report." MR 25 (1964): 320–23. In English.

Laments the "amateurish" state of Berg research and "regressive tendencies" of Reich and others regarding Berg's unpublished music.

907. ———. "Alban Berg und die österreichische Landschaft." In *40 Jahre Steirischer Tonkünstlerbund Festschrift*, 57–64. Graz: Akademische Druck- und Verlagsanstalt, 1967. In German.

Surveys Berg's attachment to nature and especially to the landscape of Styria. Quotes from letters from Berg to Yella Hertzka (27 February 1935), to Ruzena Herlinger (17 November 1935), to Helene Berg, and to Hermann Watznauer (1904).

908. ———. *Alban Berg: Versuch einer Würdigung*. Vienna, Zurich, and London: Universal Edition, 1957. Reprinted Vienna: Universal Edition, 1987. 393 p. plus unpaginated facsimile of Berg's Twelve Variations (no. 2). Several excerpts from this book appeared separately as articles. ML410.B47 R37. In German. Reviewed by Thomas M. Langner, MF 15 (1962): 401–402; Heinrich Lindlar, *Musica* 12 (1958): 58–59; Gerhard Schumann, BMW 10 (1968): 220–24; H. H. Stuckenschmidt, MEL 25 (1958): 198–99; Ronald Tidmarsh, MR 19 (1958): 240–43 (also English version).

English translation (extensively abbreviated): *Alban Berg: The Man and His Music*. London: John Calder; New York: Abelard-Schuman, 1957. 316 p. ML410.B47 R35 (1957a for American edition). Reviewed by G.A., *Monthly Musical Record* 88 (1958): 110–11; Richard Franko Goldman, *Notes* 14 (1956–57): 574–75; Rudolf Klein, ÖMZ 12 (1957): 174; Ernst Krenek, MQ 43 (1957): 403–406; William Mann, ML 38 (1957): 191–92; Donald Mitchell, MT 98 (1957): 550–51; Erwin Stein, *Tempo* 44 (1957): 4–7 (also see the responses by Redlich and Stein to this article, *Tempo*, 45 [1957]: 35–36); H. H. Stuckenschmidt, MEL 25 (1958): 198–99.

A pioneering study of Berg's life and music, analytic in orientation, with greatest emphasis on the music beginning with *Wozzeck*. Contains a facsimile of Berg's Twelve Variations for piano (no. 2), Berg's lecture on *Wozzeck* (no. 65), and a catalog of works.

909. ———. "Bergs Briefe an seine Frau." ÖMZ 21 (1966): 338–42. In German.

Reviews the recently published *Briefe an seine Frau* (no. 67), finding Helene Berg's suppression of the version edited by Franz Willnauer to be unjustified and her own edition lacking. See her response, no. 694, and Willnauer's remarks (no. 1052).

910. ———. "Letters to the Editor: Debussy and Berg." MT 108 (1967): 428–29. In English.

In the form of a letter concerning an earlier article in the same journal, Redlich outlines Berg's attitudes toward the music of Debussy.

911. ———. "Significato del dramma musicale di Alban Berg." *Rassegna musicale* 32 (1962): 217–23. In Italian.

Brief description of the text and music of *Lulu* and *Wozzeck*.

912. ———. "Unveröffentliche Briefe Alban Bergs an Arnold Schönberg." In *Festschrift Friedrich Blume zum 70. Geburtstag*,

272–80. Edited by Anna Amalie Abert and Wilhelm Pfannkuch. Kassel: Bärenreiter, 1963. In German.

> Transcriptions of six letters from Berg to Schoenberg, 1928–33. All are included in *The Berg-Schoenberg Correspondence* (no. 704).

913. Reich, Willi. "Alban Berg." *Die Musik* 22 (1930): 347–53. In German.

> A general appraisal of Berg and his music through *Der Wein*, also containing the first edition of the two settings of Theodor Storm's "Schließe mir die Augen beide."

914. ———. "Alban Berg." In Louis Biancolli, *Opera Reader*, 39–41. New York: McGraw-Hill, 1953. In English.

> Brief sketch of Berg's life and works.

915. ———. "Alban Berg, 1885–1935." In *Große Österreicher: Neue österreichische Biographie ab 1815.* Volume 11: 205–12. Zurich, Leipzig, and Vienna: Amalthea-Verlag, 1957. In German.

> Biography of the composer.

916. ———. "Alban Berg als Apologet Arnold Schönbergs." SMZ 95 (1955): 475–77. In German.

> Discusses Berg's support for and tributes to Schoenberg. Part of the text of Berg's essay "Wiener Musikkritik" (no. 63) is first published.

917. ———. *Alban Berg: Bildnis im Wort. Selbstzeugnisse und Aussagen der Freunde mit Photos und Musikdokumente.* Sammlung Horizont. Zurich: Verlag 'Die Arche,' 1959. 88 p. In German. Reviewed by U.H., SMZ 101 (1961): 57–58.

> A documentary study of Berg containing letters from Berg to Hermann Watznauer, Frida Semler Seabury, Helene Berg, Anton Webern, Willi Reich, Adolf Loos; writings by Berg, and writings concerning Berg by Schoenberg, Karl Linke, and Hans Heinsheimer.

918. ————. *Alban Berg: Leben und Werk.* Zurich: Atlantis Verlag, 1963. 215 p. Reprinted Munich and Zurich: Piper, 1985. ML410.B47 R397. In German. Reviewed by Mark DeVoto, PNM 4 (spring-summer 1966): 150–60 (also dealing with the English version); Denis Dille, *Studia musicologica* 12 (1970): 349–51; Herbert Eimert MEL 31 (1964): 269–71; Christoph Richter, MB 17 (1985): 895; Gerhard Schumann, BMW 10 (1968): 220–24; Rudolf Stephan, NZM 126 (1965): 48–49; Konrad Vogelsang, MF 18 (1965): 100–101.

English translation: *Alban Berg.* Translated by Cornelius Cardew. London: Thames and Hudson; New York: Vienna House; New York: Harcourt, Brace & World, 1965. 239 pp. ISBN 0844300780. ML410.B47 R3973 1965. Reprint: New York: Da Capo Press, 1982. ISBN 030676136X. ML 410.B47 R3973 1981. Reviewed by Mark DeVoto, PNM 4 (1966): 150–56; Peter Dickinson, *Composer* 16 (1965): 33–34; Allen F. Edwards III, PNM 4 (1966): 157–60; Peter Evans, MT 106 (1965): 679–80; Ernst Krenek, MQ 43 (1957): 403–406; Peter J. Pirie, MR 29 (1968): 61–62; Hans F. Redlich, ML 46 (1965): 353–55; Joan Allen Smith, *Opera Quarterly* 3/3 (1985): 172–74.

> A completely rewritten version of no. 919, surveying Berg's life, analyzing major compositions, and seeking the "human aspect of Alban Berg and his high spirituality." Several essays by Berg are reproduced and, in general, Reich relies in documentary fashion upon the composer's own words about his music.

919. ————. *Alban Berg: Mit Bergs eigenen Schriften und Beiträgen von Theodor Wiesengrund-Adorno und Ernst Krenek.* Vienna, Leipzig, Zurich: Herbert Reichner Verlag, 1937. 208 p. ML410.B47 R4. In German. Reviewed by J. A. Westrup, ML 19 (1938): 93–94.

> Pioneering study of Berg that surveys the composer's life and works, to which eighteen of his essays are appended. The analytic parts were written by Theodor Adorno and Ernst Krenek.

920. ———. "An der Seite von Alban Berg." MEL 27 (1960): 36–42. In German.

Personal recollections of Berg as composer, teacher, and person. Facsimiles of three sketches for *Lulu*.

921. ———. "Anton Webern über Alban Berg." NZM 124 (1963): 143. In German.

Contains a letter from Webern to the editors of *De muziek* concerning Berg (see no. 1040).

922. ———. "Aus Alban Bergs Jugendzeit." MEL 22 (1955): 33–38. In German.

Survey of Berg's early years, relying on quotations from Berg's letters of 1902 to 1904 to Hermann Watznauer and letters of 1907 to Frida Semler.

923. ———. "Aus unbekannten Briefen von Alban Berg an Anton Webern." SMZ 93 (1953): 49–52. In German.

Excerpts from five letters from Berg to Webern (dated 19 August 1918, 26 July 1920, 14 August 1920, 23 July 1931, 6 May 1934) concerning Berg's work on *Wozzeck* and *Lulu*, editorial employment for the journal MBA, and displeasure with musical journalism.

924. ———. "Berg und Webern schreiben an Hermann Scherchen." MEL 33 (1966): 225–28. In German.

Transcription of the texts of letters from Berg to Scherchen dated 22 October 1931 (concerning a performance of *Wozzeck*) and 15 October 1935 (concerning the Violin Concerto).

925. ———. "Ein Briefwechsel über Moses und Aron." SMZ 97 (1957): 259–60. In German.

Texts of letters from Schoenberg to Berg (9 August 1930) and Berg to Schoenberg (13 August 1930).

926. ———. "Les dernières oeuvres d'Alban Berg." RM 12/issue 112 (1931): 148–54. Reprinted in RM 416–417 (1989): 109–15. In French.

General description of Berg's *Wozzeck*, Chamber Concerto, and *Der Wein*.

927. ———. "Erich Kleiber und Alban Berg." SMZ 98 (1958): 374–77. In German.

Transcribes four letters from Berg to Erich Kleiber (5 October 1923; 18 November 1923; 15 November 1934; undated, probably early 1935) regarding *Wozzeck* and *Lulu*.

928. ———. "Erinnerungen an Alban Berg." SMZ 91 (1951): 1–3. In German.

From a radio lecture of 1950, personal recollections regarding Reich's contacts with Berg.

929. ———. "Persönliches von Alban Berg: Fragmente einer Chronik nach seinen Briefen." ÖMZ 16 (1961): 276–83. In German.

Reviews the contents of 148 pieces of correspondence (1929–35) sent by Berg to Reich. The theory of "complementary" rows shared by Berg and Reich is mentioned (see Hall, no. 352) as is Berg's interest and participation in the journal *23*.

930. ———. "Scherzzeichnungen von Alban Berg." ÖMZ 15 (1960): 5–7. In German.

Reproduces seven pencil drawings made by Berg upon a visit from Reich in Trahütten in 1929.

931. ———. "Ein unbekannter Brief von Arnold Schönberg an Alban Berg." ÖMZ 14 (1959): 10. In German.

Transcribes Schoenberg's letter of 28 November 1930 concerning his chagrin over not being cited as Berg's teacher.

An English translation of the letter is given in *The Berg-Schoenberg Correspondence* (no. 704): 410.

932. ———. "Versuch einer Geschichte der Zwölftonmusik." In *Alte und neue Musik: Das Basler Kammerorchester (Kammerchor und Kammerorchester) unter Leitung von Paul Sacher,* 106–32. Zurich: Atlantis Verlag, 1952. In German.

A subsection of this article ("Anton Webern und Alban Berg als Zwölfton-Komponisten," 120–23) addresses Berg. The passacaglia from Act 1 of *Wozzeck* is cited as an early twelve-tone experiment, and the Chamber Concerto, Lyric Suite, *Lulu,* and Violin Concerto are also surveyed.

933. ———. "Vom Wiener 'Schönberg-Verein': Mit unbekannten Briefen von Alban Berg." SMZ 105 (1965): 340–43. In German.

Excerpts from letters by Berg to Erwin Stein (17 February 1919, 2 June 1921, 21 July 1921) concerning activities in the Verein für musikalische Privataufführungen and Stein's relations with Schoenberg. In the letter of 17 February, Berg encloses a copy of the first prospectus of the Verein (no. 33), saying that he is its author.

934. ———. "Von Büchner und Wedekind zu Alban Berg." In *Beiträge 1970/71,* 71–77. Edited by the Österreichische Gesellschaft für Musik. Kassel: Bärenreiter, 1971. In German.

General appraisal of Berg's knowledge and adaptation of Büchner's *Woyzeck* and Wedekind's Lulu plays for his two operas.

935. ———. "Von zu Haus und unterwegs: Briefe Alban Bergs an seine Braut und Gattin Helene." *Forum: Österreichische Monatsblätter für kulturelle Freiheit* 12 (1965): 396–98. In German.

Review of and excerpts from the forthcoming volume of Berg's letters to his wife.

936. ———. "Zur Biographie Alban Bergs." *23: Eine Wiener Musikzeitschrift* 31–33 (1937): 36–39. In German.

Reich outlines his plan for the 1937 biography of Berg, suggesting that Berg, toward the end of his life, supported Reich's idea for a biographic study. Begins with excerpts from Schoenberg's 1930 tribute to Berg (no. 963).

937. ———. "Zwei verschollene Porträts von Arnold Schönberg und Alban Berg." SMZ 103 (1963): 186–88. In German.

Reproduces a drawing of the youthful Berg made by Karl Kraus and one of Schoenberg by Emil Preetorius.

938. Restagno, Enzo. ". . . E tuttavia una carriera esemplare." In Monte and Segreto (no. 851): 13–23. In Italian.

Discussion of Berg's overt and secretive expressions of love and their relation to his musical works.

939. Rich, Maria F. "Alban Berg and the Vienna of His Time." *Opera Quarterly* 3/3 (1985): 39–67. In English.

General appraisal of Berg's life and cultural milieu.

940. Rihm, Wolfgang. "Als ob Berg Geburtstag hätte." *Oper 1985* (yearbook of the journal *Opernwelt*): 48. In German.

A brief reflection on the significance and achievement of Berg, who was an idol of Rihm's youth. *Wozzeck* is praised as the "opera of the century," although *Lulu* is found boring. The "fragmentary dramaturgy" of the former work is stronger than continuous dramaturgy. Berg's works present an "essentially undialectic growth form" which rules out the arbitrary.

941. Ringger, Rolf Urs. "Alban Berg." *Musica* 17 (1963): 158–61. In German.

General appraisal and appreciation.

942. ——. "Alban Berg nur ein 'Klassiker der Moderne'." *Musica* 28 (1974): 117–20. In German.

Sees Berg as a forerunner of hypermodernist tendencies in music, including multimedia tendencies.

943. Rode, Susanne. "Wagner und die Folgen: Zur Nietzsche-Wagner-Rezeption bei Alban Berg und Anton von Webern." In *"Der Fall Wagner": Ursprünge und Folgen von Nietzsches Wagner-Kritik*, 265–91. Edited by Thomas Steiert. Laaber: Laaber Verlag, 1991. In German.

Studies Berg's correspondence with his wife, Hermann Watznauer, Paul Hohenberg, and others regarding Berg's enthusiasm for Wagner and interest in Nietzsche. This interest led to Berg's disagreement with Karl Kraus, especially after 1905 when Kraus became critical of Wagner.

944. Rognoni, Luigi. Chapter 5 ("L'esperienza lirica di Alban Berg") and Chapter 6 ("Il teatro musicale di Alban Berg"). In Rognoni, *Espressionismo e dodecafonia*, 126–87. Turin: Einaudi, 1954. Revised and expanded as *La scuola musicale di Vienna: Espressionismo e dodecafonia*. Turin: Einaudi, 1966. In Italian. English translation (Chapter 5: "The Lyric Experience of Alban Berg" and Chapter 6: "The Music") in *The Second Vienna School: Expressionism and Dodecaphony*, translated by Robert W. Mann (London: John Calder, 1977).

Berg's music—more than that of Schoenberg or Webern—is said to be rooted in the late romantic style, which constitutes a "regression" and recovery of an earlier aesthetic. Rognoni also includes Italian translations of Berg's major writings.

945. Rogoff, Gordon. "Emotional Weather: Notes on Alban Berg's Theater." *Parnassus* 10/2 (1982): 103–14. In English.

General discussion of Berg's impulse to write opera and his decision to adopt the texts of *Wozzeck* and *Lulu*. Berg is described as "an instinctive actor-dramatist. . . . The secrets in the operas are the secrets of a life otherwise half-lived."

946. Romano, Jacobo. "Musicos de hoy: Alban Berg y su ópera *Lulu* a través de una entrevista con Héléne Berg." *Buenos Aires musical.* 20/334 (1965): 5–6. In Spanish.

Interview with Helene Berg in Vienna in February 1965 (primarily concerning *Lulu*).

947. Rubin, Marcel. "Alban Berg und die Zukunft der Schönberg-Schule." *Musik und Gesellschaft* 5 (1955): 384–86. In German.

Description of the twelve-tone idea in music and its dangers. Many references to the ideas of socialist writers including Hanns Eisler and György Lukács.

948. Rudolph, Eberhard. "Alban Berg: Zum 25. Todestag." *Musik und Gesellschaft* 10 (1960): 720–23. In German.

Brief appreciation stressing Berg's humanity and resistance to the materialism and imperialistic tendencies in the society of his day.

949. Rufer, Josef. "Alban Berg: Der Mensch und der Künstler." *Das Musikleben* 8 (1955): 205–209, 251–56. In German.

General reflections on Berg as man and artist, drawn from a lecture. Quotations are made from letters from Berg to Schoenberg, 1934–35, most of which are also excerpted in Rufer 1955 (no. 951), and from Berg to Helene Nahowski.

950. ———. "Berg—Webern—Krenek." In *Musiker über Musik: Aus Briefen, Tagebüchern und Aufzeichnungen*, 195–214. Darmstadt: Verlag Stichnote, 1956. Revised as *Bekenntnisse und Erkenntnisse: Komponisten über ihr Werk* (Frankfurt: Propyläen Verlag, 1979). In German.

Contains selected writings by Berg.

951. ———. "Dokumente einer Freundschaft." MEL 22 (1955): 42–46. In German.

Texts (including facsimiles) of letters between Schoenberg and Berg, 1934–35. Also see E. Randol Schoenberg (no. 967).

952. Ruppel, Karl Heinz. "Alban Bergs Vision vom Untergang." In Ruppel, *Die Musik in unserer Zeit: Ein Bilanz von zehn Jahren*, 58. Munich: Prestel, 1960. In German.

Critiques from the *Süddeutsche Zeitung* and other periodicals.

953. Ruyneman, Daniel. "Alban Berg." *Maandblad voor hedendaagsche muziek* 5 (1935–36). In Dutch. French translation, *La revue musicale belge* 7/4 (1936): 2–3.

Tribute to Berg and survey of his work following the composer's death. The article is notable for the author's confusion on many aspects of Berg's career (e.g., "He died shortly after the triumph of his *Lulu* Suite and the premiere of this opera in Prague").

954. Saathen, Friedrich. "Rede auf Alban Berg." NZM 122 (1961): 267–68. In German.

Points to the general conception of unity among the three figures of the Viennese School as myth. Finds Berg to be the most tragic of the three.

955. Samson, Jim. "Berg and Webern." In Samson, *Music in Transition: A Study of Tonal Expansion and Atonality, 1900–1920*, 115–28. London: Dent; New York: W. W. Norton & Company, 1977. In English.

Analysis of Berg's Seven Early Songs; Four Songs, Op. 2; and Piano Sonata, Op. 1; finding "thematically derived textures and independent harmonic elements" within a late romantic tonal context.

956. Sánchez Reyes, Julio. "Alban Berg (1885–1935)." In Sánchez Reyes, *Bach, Schütz, Händel y Berg: 1985, aniversario de cuatro músicos germanos*, 189–221. Colección Autores Nacionales, series 3, number 2. Bogota: Instituto Colombiano de Cultura, 1985. In Spanish.

Sketch of Berg's life and major works. The bibliography lists eight items.

957. Schaefer, Hansjürgen. "Expression und Konstruktivität: Zum 90. Geburtstag Alban Bergs." *Musik und Gesellschaft* 25 (1975): 98–99. In German.

Brief appreciation, finding in Berg's music "suffering, compassion, and an unmistakable protest against the barbarism of the decadent bourgeois world."

958. Scherliess, Volker. *Alban Berg mit Selbstzeugnissen und Bilddokumenten.* Dissertation, University of Hamburg, 1975. Rowohlts Monographien. Reinbek bei Hamburg: Rowohlt Taschenbuch Verlag, 1975. 158, ii p. ISBN 3499502259. ML410.B47 S3. In German. Reviewed by Willi Reich, SMZ 115 (1975): 329–30; Konrad Vogelsang, MF 28 (1975): 360.

New edition ca. 1981 contains minor alterations and additions. ISBN 3499502254. ML410.B47 S3 1981.

Italian translation: *Alban Berg.* Translated by Laura Dallapiccola. Florence: Discanto Edizioni, 1981. 128 p.

A concise study that is both biographical and analytic, primarily for the nonspecialist reader. The author relies on Berg's own writings, especially correspondence. Excerpts from the Berg-Webern correspondence are noteworthy.

959. Schibli, Sigfried. "Auf dem Weg in die künstlerische Vereinsamung: Vierundzwanzig unbekannte Briefe und Postkartentexte Alban Bergs." NZM 146/4 (1985): 9–21. In German.

Texts (with commentary) of twenty-four letters and cards from Berg to Bruno Vondenhoff from 1 October 1930 to 30 July 1935. Vondenhoff led an early performance of *Wozzeck* in Gera. Also see Mrs. Vondenhoff's reminiscences of the Bergs in Maul (no. 840).

960. Schmidt-Garre, Helmut. "Berg als Lehrer." MEL 22 (1955): 40–41. In German.

Recollections from a former student of Berg, emphasizing the importance that Berg attached to variations as a formal principle of composition.

961. Schneider, Frank. "Drei Wege zu Berg: Joachim Herz über seine Inszenierungen der Opern *Lulu* und *Wozzeck*, befragt von Frank Schneider." *Bulletin des Musikrates der DDR* 22 (1985): 26–32. In German, summary in English and French.

Interview with Joachim Herz concerning his stagings in Dresden and East Berlin of Berg's two operas.

962. ———. "Kleine Berg-Wanderung." In Berg (no. 68): 5–33. In German.

This article functions as an introduction to Schneider's edition of Berg's complete writings on music. It surveys his musical output and writings. "Berg's most general theme is the defense of a music that in a traditional sense holds to the highest aesthetic, technical, and moral standard. Given the social conditions of the period, this music deals directly with the conflict between social need and professional musical interest, mediating the conflict without capitulating to it."

963. Schoenberg, Arnold. [Untitled notice on Berg]. *Die Theaterwelt: Programmschrift der städtischen Theater in Düsseldorf* 5/10 (10 April 1930): 149. Reprinted (untitled) in Reich 1937 (no. 919): 204; *23: Eine Wiener Musikzeitschrift* 31–32 (1937): 36–37; Schoenberg, "Über Alban Berg," SMZ 99 (1959): 221; Reich 1959 (no. 917): 7. In German. English translation ("Alban Berg") in Arnold Schoenberg, *Style and Idea*, 475, edited by Leonard Stein, translated by Leo Black (London: Faber and Faber, 1975). French translation ("Alban Berg") in Schoenberg, *Le style et l'idée*, 373, translated by Christiane de Lisle (Paris: Buchet/Chastel, 1977).

964. ———. "Alban Berg." In Redlich (no. 908, English version): 328–29. Reprinted in Schoenberg, *Style and Idea*, 474, edited by Leonard Stein, translated by Leo Black (London: Faber and Faber, 1975). In English. German translation: in Redlich (no. 908): 245–46. French translation ("Alban Berg") in Schoenberg,

Le style et l'idée, 372, translated by Christiane de Lisle (Paris: Buchet/Chastel, 1977).

> Both of Schoenberg's notices on Berg are filled with praise for his musicianship and strength of character. No. 964 was written in English in 1949.

965. ———. *Ausgewählte Briefe*. Edited by Erwin Stein. Mainz: B. Schott's Söhne, 1958. In German.
English translation (revised under the direction of Donald Mitchell) (*Arnold Schoenberg Letters*), translated by Eithne Wilkins, Ernst Kaiser (London: Faber and Faber, 1964; New York: St. Martin's Press, 1965). Reprinted, Berkeley: University of California Press, 1987. Italian translation, Florence: La Nuova Italia, 1969. French translation, Paris: Christian Lattès, 1983. Spanish translation, Madrid: Turner, 1987.

> Contains excerpts from eight letters from Schoenberg to Berg (dated 20 July 1922, 10 April 1930, 5 August 1930, 8 August 1931, 20 January 1932, 23 September 1932, 16 October 1933, 4 May 1935).

966. ———. [Untitled essay on Berg]. In Schoenberg, "Über Alban Berg," SMZ 99 (1959): 221–23; excerpted in Reich 1963 (no. 918): 27–29; excerpted ("Würden die Zeiten normal sein. . .") in Reich, *Schönberg oder der konservative Revolutionär*, 310–14 (Vienna, Frankfurt, and Zurich: Verlag Fritz Molden, 1968). In German. English translations ("The Teacher's Testimonial," excerpt only) in Reich 1965 (no. 918): 28–30; ("Supposing Times Were Normal," excerpt only), Reich, *Schoenberg: A Critical Biography*, 245–48, translated by Leo Black (New York and Washington: Praeger Publishers, 1971). Spanish translation ("Testimonio del maestro") in *Pauta* 4/15 (1985): 7–8.

> Originally intended by Schoenberg for inclusion in Reich's 1937 study (no. 919), but not finished in time to be included.

967. Schoenberg, E. Randol, Juliane Brand, and Christopher Hailey. "Further Berg-Schoenberg Correspondence: The Twelve Lost Berg Letters." JASI 12 (1989): 129–74. In English, letters also in German.

Translation of sixteen pieces of correspondence passing between Schoenberg and Berg in 1934 and 1935, twelve published in their entirety for the first time. Also see Rufer no. 951.

968. Schollum, Robert. "Berg." In Schollum, *Die Wiener Schule. Schönberg—Berg—Webern: Entwicklung und Ergebnis*, 64–94. Vienna: Elisabeth Lafite, 1969. In German.

A general analytic appraisal of Berg's life and works.

969. Schönberger, Elmer, compiler. *Alban Berg, 1885–1935: Documenten en commentaren.*   Musica '85.   Amsterdam: Trouw/Kwartet, 1985. 80 p. ISBN 9070675315. ML410.B47 A775 1985. In Dutch.

Anthology of writings by and about Berg translated into Dutch from earlier publications.

970. Schöny, Heinz. "Die Vorfahren des Komponisten Alban Berg." *Genealogie: Deutsche Zeitschrift für Familienkunde* 8/15 (1966): 1–10. In German.

Provoked by certain failings that he perceived in Berg's family tree as constructed by Konrad Vogelsang in his 1959 study of Berg (no. 1029), the author presents a genealogy extending back ten generations. A Postscript by Heinz F. Friederichs adds information from the study by Dieter Kerner (no. 811).

971. Schuh, Willi. "Alban Berg." In *Zeitgenössische Musik: Ausgewählte Kritiken*, 65–84.   Kritiken und Essays, volume 2. Zurich: Atlantis Verlag, 1947. In German.

Reprint of several of Schuh's reviews of works by Berg for the *Neue Zürcher Zeitung*, 1931–39.   *Wozzeck*, the *Lulu* Symphony, and the Violin Concerto are addressed, and the account of Berg's revisions in Wedekind's Lulu plays is especially detailed.

972. Schultz, Ingo. "'. . . ich bin schon lange ein begeisterter Verehrer Ihres *Wozzeck*': Viktor Ullmann und Alban Berg." *Musiktheorie* 7 (1992): 113–28. In German.

Information about Ullmann and his letter exchange with Berg, beginning in 1925 at the time when Ullmann heard *Wozzeck* performed in Prague. Letters from 1925 until 1933, primarily from Ullmann to Berg, are quoted.

973. Schultz, Klaus. "Alban Berg. Ein Aufführungsverzeichnis eigener Werk." MK 9 (1979): 91–95. In German.

Facsimile and transcription of two manuscript sheets in Berg's hand, probably prepared in 1931, listing performances of his music during the first half of that year.

974. Schwarz, Richard. "Wiener Komponisten: Webern und Berg." MBA 6 (1924): 381. In German.

A brief tribute to Webern and Berg, both known as students of Schoenberg, but both having distinctive musical voices.

975. Schweizer, Klaus. *Die Sonatensatzform im Schaffen Alban Bergs.* Dissertation, University of Freiburg im Breisgau, 1968. Freiburger Schriften zur Musikwissenschaft, vol. 1. Stuttgart: Musikwissenschaftliche Verlags-Gesellschaft, 1970. 229 p. ML410.B47 S4. In German. Reviewed by Bruce Archibald, *Notes* 28 (1971–72): 55–56; Mosco Carner, ML 52 (1971): 82–85; Wolfgang Dömling, MF 25 (1972): 569–70; Gérard Gubisch, *Revue de musicologie,* 56 (1970): 250–53; Willi Reich, *Musica* 24 (1970): 494 and MEL 38 (1971): 146; Wolfgang Martin Stroh, NZM 132 (1971): 113–14.

A study of Berg's adaptation of the principle of sonata form, primarily in his Piano Sonata, Op. 1; String Quartet, Op. 3; Lyric Suite; Chamber Concerto; *Wozzeck* (Act 2, scene 1); and *Lulu* (Act 1, scenes 2–3). The approach to sonata form in *Lulu* results from a different development from that in *Wozzeck* and earlier works.

976. Seabury, Frida Semler. "1903 and 1904." BSN 1 (1968): 3–4. In English.

Translation of Mrs. Seabury's homespun, informative memoirs of her visits in 1903 and 1904 to the Berg family at the Berghof. The original document is at the Library of Congress.

977. See, Max. "Der tragische Opernschluss: Eine dramaturgische Studie." NZM 129 (1968): 431–40, 485–93, 537–45. In German.

Comparison of tragic conclusions in operas from Monteverdi to Berg's *Wozzeck* and *Lulu*.

978. Shirley, Wayne D. "Berg Documents in the Library of Congress." BSN 1 (1968): 10–11. In English.

List of letters, musical manuscripts, and miscellaneous documents.

979. Shoaf, R. Wayne. "Variant Printings of the Berg Guides." JASI 16 (1993): 323–31. In English.

Information on the publication history of Berg's guides to Schoenberg's *Gurrelieder*, *Pelleas und Melisande*, and Chamber Symphony (see nos. 29, 32, and 35).

980. Shostakovich, Dmitri. [Passim, especially pp. 42–45]. In Shostakovich, *Testimony: The Memoirs of Dmitri Shostakovich*. Edited by Solomon Volkov. Translated by Antonia W. Bouis. New York: Harper & Row, 1979. In English.

"Mahler and Berg are my favorite composers," Shostakovich reportedly says, although he rejects any significant influence of *Wozzeck* upon his *Katerina Izmailova* or *The Nose*. The genuineness of the memoirs has been questioned.

981. Sinopoli, Giuseppe. "Von Darmstadt nach Wien." In *Zwischen den Kulturen: Neue Aspekte der musikalischen Ästhetik I*, 235–39. Edited by Hans Werner Henze. Frankfurt: S. Fischer, 1979. In German.

A wide-ranging polemic that touches briefly on Berg's relevance to the Darmstadt School of the 1950s. Because of his expressivity "Berg was, with suicidal foolishness, put in parentheses, and what was necessary for the interpretation of his music was reduced to 'good taste'."

982. Smith, Joan Allen. "Alban Berg and Soma Morgenstern: A Literary Exchange." In *Studies in the Schoenbergian Movement in Vienna and the United States: Essays in Honor of Marcel Dick,* 33–56. Edited by Anne Trenkamp and John G. Suess. Studies in the History and Interpretation of Music, volume 26. Lewiston, N.Y.: Edwin Mellen Press, 1990. In English.

Commentary and extensive quotations from the correspondence of 1925 to 1935 between Berg and Morgenstern. Among many topics discussed is Berg's search for the text of his second opera and Morgenstern's subsequent contributions to the revisions of Wedekind's plays as an opera libretto.

983. ——. "The Berg-Hohenberg Correspondence." ABS 2 (1981): 189–97. In English, synopsis and quotations from letters in German.

Report on the contents of twenty-nine letters and eighty-six postcards sent by Berg to his friend Paul Hohenberg from 1901 to 1924 (copies of the letters are located at the New York Public Library for the Performing Arts). The early letters talk of Berg's difficulties in school and of his intellectual interests. Later letters reveal Berg's ambivalence toward the writings of Karl Kraus. Also see Rode (no. 943).

984. ——. "Berg's Character Remembered." In *The Berg Companion* (no. 803): 13–32. In English.

Discussion of Berg's character based on an unpublished memoir of Soma Morgenstern, who knew the composer from 1924 to 1935. This memoir "constitutes the major insight we have into Berg's personal life." Among the topics mentioned are Berg's personal habits, religious attitudes, literary tastes, relations with Schoenberg and other musicians, and aspects of his marriage. There are also comparisons of Morgenstern's recollections with other similar memoirs, including those of Hermann Watznauer and Erich Alban Berg (see no. 693).

985. ———. *Schoenberg and His Circle: A Viennese Portrait*. New York: Schirmer Books; London: Collier Macmillan Publications, 1986. xiv, 319 p. ISBN 0028726200. ML410.S283S57 1986. In English.

An oral history conducted primarily from 1972 to 1974 with figures from Schoenberg's circle. References to Berg are found throughout, primarily of a biographical nature. Appendices deal with aspects of the Verein für musikalische Privataufführungen, including Berg's statement of objectives (no. 33, from Nicolas Slonimsky).

986. **Smith, Joan Allen, and Mark DeVoto.** "Berg's Published Correspondence: An Index." BSN 3 (1975): 11–19. In English.

A detailed index of published correspondence by Berg; includes excerpts in addition to complete letters. Organized by addressee.

987. **Stadlen, Peter.** "Berg's Cryptography." ABS 2 (1981): 171–80. In English.

Survey of compositional applications of numerical symbolism and musical ciphers, concluding that earlier composers, like Berg, probably intended such cryptic references to be inaudible.

988. **Stefan, Paul.** "Festspruch auf Alban Berg: Zum 50. Geburtstag infolge Abwesenheit des Festredners verlesen bei Feier des Wiener Frauenklub." MBA 17 (1935): 8–10. In German. Reprinted (revised and retitled "Alban Berg") in *Europäische Rundschau* 22/special issue "Musikfest Wien" (1948): 1016.

Talk for the celebration of Berg's fiftieth birthday, praising the composer's high ideals.

989. Stein, Erwin. "Alban Berg and Anton von Webern." *The Chesterian* 26 (October 1922): 33–36. Reprinted in Jarman, *Alban Berg: "Wozzeck"* (no. 155): 132–35. In English. German translation ("Alban Berg—Anton von Webern") MBA 5 (1923): 13–16. In German.

Description of Berg's Opp. 1–7, emphasizing the composer's intense motivic work and the form of *Wozzeck*.

990. ———. "Berg and Schoenberg." *Tempo* 44 (1957): 4–7. In English.

An unsympathetic commentary on Redlich's *Alban Berg* (no. 908).

991. Steiner, Ena. "In Memoriam: Alban Berg and Anton Webern." *Canadian Association of University Schools of Music Journal* 5/2 (1975): 76–92. In English, summary in French.

Survey of the personal relations between the two composers, based on their own statements.

992. Steinhard, Erich. "In memoriam Alban Berg." *Der Auftakt* 16 (1936): 4–6. In German.

An appreciation of the composer, recently deceased, pointing to *Wozzeck* as the central work in his oeuvre.

993. Stenzl, Jürg. "Alban Berg und Marie Scheuchl." ÖMZ 40 (1985): 22–30. In German.

Transcription of an undated letter from Berg to Marie Scheuchl, expressing guilt over the aftermath of their affair and an attempt to reconcile the contents of the letter with what little is known of this episode in the composer's emotional life.

994. Stephan, Rudolf. "Alban Berg." In *Die Wiener Schule heute*, 45–62. Edited by Carl Dahlhaus. Veröffentlichungen des Instituts für Neue Musik und Musikerziehung Darmstadt, volume 24. Mainz: Schott, 1983. Reprinted in Stephan, *Vom musikalischen Denken: Gesammelte Vorträge*, 186–98, edited by

Rainer Damm and Andreas Traub (Mainz: Schott, 1985). In German.

Survey of the compositional and structural elements in Berg's atonal music, especially in the Four Songs, Op. 2; Orchestral Songs, Op. 4; and Four Pieces, Op. 5. The central observation concerns the presence of unified structures (shapes and complexes). These are shared also with the twelve-tone works.

995. ——. S. v. "Alban Berg." *Pipers Encyclopädie des Musiktheaters.* Edited by Carl Dahlhaus, Sieghart Döhring. Volume 1 (1986): 279–87. In German.

Studies *Wozzeck* and *Lulu,* outlining their historical background, performance history, structure, and bibliography.

996. ——. "Alban Berg (1885–1935)." ÖMZ 40 (1985): 3–11. In German.

A general survey of Berg's life and music.

997. ——. "Alban Berg als Schüler Arnold Schönbergs: Auf den Weg zur Sonate Op. 1." In *Bericht über den 2. Kongreß der Internationalen Schönberg-Gesellschaft: Die Wiener Schule in der Musikgeschichte des 20. Jahrhunderts,* 22–30. Edited by Rudolf Stephan and Sigrid Wiesmann. Vienna: Verlag Elisabeth Lafite, 1986. In German.

Survey of Berg's study materials and early student compositions prepared under Schoenberg's tutelage.

998. ——. "Alban Berg in den zwanziger Jahren." In *Alte Musik als ästhetische Gegenwart: Bericht über den Internationalen musikwissenschaftlichen Kongreß, Stuttgart, 1985,* volume 1: 1–9. Edited by Dietrich Berke and Dorothee Hanemann. Kassel: Bärenreiter, 1987. In German.

Survey of the blossoming of Berg's career in the 1920s, the development of his style, and his merging of modernistic tendencies in compositions of his own day with earlier musical idioms.

999. ———. "Alban Berg: Festansprache zur Eröffnung der Alban-Berg-Ausstellung im Prunksaal der Österreichischen Nationalbibliothek, Wien, am 22. Mai 1985." *Biblos: Österreichische Zeitschrift für Buch- und Bibliothekswesen, Dokumentation, Bibliographie und Bibliophilie* 34 (1985): 206–13. Reprinted in Stephan, *Musiker der Moderne: Porträts und Skizzen,* edited by Albrecht Riethmüller (Laaber: Laaber-Verlag, forthcoming ca. 1996). In German.

> Speech delivered in Vienna in 1985 at the opening of the Berg Exhibit at the Austrian National Library. (Also see the catalog of the exhibit, no. 1060.) The speech emphasizes Berg's accomplishments that place him among the great masters of modern music. These include Berg's ability to synthesize several opposing musical or expressive styles.

1000. ———. *Alban Bergs Bedeutung für die Neue Musik.* Vienna: Österreichische Gesellschaft für Musik, 1985. 16 p. In German.

> A general depiction of Berg's musical style, finding a merger of high-level architectonic structures and a voice leading that is often traditional and fluid. The author reports that this brochure is available only at the Österreichische Gesellschaft für Musik and has never been generally distributed.

1001. ———. "Berg und Schönberg." In *Die Sprache der Musik: Festschrift Klaus Wolfgang Niemöller zum 60. Geburtstag,* 543–59. Kölner Beiträge zur Musikforschung, volume 165. Edited by Jobst Peter Fricke. Regensburg: Gustav Bosse Verlag, 1989. In German.

> Surveys the historical background to and the artistic relationship between Berg and Schoenberg, emphasizing both similarities and differences in musical conceptions.

1002. ———. "Drei Autographe von Alban Berg." In *Komponisten des 20. Jahrhunderts in der Paul Sacher Stiftung,* 149–56. Basel: Paul Sacher Stiftung, 1986. In German.

Description of three Berg autograph manuscripts in the Sacher Stiftung in Basel: the 1908 song "Schilflied" (from the Seven Early Songs), a piano four-hands arrangement of the Prelude from the Orchestral Pieces, Op. 6, and Berg's analytic examples concerning *Lulu* presented ca. 1934 to Willi Reich (also discussed in Reich, no. 434). The last of these is shown in facsimile.

1003. ———. "Schönberg—Berg—Webern—Klassiker?" BMW 32 (1990): 7–10. In German.

Traditional values in the Second Viennese School and the relevance of Berg and Webern to contemporary composers.

1004. ———. "Von der Planung zum musikalischen Kunstwerk: Über Alban Bergs Komponieren." In *Vom Einfall zum Kunstwerk: Der Kompositionsprozeß in der Musik des 20. Jahrhunderts*, 253–72. Edited by Hermann Danuser, Günter Katzenberger. Publikationen der Hochschule für Musik und Theater Hannover, volume 4. Laaber: Laaber-Verlag, 1993. In German.

Extensive study of Berg's compositional practices, using sketches to trace the methods of composing from the earliest written ideas progressively through a process of "filling out." Examples are drawn primarily from the sketches for the Chamber Concerto and *Lulu*. Based on a lecture of 1988.

1005. ———. "Zur Würdigung Alban Bergs." ÖMZ 35 (1980): 204–208. In German.

Evaluation of the organic element in Berg's music and the sources of his distinctive style.

1006. **Straus, Joseph N.** *Remaking the Past: Musical Modernism and the Influence of the Tonal Tradition.* Cambridge, Mass., London: Harvard University Press, 1990. ix, 207 p. ISBN 0674759907. ML 197.S767 1990. In English.

Passing analytic references to the Lyric Suite (pp. 144–49), Violin Concerto (78–82, 139–44), and other works by Berg.

1007. Stravinsky, Igor, and Robert Craft. "Schoenberg, Berg, Webern." In Stravinsky and Craft, *Conversations with Igor Stravinsky*, 76–82. Garden City, NY: Doubleday, 1959. In English.

Personal and artistic reflections by Stravinsky, who finds Berg to be a "gifted constructor in form. . . . The essence of his work is thematic structure."

1008. Stroh, Wolfgang Martin. "Alban Berg's 'Constructive Rhythm'." PNM 7 (1968): 18–31. In English. German translation ("Alban Bergs 'konstruktive Rhythmen'," in *Die Wiener Schule*, 207–24, edited by Rudolf Stephan (Darmstadt: Wissenschaftliche Buchgesellschaft, 1989). In German.

Deals with rhythmic motives throughout Berg's oeuvre and the tendency for prominent rhythmic figures to take on symbolic meaning.

1009. Stuckenschmidt, H[ans] H[einz]. "Alban Berg." In Stuckenschmidt, *Schöpfer der neuen Musik: Portraits und Studien*, 180–91. Frankfurt: Suhrkamp Verlag, 1958. In German.

General account of Berg's life and works.

1010. ———. "Eine fragwürdige Berg-Ehrung." MEL 22 (1955): 109–110. In German.

Review of Berlin observances of Berg's seventieth birthday.

1011. ———. "Gebändigte Emotion: Eine Analyse anläßlich des 80. Geburtstags von Alban Berg." *Forum: Österreichische Monatsblätter für kulturelle Freiheit*, 12 (1965): 88–91. Reprint (abbreviated) in *Opernwelt* 12/1 (1971): 20–21. In German.

Taking his departure from a conception of the music of *Wozzeck* as expressionistic, the author analyzes its harmonic and dramaturgical aspects and finds precursors to its harmonic language in the Four Songs, Op. 2.

1012. ———. "Der Komponist Alban Berg und sein Lebenswerk für die moderne Musik." *Universitas: Zeitschrift für Wissenschaft, Kunst und Literatur* 25 (1970): 1129–34. In German.

General appraisal of Berg and his music for the nonspecialist, well-informed reader.

1013. Sulzer, Peter. "Alban Berg." In Sulzer, *Zehn Komponisten um Werner Reinhart: Ein Ausschnitt aus dem Wirkungskreis des Musikkollegiums Winterthur, 1920–1950,* volume 3: 151–65. Winterthur: Stadtbibliothek; Zurich: Atlantis Musikbuch-Verlag, 1983. In German.

Texts of eleven letters from Berg to Werner Reinhart (1926–35), plus other correspondence from other writers concerning Berg.

1014. ———. "Schönberg—Webern—Berg—Krenek." In Sulzer, *Zehn Komponisten um Werner Reinhart: Ein Ausschnitt aus dem Wirkungskreis des Musikkollegiums Winterthur, 1920–1950,* volume 1: 95–220. Winterthur: Stadtbibliothek, 1979. In German.

Lengthy study of the personal and artistic relations of the four composers with Werner Reinhart.

1015. Suppan, Wolfgang. "Alban Berg in der Steiermark: Mit allgemeinen Bemerkungen zur Berg-Rezeption." *Mitteilungen des Steirischen Tonkünstlerbundes* 90 (1986): 245–51. In German.

Text of a lecture in May 1985 for the Kulturkreis Deutschlandsberg. The author reports on Berg's connections with Styria and interprets his music essentially as a "code of emotional states" rather than as an abstract musical structure.

1016. Sutcliffe, James Helme. "Frau Berg." *Opera News* 33/24 (1968–69): 12–13. In English.

An interview by the author with Helene Berg, including homespun recollections.

1017. Szmolyan, Walter. "Alban Bergs Tätigkeit im 'Schönberg-Verein'." ABS 2 (1981): 224–31. In German.

Berg was probably the central figure, both as a musical director and administrator, in Schoenberg's Verein für musikalische Privataufführungen. His diverse activities are outlined, based on information from documents preserved in the Berg Collection of the Austrian National Library and from materials in Schoenberg's legacy.

1018. ——. "Helene Bergs Vermächtnis." ÖMZ 32 (1977): 169–79. In German.

Excerpts from Helene Berg's will and its codicils, especially as regards the founding of the Alban Berg-Stiftung, her wishes that Act 3 of *Lulu* never be completed, performed, or further studied, and the disposition of Berg's manuscripts and correspondence. Opinions by leading musicians concerning the completion of *Lulu* are cited.

1019. ——. "Schönberg und Berg als Lehrer." ÖMZ 29 (1974): 291–97. In German.

Concerns Gottfried Kassowitz's studies with Schoenberg and Berg, quoting from letters by both to Kassowitz. Those from Berg are dated 16 March 1920 and 4 January 1923.

1020. ——. "Schönbergs Wiener Skandalkonzert." ÖMZ 31 (1976): 293–304. In German.

The history of the concert in Vienna of works by Schoenberg and his students (31 March 1913), when two of Berg's songs from Op. 4 were first heard. Based on press reports of the concert, the author concludes that songs nos. 2 and 3 were the ones performed.

1021. Tarakanov, Mikhail Evgen'evich. *Muzykal'nyi teatr Al'bana Berga* [The Musical Theater of Alban Berg]. Moscow: Sovetsky Kompozitor, 1976. 558 p. ML410.B47 T4. In Russian.

Detailed musical and historical study of *Wozzeck* and *Lulu* covering the plays by Büchner and Wedekind, Berg's vocal idiom, and his treatment of themes, harmony, and form. A bibliography lists twenty-eight items.

1022. Thomas, Gavin. "An Affair with Numbers." MT 133 (1992): 137. In English.

Primarily a review of Berg performances in London.

1023. Thompson, Oscar. "Alban Berg, Composer of *Wozzeck,* Is Dead." *Musical America* 56/1 (1936): 8, 17. In English.

An obituary that is decidedly cool toward Berg's importance in the history of music. Except for *Wozzeck,* Berg is deemed "a lesser Schönberg."

1024. Tortora, Daniela. "Alban Berg: Un'eredità irrisolta." In Monte and Segreto (no. 851): 543–58. In Italian.

History and assessment of attitudes toward Berg among modernist composers following World War II.

1025. Ullmann, Viktor. "Alban Berg." MBA 12 (1930): 50–51. In German.

Great praise for Berg and his music, especially in his mastery of form. Divides Berg's works into three periods: those through Op. 3, Opp. 5–6, and a final "period of mastery" beginning with *Wozzeck.*

1026. "Unbekannte Briefe von Reger, Pfitzner und Alban Berg." *Musik und Gesellschaft* 7 (1957): 340–43. In German.

Reproduces a letter from Berg to Gustav Havemann (14 October 1929) concerning a forthcoming performance of Berg's String Quartet in Vienna.

1027. "Unveröffentliche Briefe an Alfredo Casella." MEL 34 (1967): 45–51. In German.

Transcription and facsimile of a letter (17 October 1930) from Berg to Casella, responding to Casella's praise for *Wozzeck.*

1028. Vogel, Johann Peter. "Das Lied 'Nachts' von Hans Pfitzner: Ein Nachwort zur Kritik Alban Bergs an der *Neuen Ästhetik.*" In *Symposium Hans Pfitzner Berlin 1981,* 217–37. Edited by Wolfgang Osthoff. Veröffentlichungen des Hans Pfitzner-Gesellschaft, volume 3. Tutzing: Hans Schneider, 1984. In German.

Analysis of Pfitzner's song "Nachts," Op. 26, no. 2, to which Berg referred in his essay on Pfitzner (no. 34).

1029. Vogelsang, Konrad. *Alban Berg: Leben und Werk.* Hesses Kleine Bücherei, volume 5. Berlin-Halensee: Max Hesses Verlag, 1959. 88 p., table. ML410.B47 V6. In German. Reviewed by Willi Reich, MEL 29 (1962): 152.

Concise study of Berg's life and works, the latter dealing only with music beginning with the Orchestral Pieces, Op. 6. Abbreviated work list, discography, and bibliography.

1030. Vogt, Harry. "Alban Berg auf Schallplatten." ÖMZ 40 (1985): 69–71. In German.

Discography.

1031. Vojtěch, Ivan. "Arnold Schoenberg, Anton Webern, Alban Berg: Unbekannte Briefe an Erwin Schulhoff." *Miscellanea musicologica* (Prague) 15 (1965): 31–83. In German.

Transcribes the contents of twenty-one letters from Berg to Schulhoff (1919–26) plus a letter from Berg to V. V. Šak (1 November 1920). These mainly concern performances by the Prague branch of the Verein für musikalische Privataufführungen, but they touch on other issues as well. One of the letters, revealing Berg's feelings of dejection following the end of World War I, is translated by DeVoto (no. 730).

1032. Volkov, Solomon. "Alban Berg über die Kunst für das Proletariat: Ein unbekannter Brief Bergs an Boris Asaf'ev." SMZ 118 (1978): 30–31. In German.

Transcription of and commentary on a letter from Berg to Asaf'ev (5 August 1929) in which Berg makes light of being called a "proletariat" composer.

1033. ——. "Ein unbekannter Brief Alban Bergs." ÖMZ 34 (1979): 559–61. In German.

Transcribes and discusses a letter from Berg (9 August 1927) to the Russian opera producer Josef Lapitzky concerning a prospective performance of *Wozzeck* in Moscow and touching on Berg's social views. Berg enclosed a copy of an article on *Wozzeck* by Alexander Landau (no. 179), which he endorses as expressing his own views.

1034. Wagner, Manfred. "Alban Berg und die *Musikblätter des Anbruch.*" ABS 2 (1981): 216–23. In German.

A survey of writings by and about Berg in MBA.

1035. Walden, William Glenn. "Historical Tradition in the Pre-Serial Atonal Music of Alban Berg." Dissertation, Louisiana State University, 1988. UMI order no. 8819989. 271 p. In English.

Study of compositional techniques and traditional forms emphasizing Berg's Opp. 3–6 and Chamber Concerto.

1036. Walker, Arthur D. "An Alban Berg Discography." BSN 3 (1975): 8–10. In English.

List of commercial recordings subdivided by composition.

1037. Weber, Frieder R. "Der literarische Gehalt von Bergs Musikdramatik." MEL 35 (1968): 144–49. In German.

Finds the treatment of societal, psychological, and erotic issues in *Wozzeck* and *Lulu* to be realistic at a time when traditional opera was still concerned with illusion, symbolism, or aestheticism. Berg's innovative choice of text in these operas reflects his own personal engagement with these realistic concerns.

1038. Weber, J. F. *Alban Berg.* Discography Series, no. 14. Utica: Weber, 1975. ML156.5.B45 W4. In English. Reviewed by Donald McCormick, *Notes* 36 (1979–80): 889–92.

Discography of commerical recordings.

1039. [Webern, Anton]. "Aus dem Briefwechsel." *Die Reihe: Information über serielle Musik* 2 ("Anton Webern") (1955): 20–28. In German. English translation ("From the Correspondence"), *Die Reihe* 2 (1958): 13–21.

Letters to and from Webern. The texts of letters from Webern to Berg (21 December 1911, 1 August 1919) and from Berg to Webern (12 October 1925, 8 December 1927, 19 August 1932) are given.

1040. ——. [Letter to the Editor]. *De muziek* 5 (1930–31): 22. Reprinted in Reich (no. 921). In German.

Webern was invited to write on Berg for a special issue of *De muziek* in 1930. In this letter to the editor, Paul F. Sanders, dated 17 September 1930, he declines, saying only that Berg's *Wozzeck*, like all of Berg's music, springs from "the most sacred inspiration, for all eternity."

1041. Weigl, Hans. "Ein Brief von Karl Kraus an Smaragda Berg." *Kraus-Hefte* 14 (1980): 1–2. In German.

The author purchased documents from the estate of Smaragda Berg from a Viennese antiquarian dealer. These included a photograph of Kraus, a drawing by Kraus of Smaragda, and a letter to her from Kraus in which he declines to use a contribution that she had submitted to *Die Fackel* having to do with the failings of the Viennese press.

1042. Weimann, Margareta. "Alban Bergs Handschrift." MEL 27 (1961): 372–76. In German.

Analysis of Berg's personality through his handwriting. Letters and cards to Paul Königer (24 July 1912, another undated) and to Ruzena Herlinger (June 1930) plus notes from the early 1930s are analyzed. The writing from 1912 shows "strongly neurotic characteristics."

1043. Wellesz, Egon. "Alban Berg." *Monthly Musical Record* 66 (issue no. 774) (1936): 27–28. In English.

Memorial tribute to Berg from a personal acquaintance, surveying the composer's final illness and his late works. Wellesz expresses the hope that *Lulu* will soon be completed and performed.

1044. Werle, Fritz. "Zwei Künstlerhoroskope." MBA 9 (1927): 163–69. In German.

Constructs a horoscope for Berg and for Schoenberg. For Berg one must often turn to Jupiter for answers. The author finds much of Berg's musical style reflected in his stars.

1045. Westergaard Madsen, Jens. "Rytmiske fænomener i Alban Bergs produktion." *Musik & forskning* 3 (1977): 38–66. In Danish, summary in English.

Survey of innovative rhythmic procedures and styles in the music of Berg, including polymeter, the concept of *Hauptrhythmus*, rhythms governed by numbers, and palindromic rhythms.

1046. Whittall, Arnold. Chapter 7 ("Alban Berg"). In Whittall, *Music since the First World War*, 143–56. London: J. M. Dent, 1977. In English.

Analytic observations on Berg's music from *Wozzeck* to *Lulu*.

1047. ———. "The Theorist's Sense of History: Concepts of Contemporaneity in Composition and Analysis." RMA 112 (1987): 1–20. In English.

Reflection upon the analysis of modern music possessing retrospective tendencies. Berg's Violin Concerto is one work discussed.

1048. Wildgans, Friedrich. "Alban Berg zum 75. Geburtstag." ÖMZ 15 (1960): 2–5. In German.

A brief tribute.

1049. Wilkey, Jay Weldon. "Certain Aspects of Form in the Vocal Music of Alban Berg." Dissertation, Indiana University,

1965. UMI order no. 6510911. 2 volumes. 146, 134 p. In English. Reviewed by Fred Hauptman, *Current Musicology* 12 (1971): 113–15.

General study of Berg's life, music, milieu, serial practices, and ways of relating words and music.

1050. Willnauer, Franz. "Alban Berg in seinen Briefen." ÖMZ 20 (1965): 110–11. In German.

Transcription of Berg's letter to his wife (3 August 1923), extracted from the forthcoming no. 67.

1051. ——. "Alban Berg über Musik und Musiker." NMZ 127 (1966): 128–35. In German.

A survey of musical topics and insights contained in the 1965 volume of Berg's letters to his wife (no. 67).

1052. ——. "Forum des Lesers: Weggebliebene Anmerkungen zu Alban Berg." *Forum: Österreichische Monatsblätter für kulturelle Freiheit* 12 (1965): 446–47. In German.

Willnauer states his case as to his editorial work on Berg's *Letters to His Wife* and Helene Berg's last-minute rejection of his edition.

1053. "Worte aus dem Ausland über Alban Berg." MBA 18 (1936): 9–11. In German.

Excerpts from obituaries by Ernest Ansermet, Henry Prunières, Aloys Mooser, Guido Gatti, and Erich Steinhard.

1054. Zauner, Waltraud. "'Meine tiefe und aufrichtige Verehrung für Ihre Person und Ihr Werk': Briefe an Julius Bittner." ÖMZ 44 (1989): 70–80. In German.

Transcription and facsimile of a letter from Berg to Bittner (9 April 1924) containing Berg's birthday greetings and praise.

1055. Zillig, Winfried. "Alban Berg und die Wiener Schule." In Zillig, *Variationen über neue Musik*, 140–48. Munich: Nymphenburger Verlagshandlung, 1959. In German.

> Surveys Berg's life and music, mainly emphasizing *Wozzeck*.

Exhibition Catalogs

1056. Festival Berg. *La musica di Alban Berg: Mostra realizzata dal Centro di Drammaturgia del Théâtre National Opéra de Paris.* Milan: Edizione del Teatro alla Scala, 1979. 234, 38 p. In Italian.

1057. Hell, Helmut, Sigrid von Moisy, and Barbara Wolff, compilers. *Quellen zur Musikgeschichte des 20. Jahrhunderts: Alban Berg und die zweite Wiener Schule. Musiker im amerikanischen Exil. Bavarica.* Catalog of an exhibition sponsored jointly by the Bayerische Staatsbibliothek (Munich) and the Houghton Library, Harvard University (Cambridge, Mass.). Ausstellungskatalog der Bayerischen Staatsbibliothek, volume 45. Cambridge: Harvard University; Munich: Bayerische Staatsbibliothek, 1988. 138 p. In English and German. Reviewed by Dave Headlam, *Notes* 47 (1990–91): 1139–42.

> The exhibition featured items concerning Berg primarily from the legacy of Rudolf Kolisch (at Harvard University) and from the former archive of Hans Moldenhauer (acquired in part by the Bayerische Staatsbibliothek).

1058. Hilmar, Ernst, compiler. *Schönberg, Webern, Berg.* Vienna: Bundesministerium für auswärtige Angelegenheiten, 1985. 8 p. In German.

1059. Hilmar, Rosemary, editor. *Alban Berg (1885–1935): Klassiker der Musik des 20. Jahrhunderts.* Vienna: Bundespressedienst, 1984. 61 p. ML410.B47 H48 1984. In German.

English translation: *Alban Berg (1885–1935). Classic Composers of Twentieth Century Music.* Vienna: Austrian National Library, 1984. 60 p. Also translated into French and Spanish.

1060. Hilmar, Rosemary (compiler and author of text), and Günter Brosche (organizing and general administrative editor). *Alban Berg, 1885–1935. Ausstellung der Österreichischen Nationalbibliothek Prunksaal, 23 Mai bis 20. Oktober 1985.* Vienna: Universal Edition, 1985. 240 p. ISBN 3702401768. ML141.V4 B53 1985. In German with "Synoptic Guide" in English.

Descriptive catalog of an exhibit concerning Berg at the Austrian National Library in Vienna in 1985. The exhibit displayed items from the Berg Collection at the library and from other sources, including letters, manuscripts, photographs, and memorabilia, each of which is described and often excerpted or illustrated.

1061. *Der künstlerische Nachlaß Alban Bergs: Festakt zur Übernahme des Bestandes.* Vienna: Austrian National Library, 1977. 20 p. In German.

Program for the ceremony on 5 December 1977 marking the transfer of Berg's legacy to the Austrian National Library. An exhibition of thirty-four items from this legacy is cataloged by Rosemary Hilmar.

1062. Schoenberg, E. Randol, compiler. "Alban Berg—Arnold Schoenberg Exhibit at the Arnold Schoenberg Institute. August-December 1985 in Honor of the Alban Berg Centennial." *JASI* 9 (1986): 236–59. In English.

The exhibit contained forty-two items, primarily from the Archives of the Arnold Schoenberg Institute.

1063. *Schönberg—Webern—Berg: Bilder, Partituren, Dokumente. Museum des 20. Jahrhunderts, Schweizergarten, Wien III, 17. Mai bis 20. Juli 1969.* Vienna: Bruder Rosenbaum, n.d. (1969). 118 p. N1688.A53 no. 36. In German. Reviewed by Dika Newlin, *Notes* 27 (1970–71): 488–89.

The exhibit (188 items) contained autograph manuscripts, paintings and drawings, scores, letters, photographs, books, and programs by Schoenberg, Berg, and Webern.

1064. *Schönberg/Webern/Berg: Portretten, partituren, documenten. Haags Gemeentemuseum 29 februari-28 april 1969.* Unpaginated. ML141.H14 S3. In Dutch.

The exhibit (167 items) contained mainly pictures of and by the three composers. Many of these are illustrated. An essay by Werner Hofmann, "Beziehung zwischen Malerei und Musik," is appended.

Index

Numbers in this index refer to items in the bibliography.

Authors, Editors, Translators, and Reviewers

Aber, Adolf, 70
Ackere, Jules E. van, 664–65
Adensamer, Eva, 666
Adorno, Theodor W., 71–75, 306–307, 470, 493, 512, 553–54, 564–65, 619–21, 667–76, 679, 919
Agea, Francesco, 308
Albéra, Philippe, 686
Alcaraz, José Antonio, 680
Altenberg, Peter, 1, 9, 681
Andréani, Eveline, 76
Andrews, Hilda, 77
Angermann, Klaus, 150
Ansermet, Ernest, 1053
Antesberger, Günther, 78
Apostel, Hans E., 13, 19
Apter, T. E., 79
Archibald, Bruce, 297, 543, 599, 682, 975
Ardoin, John, 80
Arndt, Michael, 134
Ashby, Arved, 513
Ashton, E. B., 836
Åstrand, Hans, 311
Ayrey, Craig, 623, 648
Bach, David Josef, 82, 683

Bachmann, Claus-Henning, 312–13
Baier, Christian, 684
Banda, Daniel, 685
Banks, Paul, 704
Barcaba, Peter, 566
Barilier, Étienne, 686
Barraud, Henry, 83
Bartosch, Alex Hans, 314–15
Bauer, Hans-Joachim, 567
Bauer-Mengelberg, Stefan, 687
Baum, Oskar, 41
Bean, Calvert, 472
Beaujean, Alfred, 688
Beck, Joachim, 84
Bek, Josef, 689
Bellingardi, Luigi, 690, 780
Bennett, Clive, 316
Berg, Alban, 21–69
Berg, Erich Alban, 691–93
Berg, Helene, 694
Berger, Gregor, 568
Berio, Luciano, 85
Berl, Christine, 695
Berra, Donata Schwendimann, 86
Berry, Wallace, 483
Bierbaum, Otto Julius, 1
Bischof, Rainer, 696

Subjects

A Concordance of Titles of Berg's Music

About the Author

BRYAN R. SIMMS is Professor of Music at the University of Southern California. He is a graduate of Yale University and has taught also at the University of Denver. He specializes in music and music theory of the twentieth century. In addition to writing articles and reviews, he is the author of *Music of the Twentieth Century: Style and Structure* (New York: Schirmer Books, 1996) and *The Art of Music: An Introduction* (New York: HarperCollins, 1993).